Dear Mary,

Best Wishes!

CHOOSING LIGHT

Viral Dalal

VIRAL DALAL

Over Darkness, choose Light!
Always!

CHOOSING LIGHT

ISBN: 978-0-9985917-1-1
Printed in the United States of America

Eye Of The Tiger
Theme from ROCKY III
Words and Music by Frank Sullivan and Jim Peterik
Copyright © 1982 Sony/ATV Music Publishing LLC, Rude Music,
Three Wise Boys LLC, WB Music Corp. and Easy Action Music
All Rights on behalf of Sony/ATV Music Publishing LLC, Rude Music and Three Wise Boys LLC
Administered by Sony/ATV Music Publishing LLC, 424 Church Street, Suite 1200, Nashville, TN 37219
All Rights on behalf of Easy Action Music Administered by WB Music Corp.
International Copyright Secured All Rights Reserved
Reprinted by Permission of Hal Leonard LLC
Used by permission of ALFRED MUSIC

Photographs appearing on pages 304 and 305
are used by permission from International Rescue Corps, UK.

Photograph appearing on page 305
of Viral Dalal, with a dust mask is used by permission from The Associated Press.

Photograph appearing on page 306
with Dr. Adams is used by permission from Fairleigh Dickinson University.

Cover design by George Foster:
www.fostercovers.com

Editorial development and creative design support by Ascent:
www.itsyourlifebethere.com

Follow Viral Dalal:
www.viraldalal.com   ViralDalalLive   @ViralDalalLive

Mom, Dad, Bhai,
I am, because of you.

To
Pi, Sweetie Pie and Margi,
with love.

and to
The brave men and women of the International Rescue Corps,
with deepest gratitude.

Rising up, back on the street,

Did my time, took my chances,

Went the distance, now I'm back on my feet.

Just a man, and his will to survive.

—EYE OF THE TIGER, SURVIVOR

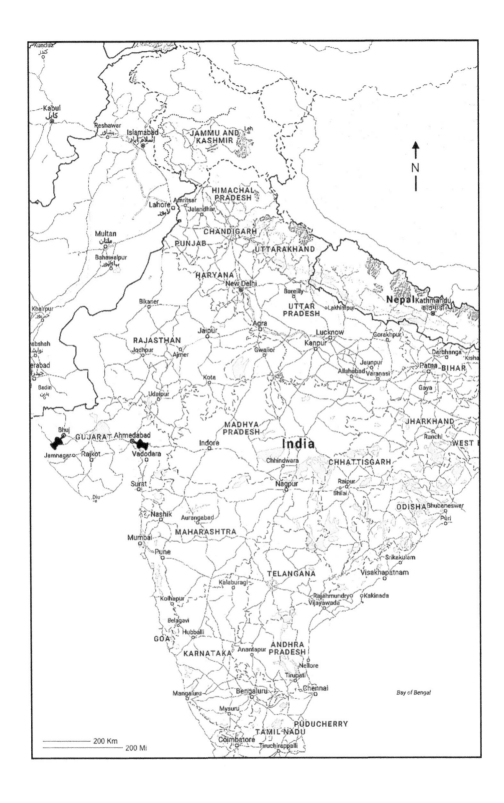

CONTENTS

1

THE PRECIOUS CARGO

"It is during our darkest moments that
we should focus to see the light."

—ARISTOTLE ONASSIS

Christmas Eve 2000
Newark Liberty International Airport, New Jersey

Would all my bags get on the flight?

I looked at my watch for the third time in a minute, as I eagerly waited in line at the Alitalia airlines check-in counter. It was 4:37 PM. With two overweight hard-case suitcases and a carry-on bag, all I could think of was that some of the precious gifts I'd bought might not make it on the plane and that I'd have to abandon them here at Newark airport. If so, what would I do with them?

I was eager to return home to my family, and 27 hours away from meeting them. While I waited, every single minute felt like ten, and I wondered how I could contain my excitement any longer. It was my first time being away from my family—more than 15 months—and this was the day I had been waiting for since October, when I had bought the return ticket to my home country of India.

The people in front of me moved and the line to the ticket counter advanced a little. I calmed myself. It was more than two hours until flight time, and I would make the flight for sure.

9

While I waited I thought about the way life had been good to me as a student here in America. I had made a number of great friends and enjoyed my studies. But I was looking forward to making the best of my winter vacation, spending the holiday with my family.

And here was the reason for my anxious feelings.

In my heart I deeply missed them and wanted to be home—and right now all I could feel was joy at the thought of being back among all the people I loved. The only concern at the moment was that of the excess weight in the suitcases—about ten extra pounds in each of the bags. I would be heartbroken if any gifts I'd purchased for everyone had to be removed. I had no cash left with me to pay for the extra baggage weight. Likewise, my first and only credit card was maxed out.

"Next in line!" the middle-aged man behind the ticket counter called.

Stepping up, dragging my cases behind me, I greeted him with a smile. Maybe the smile would help my cause if I ran into a problem.

"Hello, sir!" I said, handing over the ticket and passport.

The man across the counter had a big square face, and he looked down at the papers I slid to him. I kept a relaxed facial expression even though I was nervous.

He looked bored or unhappy, I couldn't tell which.

"Going to India?"

"Yeah," I replied brightly, forcing myself to smile.

"Can you please place both the bags on the scale for me?" he said, nodding to the low, silver platform adjacent to his seat.

I pretended to pick up the large green suitcase effortlessly, and set it down as lightly as possible on the scale. Then I hauled over the brown suitcase and placed it on the scale while the ticket agent was busy pressing keys on his computer.

"Can I get a window seat, please?" I said, hoping to divert his attention from the weight gauge, which had shot up instantly.

"Let me see if I have one available."

"Can you please make sure that it is not over the wings? I want to have a better view if possible."

"Let me check," he said without looking at me. . .or, more importantly, at the scale.

"Are you a student?" he asked absently.

"Yeah, I am going to India for the first time in one-and-a-half years. My entire family is there."

At that moment, he glanced at the weight gauge and slowly raised his eyebrows.

"Let me guess. You're taking home gifts for your family."

I swallowed hard. "Yes, sir, I am."

"*A lot* of gifts?"

"Yes. You see I have my father and mother, a brother and sister-in-law and their child, and. . ."

"Have a good trip!" he interrupted, then he smiled and handed back my passport along with my boarding passes. "I'll tag these through to your final destination. Gates are on the right side of the counter," he concluded, pointing.

"Thank you, sir!" I said, relieved.

"You can collect your bags full of gifts in India," he said, as a baggage handler swung my bags onto the conveyer belt.

I couldn't believe my luck. Now all I had to do was endure my own growing impatience and desire to see my family.

Making my way around the lines of other passengers, I headed toward the far end of the long ticket counter, smiling. I suspected the airline official understood the significance of gifts in India, and especially when someone was arriving from a foreign country. Everyone that I knew in India loved "imported" goods, be it chocolates, clothes, shoes, toys, books, electronics or anything else. These things were rare and always cherished by everyone who received them.

"I am going to Indiaaaaa, man!" I said as I rejoined my room-mate Alpesh and my friend Maulik, who had come to drop me at the airport.

"I'll meet you at your home," Alpesh said, as we headed toward the security checkpoint. Both of them would be heading back to India shortly as well.

"Yes! I'll see you soon. Have a great trip."

"Safe travels, Viral. I hope your time with your family is fantastic."

At the security checkpoint, we parted company, and I soon found the assigned gate. Finding a seat by one of the pillars in the waiting area I took out my small spiral pocket diary. On the three-page long list, everything was checked. Now, at last, I was breathing easy.

Next stop, India. My family would be waiting.

Now, too, I could chuckle about all that I'd stuffed in my suit-cases. I really had overdone it. But there was a good reason.

Two bags were crammed with toys for my two-year-old nephew; boxes of chocolate bars; colognes for my father, mother, brother and my sister-in-law; nail polishes; pens, pencils, silk ties, shirts, trousers, a winter jacket, wine, a decorative crystal vase, eight large crystal goblets, crystal serving trays, candles. . .and other innumerable little things that I had squeezed into the little spaces in the suitcases. There hadn't been enough room in the suitcase for my own things, but I was okay with that. This visit was not about me; it was all about them. Seeing them, being with them.

I knew that I was going to have the best time during this five-week vacation. I wanted to live the way I used to live before, do what I used to do, enjoy the way I enjoyed life with my family, relatives and my friends. Now that I was headed home I realized how much I was longing to relive and recreate the good times I had been missing.

Most of all I wanted to tell my parents that I was now on my own two feet. That all their help and support was paying off, as I was launching my own life. They had worked so hard and done so much to help me start my own life. And now I wanted to tell them all about America and how I was doing here. The truth was that being on my own two feet did not matter to me if they were not looking.

Yes, the reason I had overdone it with gift buying was that I loved and missed my family. They had done so much for me in my life. Sending me to America also required such big sacrifices by my parents. Even if gifts were not customary, bringing them gifts would have been the least I could do. All I wanted was to be able to please them with something that they would love.

But the gifts were more than tokens of affection—they were like an offering really. In my mind's eye as I began to envision my family members one by one, there was something else I could not quite wrap my head around. A sort of brightness that filled me whenever I thought of them that was more than the glow of remembering the loving, wonderful things they had done for me and that we had done together. It was bigger than any one experience with my family, and I couldn't quite put my finger on it. . .

Noise distracted me from my thoughts, and I put my list away and looked around at the other passengers now filling the waiting area. A mom and dad, with three young children in-tow and young passengers who looked like students heading back home. I felt warmth for them. A deeper sense also began to grip me.

Family is what my trip was about. That was *all* it was about.

Apart from spending time at home, our plan was to visit

various cities in India and spend time at one of the resorts by the ocean, but all that really mattered to me was that we would all be together again. Very soon I would be telling my family how everything seemed to be falling in place as per plan, and everything was happening in my favor. Life was amazing for me, and in 26 hours, now, it was about to be even more wonderful.

I had met people who were not close to their families. I couldn't understand how that was even possible. I felt sad for them. And sometimes when I talked about my family I got looks of skepticism. Feelings and care always took precedence over everything else in our family, truly, and we were a genuinely tight-knit clan. It was something special that happened when we were together; I never could define it. All I knew was that I did not need anything if I was around them.

We always tried to find reasons to celebrate life, whether it was a birthday, an anniversary or even a small achievement. Since I had been studying in the U.S., I'd missed all such events. My father had bought a new car, my little nephew's second birthday had gone by, various get-togethers had taken place and many festivals and holidays had passed by.

I was going back to my parents, who had taught me everything that I knew to that point. They were the ones who had built the strong pillars of the beliefs that I lived by, and who taught me how to live.

"If you have the will, you will find a way," my mother would always say, when she thought I needed a push, or when I was about to give up. I had heard this from her since I was a child. Every time I had given up hope, I remembered her words and moved forward. It had always helped.

She had always told me, "You have a sharp mind like your father, Viral. If you focus on anything that you want, I know that you can achieve it." Whenever she said this I felt great. Her trust in me made me trust myself even more. Also I felt great because I was being compared to someone whom I had utmost respect for. My father.

Likewise, whenever my father offered a bit of life guidance, I remembered and treasured it. While growing up, I had learned a lot from what he said, and even more watching his conduct and his actions.

"Nothing in the world can stop you if you have a strong will," he would often say.

I believed in what he said with all my heart, and I worked very hard to follow what he told me, and also to please him. Whenever I remembered his words of guidance, it gave me strength to move ahead.

"Right actions will move you toward where you want to go in life. Act," he would insist.

"Ladies and gentlemen, we will be boarding the aircraft shortly. Passengers who are travelling with small children or who need help. . ."

No, my elation at returning home was not just because we had celebrated the events of life together. And it wasn't just because I had learned life's great lessons from my parents, who had taught me the way to be happy in life. Though I wanted to experience these wonderful things with them again, for sure.

But the deeper sense that held me was this: We were all a part of each other. When you are part of a family that loves and cares about and for each other, you are woven into the fabric of each other's lives. And that is what we were. One fabric. Indivisible. That's the feeling that was rising in me again.

If only that could have remained true. . .

While I waited to board an airliner that would take me back to the arms of everyone I loved, unbeknownst to me or anyone else, a terrible event was in the making.

Miles beneath the earth's crust, and only a few hundred miles away from where I was headed, a monstrous amount of pressure had been building up for decades between the Eurasian and Indian tectonic plates. These mammoth tectonic plates deep underneath the earth's surface had been pushing against each other with tremendous force, and this pressure could not hold much longer.

But for the moment, all I knew, of course, was that thousands of miles away, my whole family was as eager to see me as I was to see them.

I was thinking about how exciting it was going to be, to share the details of my experiences in the last 15 months in the U.S. I was thinking about how incredible it was going to be to talk about my first job in New York City. How wonderful it was going to be to look deep into my parents' eyes.

"We will begin boarding momentarily. Please have your passports and boarding passes ready for the agent at the gate."

I did not know that the path of my life was about to be altered forever, and that everything I'd been taught about love and life was going to be tested. Not in my wildest dreams could I have imagined that my family and I were about to walk into the path of terrifying destruction.

2

ROOTS

"We do not remember days, we remember moments."

— CESARE PAVESE

The airliner was now far out over the Atlantic, and as I alternately dozed and read, images of my family kept rising to interrupt my distractions.

Given the overwhelming amount of gifts I was lugging home I felt like Santa in his sleigh. I loved gift giving, and I was anticipating how great it would feel to surprise my family and how each person would react.

One face kept coming to mind first and foremost.

She was everyone's best friend in the family. Whenever I thought about her, I would smile, recall something wonderful she'd done for me, something wise or comforting from our last conversation. She was the one who made all of us laugh, and the one who connected us all.

"She" was my mother.

When I was younger I wondered how the three of us males would even interact if she were not at home all day, taking care of the house and caring for us. Luckily, we never had to face such a situation—that of being men, left to our own devices—because my mother was always there for us. In a very traditional Indian way, her realm was the home and she ruled and planned and cared for the house and us like a domestic monarch.

She was an extremely soft-hearted person, and yet she instilled strength into us when my elder brother Roshan and I were fearful. She was the one who cried when her children were in pain, and she was the one who had taught both her children how to love and care for each other.

I pictured my mother in her colorful and elegant *saree*, pressed and crisp. Her eyes would be glistening with tears of happiness. Whether it was about giving up her career to take care of her family or her little or big dreams, her sacrifices to bring us up were endless.

She was the one who made sure that we were well fed and clean and provided for, but more importantly, she was the one who took care of us, and showered upon us the love and the affection that we needed the most. She did not ask for anything for herself, but prayed constantly only for *our* wellbeing. Her family was her life.

It gave me a sense of inner buoyancy to think of her now, how she must be excited about my return.

"The house is going to feel so empty after you are gone," she had repeated several times before I left for the U.S. And she'd had tears in her eyes the last time I'd seen her at the airport in Ahmedabad. I knew then how difficult it was for her to hold back her tears. She had been thrilled that I was moving ahead in my life, but still grieving the fact that her youngest was leaving.

We often spoke over the phone after I settled down in the U.S., and every single time that we spoke, we ran short of time. We often talked about my life in the U.S., and then about the grueling cold winter, the long walks back and forth from the college in New Jersey, the antics of my roommates, the self-cooked food, and the dirty dishes. I never told her that I deeply missed everyone. That was understood.

"I know you are tough and that you'll manage. Don't skip your meals, and don't worry about money. Your father will be more than willing to send money to you if you need it," she would dote and direct at the same time.

Looking out the window from 32,000 feet, I thought about my overstuffed suitcases again and their precious cargo. I hoped she would like the beautiful brushed golden wristwatch I had bought for her. I knew that the crystal glass decorative pieces would please her, since she loved to decorate, and I was also sure that she was going to like the large crystal goblets even though she never drank alcohol. She would use them for juice or other soft drinks at our family meals. I'd picked up various perfume gift sets for her and hoped that she would like them, too.

I also knew what she was going to say once she opened her gifts. She would tell me, "You shouldn't have spent so much money. I have everything I need. My two sons are my gifts." I had heard those words many times before.

Another image loomed in my mind now.

I pictured my father now, his tall frame sitting on the sofa in our living room wearing an oxford check shirt and jeans, with a newspaper in his hands. I could picture his wide shoulders, and the beard that covered most of his face, but which could never hide his expressions. Most of all, I clearly pictured his deep piercing eyes and the way they would look straight into mine, as if reading my mind and my soul.

When I spoke to my father, the conversations were very different than with my mother. Even thousands of miles away, I would first straighten my back and sit up straight if my father was on the phone.

When I was in the U.S. we would talk about my studies, and then my exams and about my day-to-day life in the U.S. We would often also talk about our new car, which was always exciting. Even though the conversations were to the point and not very long, I always looked forward to them. I always learned something.

"Be tough. If you have self-discipline and self-control, you can achieve anything," he would often say.

"When you pray, show gratitude first. If you ever ask for something from God, ask for the path to knowledge. Because *that* is all you need."

"Study hard, and get all A's," was his usual closing.

The personality and presence of my father was such that anyone who met him even once would remember him very distinctly, and more importantly would remember the words he spoke. People did not just remember him because of his tall and lean stature and his well-suited beard, but it was primarily because of his vast knowledge and his genuine warmth toward them. He was man of few words and spoke only when necessary and when he spoke, it made sense, and people always listened.

"You can't always prevent problems from happening. More important is to make yourself capable of handling them," he would often say.

A different sense filled me when I thought about my dad. Resilience. Determination. Forward momentum.

I enjoyed being in his company immensely even though I was scared of him when I was younger. I always stayed by his side and learned from him, because I wanted to be like him.

I had seen him pray in the morning before leaving for work each day. And I remembered once when my mother had asked him about his belief in God, and he had replied without hesitation.

"Always respect the Creator. You should respect everyone else, but you don't *have to* bow down to anyone other than the Creator— and your mother and your father," he'd added, "only because they made you."

Both my elder brother Roshan and I were also brought up to understand our Hindu religion and what specific rituals meant, even though there were many "modern" Indians who ignored the ancient faith. My parents would have none of that. "You do not follow what everyone else does," they told us.

I'd had a tough time picking the presents for my father because I knew that he had a distinct preference for everything that he used. I had bought a wristwatch for him, too, and also I had bought two neckties, colognes and an expensive, silver metal Cross pen. I knew that he'd like the pen since he collected them and would love to add another one to his collection, which he safely kept inside the locker in his metal cupboard.

I had heard from my mother that he was quite eager and looking forward to meeting me at the airport. I could hear it in his tone when I spoke to him the last time, even though he did not mention it.

I wasn't sure how he would react after seeing the gifts that I had gotten for him, but I thought that he would look at each of the gifts closely, and then he'd take something out from his cupboard and show me what he had bought when he visited the U.S. in the '70s. I also knew that he was going to use all the gifts sparingly and with immense pride.

As the string of thoughts about my family continued, the smiling face of my brother Roshan came to mind. *Bhai* (brother) as I called him, had a smile that could easily win anyone's heart. He was a very genuine guy, who happened to be quite knowledgeable and who had a great sense of humor. He was my support system for anything and everything that I needed, and I had looked up to him my whole life for guidance. He was the smarter one.

Roshan and I were very different. He was soft spoken and calm, while I considered myself tough and wouldn't settle for anything less than what I wanted. He was easy going, I was not.

Our interests were as different as our personalities and our looks. He liked reading books and spent more time learning. I preferred being outdoors and liked spending time around the garage, our cars and my motorcycle, or somewhere else outside in the sun.

Our differences were probably the reason why we fought a lot when we were younger. Although oddly enough, as we matured our differences became our strengths and brought us closer than we had ever been before.

Everyone loved Roshan dearly because of his pleasant personality, his easygoing attitude and just for who he was. As for me, I was constantly amazed by his vast knowledge about various subjects.

"How do you know so much, *Bhai*?" I asked him often.

"Everyone knows this much," was his standard response.

When I thought of Roshan now, I felt the spirit of fun and an ability to face anything with good humor. Also a sense of respect for the powers of the human mind.

Even though my next semester was scheduled to start the following year on January 29th I had planned on returning to the U.S. a week later. I wanted to be with Roshan on February 3rd—his 30th birthday. The celebration would be fantastic.

We had a special family custom for celebrating birthdays, and thinking about Roshan's upcoming 30th made me remember the last time we'd celebrated my mother's birthday together.

It went down like this.

Once everyone had gone to bed, late in the evening when the lights were out, I frantically looked for scotch tape, a pen and scissors. It was 11:30 PM the night before my mother's birthday, and I scrambled beneath the dim study lamp on my table to wrap mom's present and write something extra special on the birthday card.

Even though the other rooms seemed dark and quiet, I knew that similar preparations were underway there as well.

At midnight, Roshan, my sister-in-law Jaishree and I stood outside my parents' bedroom door in darkness.

Roshan lifted his hand and knocked.

"Come in!" Mom called. She was awake.

The light switched on as soon as we entered, calling, "HAPPY BIRTHDAY, MOM! "MANY, MANY HAPPY RETURNS OF THE DAY!"

She rose from the bed, and we shook her hands, hugged her and then bowed down to touch her feet as a mark of respect.

In India, touching the feet of your parents, elders or a learned person is considered a form of respectful salutation. When you bow down and touch someone's feet, you get blessings from them. It is considered that even the dust from a learned person's feet is something that you gain from, and thus you should bow down and touch their feet.

Mom blessed us all, and then from the quiet sanctuary it had been, our home was suddenly full of noise and laughter.

My father—the one who had introduced the habit of wishing birthdays at midnight in our family—was still pretending to awaken from a deep sleep.

Happy to see us all, and to receive gifts, my mother resisted opening them for several minutes as we all tried to guess what was inside. But the size of the gift inside was always much different than the box itself, which made it impossible to guess. That was part of the fun. As expected, my father also took out another present from behind his pillow, then pulled out a birthday card from underneath the mattress, while mother was still working on opening the gifts.

I could never forget the look in my mother's eyes—one of curiosity, surprise and happiness combined—when she opened our gifts. I loved to see that expression on everyone's face—every time we celebrated a birthday.

That night we spent time celebrating with some pastries, ice cream and beverages, while talking about the gifts and discussing plans for the next day.

We retired to bed only after 2:00 AM after mother forced us to go to our rooms.

The next day phones continued to ring off the hook as friends and relatives called to wish my mother a happy birthday. That evening we celebrated at one of the finest restaurants in town, at a candlelit dinner table. It was one of the most beautiful evenings that we spent together.

The sense that filled me now was one that spread out in a bright embrace for my whole extended family of aunts, uncles, cousins. In fact, I was one thread in a fabric that surrounded and held me. I felt deeply grateful for them all.

So birthdays were very special in our household, and I was expecting a similar evening on Roshan's 30th.

I settled my thoughts again on him. . .and on his young family.

The last time we spoke over the phone, he told me, "When you come home, we'll go around the city. You will be amazed how much it has changed in the last year. I'll also show you my new office."

Then he said something that deeply moved my heart. "You are missing the most precious moments of seeing a child grow up, Viral!" He was referring to my nephew, Shalin.

I felt a lump in my throat. "Yes, I'm sure that's true."

Now, I was confident that Roshan was absolutely going to love everything that I got for him. He surely would tell me to save money first and not "waste" it over gifts. He would probably ask me if I would like to keep any of the presents for myself. And I knew that he wasn't going to be particularly happy to learn that I had quit my job only so I could see everyone. I knew that his wife—my *Bhabhi* (sister-in-law) Jaishree would be shocked to learn about my decision to quit the job as well.

I had been able to speak to Jaishree *Bhabhi* only rarely while I was overseas, and whenever we talked we spoke mostly about Shalin, my two-year-old nephew.

"Viral *Bhai*, Shalin knows that you are coming home soon. He is sitting in his grandma's lap right now and trying to mimic what I am saying," she said the last time we'd spoken.

Knowing that she liked pretty things I had bought for her a silver handcrafted jewelry box, and a makeup kit along with various other small gifts that I was sure she was going to love.

The biggest and the most exciting portion of my gifts were the toys, though: the "Mask" doll, a set of 30 toy cars, a large bag of Lego blocks, a musical toy TV and a few other smaller toys. I knew that Shalin was going to go crazy over his *Chachu* (uncle) arriving from America with bags full of goodies.

Thinking of Shalin now made my heart swell with the sense of the ongoing life of my family, the stream of generations that I could imagine passing on our heritage and wonderful traditions.

At the moment, of course, I just wanted to bring delight to that little, sweethearted nephew of mine. Just like I wanted to talk my heart out to my parents, things I couldn't express over the phone.

I wanted them to feel what I felt, and I wanted to feel what they felt when I was away. Mostly, I wanted to once again experience the oneness that we all shared.

25

I shifted in my seat looking at the wristwatch that my father had sent to me on my last birthday when I was in the U.S.

In the darkness I looked at the glow on the watch's face.

All the happiness I was imagining was only hours away.

I could hardly wait.

3

HOME

"Home is where the heart is."

— PLINY THE ELDER

Is it possible to have an insight into the future? Are we given signs and omens that portend events to come?

Time was dragging at Milan-Malpensa airport in Italy, as the layover between my flights dragged on due to very heavy snow. With most stores at the airport closed due to Christmas holiday, I sat in the lounge, having nothing to do, but watch the same program looping on Fashion Television for hours. I paced and drummed my fingers, waiting for the connecting flight to depart as I walked around and around the deserted terminal like a caged animal.

"Change the situation. And when you cannot control things that are outside yourself, focus your energy in the right direction. Persist."

The words of my father came to me.

Sooner than I knew I would need this wisdom more than I could imagine.

Taking a deep breath, I calmed myself and found another bench. There, I forced my mind to focus by jotting a list in my little notebook of all I wanted to do while I was at home in India. The

27

snow continued to fall outside the huge windows, and I imagined:

- Visiting the town of Nathdwara, and the holy shrine of Shrinathji.

- Seeing Roshan's new office.

- Visiting the new multiplexes and restaurants that had cropped up in the city.

- Visiting the oceanside resort near the town of Bhuj.

I smiled a little at the way my own mind worked: If I had a plan I was happy. Just having time on my hands, with nothing to do to direct my physical and mental energies, always made me restless. Planning events and imagining time spent with my family helped to channel those energies. We would walk on the beach in the early morning, collect shells. And this time it was going to be all the more fun when Shalin would join us.

For all my restless energy, I wanted nothing more than to be settled in the heart of my whole family—which, by extension, was quite large.

Uttrayana, the Festival of Kites, was only days away, and I was quite eager to visit my grandmother's home where we cousins and relatives would meet and fly kites all day long, and when everyone in the city would pitch themselves on their rooftops flying kites as well.

Uttarayana, which means the northern movement of the sun, refers to transmigration of the sun from the zodiac sign Sagittarius to zodiac sign Capricorn. It is considered an auspicious time.

All through the day there would be kite wars, music and food. The sky would be filled with red, blue, orange, yellow, white and rainbow-colored kites of every kind, and from the rooftop all the strings would look like nerves interconnecting everyone in the whole city, like the web of the sun god's net. Aunts and uncles, cousins, cousins of cousins would all be there playing games into the night, just like old days.

Again, my thoughts turned to my monther and her great, soft heart into which I would be enfolded. How amazing it was going to be to see the happiness in her eyes when she would first catch sight of me at the airport.

She is going to be so, so happy to see me. . .

I recalled the many beautiful hours that I spent talking to my mother after everyone else went to bed. I would pour out my heart about my dream of going to the U.S., about how I would cope in the new environment, and about what I wanted to do in life. With great patience and utmost interest she would carefully take in all my thoughts and ideas and emotions.

"How did you gain so much knowledge, Viral? You never even liked going to school," she had often said.

Another heart would be waiting for me, wide open as well.

My father, the strongest man I knew, would try to hide his emotions by trying hard to keep a straight face—though happiness would be written all over him. He would give me a firm handshake and probably make a precise observation about me. I was desperate to hear something from him.

Still the snow fell. I struggled with the feeling that I had no control, ignoring the message "when you are not in control of such things, persist."

By the time we boarded the flight, anxious energy had exhausted me. I slept for more than seven hours, as the airliner cut through the skies toward Ahmedabad.

It was about 5:00 PM Indian Standard Time when the plane finally touched the ground. Never before had I experienced such excitement in my life. I found it very hard to remain seated until the plane finally came to a halt and the doors were opened.

My family was now just a few hundred feet away.

Ahmedabad airport felt very small and crowded as soon as I entered the building. The conveyor belt near the exit gate, rattling away, seemed even smaller. The familiar mosaic tiles on the ground seemed old, and scents of coffee from nearby vending machines filled the air. In the throngs waiting for planes to arrive, people were holding rose and marigold garlands, and some held nameplates.

And in a moment I saw them from inside the building. From the center of the crowd there was my mother, waving frantically, with Roshan at her side. In another moment, my luggage arrived on the conveyor belt, and I loaded it on a cart and hurried toward the exit gate.

And then came the moment that I had been desperately waiting for. I found myself surrounded by the circle of love I had longed to feel again—Roshan, Jaishree with Shalin in her arms, and right behind them, my mother.

Dropping the handle of the cart, I bowed down and touched my mother's feet. Then I stood and wrapped her in my arms, loving the gentle scent of her favorite perfume.

"I am here," I said softly.

"I am here, Mom!"

She squeezed me tightly, then stepped back to look at me, still holding my hands. Inexpressible joy permeated her face. Her eyes were moist and filled with happiness. I held her by the shoulder and gently touched my forehead to hers.

I felt all the love I had been missing pour into me.

Then I turned to Roshan and threw my arms around him as well. "*Bhai*! You look just the same," I said while I continued to shake his hand. His smile hadn't changed.

In that moment, I felt the joy and fun leap up within me. We were going to have a great time, my brother and I!

He grinned. "Maybe you gained some weight?"

Jaishree *Bhabhi* was holding little Shalin in her arms. "Shalin, look who is here."

I could not believe how he'd grown. It underscored for me the time I'd been away and, worse, what I'd missed. I vowed I would make up for lost time by packing in as much family time as possible. Every minute with them would be precious.

Reaching out one hand to Shalin, I said, "Do you know who I am?" and brushed my fingers on his little, soft cheeks.

He looked at Roshan and then at me, and said, *"Chachu."*

"He knows me, *Bhabhi*!" I exclaimed, taking the little guy in my arms and looking in his big, brown eyes.

Yes, I was home. The idea that my flight delays had been an omen was gone now. Everything was going according to plan.

But not quite. Someone was missing.

I turned to my mother. "Where is Papa?"

"He came to Ahmedabad from his plant in Bhuj a day before your flight was due. But then your flight was delayed and delayed, and we did not even know your expected day of arrival. We were told that it could take longer than 24 hours."

"And then something urgent came up at work, so your father had to travel back to Bhuj. He was very sad and felt torn, but I forced him to go."

This was a blow, and my heart sank.

My father had started working in Bhuj, a town that was about 400 kilometers from our home in Ahmedabad, only a few years ago. The best way to travel to Bhuj was by bus since it was an overnight journey. After working with the Government of India as a scientist for more than 30 years, he had joined as a deputy general manager at a plant in Bhuj that specialized in extracting bromine from the salt marshes.

Despite my heavy disappointment, I knew that for my father to miss this reunion, something greater had to have taken precedence.

I breathed a deep breath. So everything was *not* going according to plan. At least not my plan.

"We'll call him from the car," my mother hastily assured me.

Though absent in person, my father was present in spirit. Out in the parking lot I spotted our car from a distance. It had been polished like a gem and it looked as good as new.

"Your father spent all day cleaning the car and waxing it," my mother said.

"Then he put the car cover over it to keep it from getting dusty, and instructed Roshan to uncover the car only when we were ready to leave for the airport."

"He hasn't changed," I smiled.

We made our way through streets clogged with motorcycles, cars, trucks, buses, auto rickshaws and even camel carts. Everyone was trying to get somewhere, causing chaos and a big traffic jam at a roundabout. Everyone honked, and managed to move where they wanted to go. I saw the usual scene of people running red lights and the local cops chasing with their wooden staffs. *India*—it felt great to be home. America had been a wonderful experience, but there I'd been on new and unsure footing. Here, I felt like I was on solid ground again.

Very soon, that feeling would vanish.

At home, Prabhu, our helper, swung open the main gate with a wide smile. From the main gate, I could see the clay roof tiles and that the large teak wood entrance door open.

Almost immediately after stepping inside, mother handed me a newspaper. "See! This is how your dad feels about your return."

Unfolding the newspaper. I was shocked to see my picture and a headline that read: "WELCOME." Beneath my picture was the message: "Our heartiest welcome to Viral returning from the United States. –Dalals"

More evidence of my father's presence.

"Your dad was very happy with your achievement abroad," she added, "and *very* excited about your returning home. He didn't even tell us about this message in the newspaper."

In a few minutes, my mother was able to connect to my father's cellphone—not always easy at the remote location where he worked.

My father's voice, though always measured, could not quite contain his excitement. "How are you!"

"I'm doing great, Papa!"

"I saw the car! It looks as good as new. I couldn't find even a speck of dust on it," I teased.

"That is how a car should be," he said, not missing a beat. "We are not the kind of people who change cars every year. One should maintain what one possesses—that in itself is good enough to maintain a good standard of living."

I chuckled to myself. That was my dad, never missing an opportunity to impart wisdom. More than cars and belongings, however, I knew that he valued family. And so did I.

"When are you coming to Ahmedabad?"

"I will be home at the end of the week—only a couple of days from now—and then we'll be together."

"We would have met yesterday if my flight was on time!" I said in a disappointed tone.

"Over acts of nature, we have no control."

There it was again, Dad offering me his wise perspective. But I let the words slip by. At the moment, I just wanted to see and be with my father, though that would have to wait.

"I will talk to you during the day tomorrow," he added, sounding wistful. "Unfortunately I cannot leave what I'm doing. I'm needed here."

I knew his work was demanding, and it was beyond his power to change that. I knew that it had to be something very important; if not, he would find his way to see me.

"Yeah! I may wake up late tomorrow, though. Call a little later if you can."

Later that evening, after a sumptuous dinner prepared by my mother, we all chatted late into the evening.

It had been difficult to explain my experiences during phone calls from the U.S. I didn't know where to start, but I wanted everyone to see America through my eyes.

As always, Mother wanted to know about my wellbeing. "Were you safe there? Were you comfortable?"

"During my initial few months, you cannot imagine how cold it was compared to here in India. I would walk through snow to the bus and at times my nose, cheeks and my chin would freeze on my way to college and work."

Mother looked dismayed. Time to change the subject, quickly.

"But I was happy, as always!" I hurried on.

"And he's gained weight." Roshan threw in another light-hearted jab, and we all laughed.

"At least you're safe with us now," Mother replied.

Safe. If only that had been the case.

Soon my eyes were falling shut.

I walked upstairs. Between the first and the second flight of stairs we had the *Pooja* (worship) room. Pausing I looked inside. Nothing had changed since I had left. On the clean white marble floor, a wooden Hindu temple that had pictures and idols of various deities stood in the exact same place as before. There were the pictures of my paternal and maternal grandparents who had passed.

Roshan had followed me up, and in a moment I reached my bedroom. On the door were various stickers I'd placed years before: "I have the Power" and "I never sleep." Inside, on the wall right above my bed was a poster of a Ferrari F40 in racing red, and a yellow Ferrari Dyno 246 GT poster was still pinned on the brown soft board above the study table, a large poster of Arnold Schwarzenegger pinned high up on the wall. Every single thing in the room was exactly the way I had left it.

"Shalin loves your room," Roshan said.

"He is always delighted to be here, and seems to love the wall posters, and especially the red Ferrari," he added.

"I'm sure he loves it. I love it!"

What I loved most about the moment was that it reinforced the fact that certain things never changed. I could always return home and, predictably, the love of my family would always be there for me.

With these comforting thoughts I lay down and slept under my parents' roof, with my family nearby. . .for one of the last times ever.

4

THE ACCIDENT

"One never knows what each day is going to bring.
The important thing is to be open and ready for it."
— H E N R Y   M O O R E

There are days in your life that you come back to, perhaps not so much because they are special, but because they are typical—because they capture a moment in time that holds all the loveliness of your life as in a picture frame. . .and because that loveliness vanished before you really knew exactly what you had.

My first morning home I felt as if someone had covered me with a thick blanket while I had been in deep sleep. When I uncovered my face and partially opened one eye I saw the tall figure of my father standing near my feet. Excited and disoriented, I tried to get up quickly. "Dad! How come you are here?"

He waved me back. "Go to sleep. Get your rest. It's only 7:00 AM." He turned and left the bedroom, closing the door behind him. But it felt incredible that he was here now, and that he had come upstairs just to see me. Thrilled, I ditched the idea of sleep, leaped up and dressed in anticipation.

My whole family was together now. What other beautiful gifts would this day bring me? And this time in India?

From the halfway landing of the stairs I saw my dad sitting on the sofa, while Roshan and Jaishree sat with him. He wore a checked shirt and dark blue trousers with his classic handsewn lug shoes. A few cups of tea were kept on the circular coffee table for everyone.

"Good morning, Papa! What a surprise!"

I bowed down to touch his feet. We shook hands, and then held onto each other's hands for a few moments. Father's grip was as firm as it had always been and the roughness of his palm unchanged.

"Weren't you going to come after two days? I thought I was dreaming!"

He controlled his smile and looked at me with his penetrating eyes as I sat near him.

"But Dad, you were here the day before yesterday and then you went back the same day to Bhuj, and then again you travelled 400 kilometers to be here this morning," I said with amazement.

Mom said, as a matter of fact, emerging from the kitchen, "He has come just to see his younger son, but he wouldn't admit it." Turning to Dad she added, giving him a mock scolding, "At least some times you can express that you love your children."

"Come on now, what's there in it," Dad said distractedly, picking up a magazine from the coffee table and flipping pages.

I knew that Dad's heart was tender toward us all. But that if he gave into emotion there would be tears. As a strong Indian man, he was not going to let that happen. But the newspaper ad and all the kilometers he'd logged just to see me said more than enough.

"He is not going to change," Mom said, smiling and shaking her head.

We spent the next hour talking about my experiences in America.

"New York City is simply unbelievable, Dad!" I said.

"There are miles-long tunnels running under the Hudson River. . .and you have to see the huge bus station on the third floor of the building. You have to see it to believe it."

"Yes, the Yankees are a hundred years ahead of us. I had a similar experience in Canada and in Europe back in the '70s."

Roshan and Jaishree listened in amazement to my descriptions of Times Square, the Empire State Building, the World Trade Center and other places that I had visited.

Then we moved on to family things. My family was like a holiday gift, full of news great and small that I couldn't wait to open. They talked about the new things that Shalin had learned, new developments in the city, and the new cars on the road.

We talked about Aamir Khan, one of the biggest movie stars of the country, who happened to stay in the same building where my mom and dad stayed in Bhuj.

"I heard that you all met Aamir Khan. And that he came to our home, too, Mom."

"Yes, he had come home, and we had a good chat with him over tea. He was staying in the building along with his large crew for a few months while they shot his upcoming film, *Lagaan*.

Later, this film would be nominated for an Oscar for Best Foreign Film.

All the news, all the talk and catching up—it all felt wonderful, just like old times.

Later that evening, I opened my overstuffed suitcases and presented the gifts to everyone. They were met with invaluable expressions that I find hard to put into words.

I had never before presented gifts to everyone in the family at the same time. I realized that the real gift, beyond watching the curiosity and surprise on each one's face, was *joy*.

The suitcases kept emptying, and the room kept filling.

Shalin, however, had gone crazy with delight.

"Don't show him all the toys at once, he's losing it," said Roshan, smiling. The Mask doll seemed to be his favorite.

We all had the non-alcoholic red wine in the crystal goblets that I had brought. With the taste of cheese crackers and sweet Hershey's chocolate on our lips—not a big deal in America, but a treat in India—we called it a night.

This is what I'd come home to experience—this spirit of deep, deep happiness that tied us all together. That was *my* gift.

For all the brightness, one shadow would fall during the next few weeks. A near tragedy.

Each day I would wake up late, put on some music, take morning tea while reading the newspaper, sit in the lawn chair catching sun for hours and play with Shalin. Then I would make phone calls to friends and relatives, share news and laughs, eat out at new restaurants or go for movies with friends and family. I would spend most of the evenings with my close friend Sidhant.

I also shopped for kites and threads as the festival of kites was approaching fast.

Manja the thread used to fly kites, is specially made with granulated glass pieces to facilitate kite wars. People get the kite threads intertwined and then pull on the thread until one breaks. The winners will shout, *"Kaypo che!"* ("I cut the kite!") and other local slang from their rooftops. This was the day I was waiting for.

Each day, then, was its own special gift. And yet, something began to dawn on me.

Before long, it's all going to come to an end. I'll have to go back to America.

Then my father's voice would break into my gloomy thoughts.

"Don't let worry about the future infect the present. The present moment is all we have, Viral".

As a Hindu, my father understood that life is fleeting and transient. All things rise, and pass.

On the morning of January 8, 2001, I was sitting in a lawn chair outside, sipping tea when I heard the phone ring inside the house.

In a moment, my mother shouted in a distressed voice.

"Viral. Come quick."

I sprinted to the door, where she met me, aghast. "Roshan has been in an accident!"

A jolt of fear went through me and a hundred terrible images leapt to mind.

"Where is he?"

"You have to go immediately," she said, wringing her hands.

"He is in a doctor's clinic near Rajen uncle's office!"

Rajen uncle, our next door neighbor, had an office about 5 kilometers away. I ran upstairs to put shoes on, took the car keys and rushed toward the garage.

When I reached the office building, I sprinted toward the stairs and took them two at a time. My mind was burning.

I'm going to beat the crap out of anyone who hurt my brother.

Inside the office, in an examining room, Roshan was lying on a bed with bandage on the bridge of his nose and some ointment on his eyelids.

"You came so quickly!" Roshan smiled, when he saw me.

"What happened? Who did this to you, *Bhai*?" I demanded, studying his face. Small bruises had formed.

He paused. "Viral, calm down. It was a *manja*," he said, adjusting the bandage on his nose.

A manja?

A young doctor, with a stethoscope around his neck, entered the room and greeted me with a smile and a handshake.

"Roshan is fine, but I don't think the poor kite faired very well."

As Roshan listened with a sheepish look, the doctor explained that a stray kite thread had fallen and draped itself on the road where Roshan was riding his two-wheeler. The thin, glass-laden string had caught him just beneath the eyes.

"It could have done a lot more damage if he wasn't wearing his glasses. As it is, he doesn't need stitches. He just needs to apply an ointment that will bond the skin quickly and stop the bleeding on his nose bridge and eyelids.

"I would call him very lucky," he said, squeezing Roshan's shoulder.

Rajen uncle, who had been instrumental in getting Roshan treated so quickly, entered the room just then.

"Very lucky indeed," he added.

We thanked him for his help. . .and I could not help but think, *what if Roshan had been blinded. Or worse—thrown from his vehicle and seriously injured or killed.*

No. I would not let myself think of such things. How would I go on if something that terrible happened to my brother? To anyone in my family?

Back at home, Mother was waiting, her face a study in anxiety. . .

"How did the accident happen?" she asked, once we went inside and she could examine his scrapes and bandages.

"I was going at a steady pace on my two-wheeler when suddenly in the middle of the road a kite thread came from nowhere. There must have been someone trying to fly a kite on the other side of the road. The abrasive thread got stuck under my chin, cutting my throat!" he said, pointing to the red scratch marks on his neck.

"Before I could apply the brakes, the thread got tightened around my neck, and I lost balance as I struggled to remove the string with one arm. As I was falling to the ground, the string got stuck near my nose bridge and slipped under my glasses, cutting through the skin and the eyelids."

This incident made me realize how unaware we all are of how quickly the invisible cord of life can snap. I felt a bit shaken. What if something happened to someone in my family while I was away in America? Did I really want to go back?

Somehow the stalwart face of my father surfaced in my mind.

"A person must always find the strength from inside to go on, no matter what happens. Even when tragedies occur—and they always do—you must stay connected to the great force of life that's inside you."

I thought about the great life force—*prana*—the energy that supports all life. As a young man, full of energy and curiosity, I was not very introspective. Not really much at all, in fact. Not like my father. The surface of life interested me—cars, bikes, sports, movies, fun with friends, a career. . .I could feel the energy of life in me, for sure, I just never thought about "staying connected" to it, what that meant or what would happen when it let go of your body.

I thought about purpose, too—*karma*. As far as I knew I was here on earth to become an engineer. That was it. As for some greater purpose, well, maybe that would someday reveal itself. In time. . .

At the moment, I was just glad the shadow of tragedy had not fallen on my family's path. I now once again focused on the happy possibilities ahead.

Roshan's wounds continued to heal, slowly. And not long after that incident, we all visited the temple town of Nathdwara, about 300 kilometers away from Ahmedabad, where the principle shrine of Shrinathji was located.

Belonging to the Vaishnava sect, we worshiped Lord Krishna. Shrinathji is a form of Lord Krishna.

On the way home, we also visited the royal palaces in the city of Udaipur, enjoying each other's company just a bit more, I thought, because of Roshan's close call.

But that event was quickly, happily fading into the past. Every plan was turning out to be better than what we had hoped for, and I couldn't ask for anything more.

And yet I knew that there was still more out there—something that my father was planning. A wonderful family surprise. . .

5

JANUARY 26, 2001

"Every second is of infinite value."
— JOHANN VON GOETHE

My father had returned to Bhuj once again, and he had planned so that all of us could again be together during the long holiday weekend. The 26th of January is the Republic Day of India, and January 26, 2001, happened to be on a Friday. Our plan was to spend the weekend at our home in Bhuj and also visit a resort near Mandvi beach. We would then celebrate Roshan's big 30th birthday together in Ahmedabad.

This was the first time when we all were going to be together in Bhuj under one roof, and I had no doubt that we all were going to have an incredible time together.

I had packed everything in a tote bag, making sure to bring my swimming trunks as well as my leather jacket. I knew that it was going to be cold during the night and hot during the day in Bhuj. I carried my cellphone, even though I did not use it much and if necessary I could always use Roshan's or my father's phone.

We might have taken regular buses, but instead we were travelling in a sleeping coach so we would get enough rest during the night. Once we all settled in our berths and while the bus moved through the city onto the highway and into the darkness, I was sitting on the upper berth, looking at the traffic through the large window.

I am going to miss all of this, I thought, unaware of the fact that I was only one day away from the time when my life was going to change forever.

When the bus reached Jubilee Ground station in Bhuj, we were only too happy to have the grueling, 400-kilometer road trip behind us.

The wonderful gift Father had planned for us all was a vacation in this ancient town, not far from the Arabian Sea.

Bhuj itself was the headquarters of the Kutch district in Gujarat, the largest district in India, and was founded in the year 1510 by a local ruler named Maharao Hamir. Because of Gujarat's unique ecosystem, it had become the locale of several wildlife sanctuaries. One was a combination of both desert and forest, the only one of its kind in India.

As we moved through the streets I was inspired by a few of the architectural attractions.

Bhuj's rich cultural heritage included the first Swaminarayan Sampraday temple, a center for religious instruction, and also a center of social services where alms, medicines and clothes were available to the poor and needy.

There was also the Prag Mahal, a palace named after Rao Pragmalji II, who commissioned its construction in 1865. The palace was made of Italian marble and sandstone from quarries in Rajasthan, and its main hall was filled with the mounted heads of exotic animals from the days of the great hunts. There was also a 45-foot clock tower, and from its top you could see the whole, colorful town.

It was a place of such interest.

I made a mental note. Perhaps I would climb this tower and get an overview—maybe even see all the way to ocean.

"This is a big building," I commented, when we reached the eight-storey structure where my parents had rented an apartment. It was new, and very attractive.

"It's the tallest building in the town," Mother replied proudly, as a thin older man with a white mustache greeted us at the gate. "*Namaste Memsahib* (Madam)," he nodded.

"His daughter will work for us, taking care of Shalin," she explained.

Jaishree smiled. Though she was a very attentive mother, like so many Indian women, I knew she would be happy to have help for her little bundle of constantly moving energy.

In India, the first floor is one level above the ground, which is called the ground floor. Our parking area was on the ground floor. On the second floor was our Apartment 208. We were greeted inside by a neatly printed card placed on the center table that read, "WELCOME TO YET ANOTHER HOME"—my father's doing. Though he'd had to fly to Mumbai for business, he'd be joining us this afternoon.

Mother smiled. "Your dad thinks of every single detail."

Roshan and I set down the bags and looked around, while Shalin immediately ran off exploring the rooms.

The living room was large, with a shining, brown granite floor. A large sofa and two smaller ones were arranged nicely around a glass-topped table, and in the corner was our old television set that we watched growing up. The two corner tables sported ethnic wooden carved pieces. A half wall, with a granite top, divided the dining area from the living room, which was decked out with brand-new appliances. And then I saw a wooden mail holder hanging by the wall, holding letters that I had sent in the past year.

Excitedly, I picked up my own letters and started reading them. Roshan, hearing a small crash in one of the bedrooms and Shalin's "uh-oh," went off in search of his little imp. "I hope he hasn't broken something here."

"There is nothing here I am worried about," Mother replied. "Having my whole family with me is all I need. Possessions are only things. Not as important as all of you."

I went in search of the bedroom where I'd be staying, eager to change clothes and eat breakfast. The plan was to put a mattress on the floor for me in the master bedroom and let Roshan's family take the second bedroom.

While I was longing to be here, I also felt a little wistful. The visit home was speeding by too fast. With only days to go before I left for the U.S., I felt a touch of nostalgia, not wanting this time to end. If only I could make this last.

Later, when we'd collected my father, we discussed our plan to visit the Mandvi beach and a resort on the Arabian Sea, where we would spend the next day. I was eager to spend time at the beach with the whole family. I imagined Roshan and I swimming and splashing in the surf, like kids again along with Shalin.

Mother and Jaishree were cleaning up the kitchen, and Mother looked a little stressed from the bus trip and preparing the meal.

"You should rest a bit," I offered. "This is your vacation, too."

She waved me away. "I'm fine."

But she looked tired.

"I want to show you something," Father said, motioning to me.

Downstairs, in the parking space under the pillars of the building, he walked me through all the features of our new family car. I was glad to be with him, enjoying his company.

This is so like Dad, I thought. *Proud of what he's worked to provide for us. Nothing changes. We'll be doing this exact same thing 30 years from now—only the cars will be different."*

Later that evening after a nice meal at the elegant Prince Hotel, we were having a good time playing with Shalin while driving back home. Once again I noticed Mother, who looked tired. Contented, but tired.

"We've kept up such a busy schedule. You're all going to be so happy when I'm gone," I said jokingly.

Mother's face went blank and I saw a tear in her eye. "You kids will never understand," she replied. "You will only know how much we love you, when we are no more."

That was Mother. So sensitive toward her family. I felt a twinge of remorse for hurting even, though I hadn't meant to.

Quickly I apologized, and the fun and laughter resumed, going on late into the evening.

Shalin, who'd napped earlier, was in rare form, dancing and darting at me. I'd grab and tickle him, bringing shouts of laughter, then he would hide behind the bed and we would play peek-a-boo, again and again.

With all of us talking at once the apartment was filled with happy noise once again.

It all felt so safe and secure.

After everyone went to bed that evening, as was my habit I went outside in the living room and flipped channels on TV until 2:00 AM. Knowing I had to wake up before 9:00 AM, though, I forced myself to sleep.

Waking groggily the next morning, I could hear my dad and mom's voices, with the musical sound of Shalin's young voice in the background. Turning over on the mattress that had been laid on the floor for me, I thought, it must be close to 8:00 AM, as I could see the bright sunlight from the bedroom window. It seemed like someone had already opened the window curtains. I wanted just a few more minutes of sleep.

From out in the kitchen I could hear Roshan's voice. "Mom, Shalin was playing till 1:00 AM with Viral. It was fun watching them play."

My mother must have said something about little boys needing to get to bed at a reasonable hour. I heard Roshan chuckle. "But Shalin was not ready to go to bed!"

I pulled the covers up over my eyes to keep out the morning light. Everyone seemed to be having breakfast or morning tea out in the adjoining dining room. I could hear my mom laughing and talking to Shalin in a baby's tone. I knew that any moment my dad would come and wake me up.

Not even a minute had passed, and there was Dad.

"Viral, get up!" he ordered.

I pretended to be wide awake.

"Give me just another 10 minutes, Papa, I was up late last night."

"Get on the bed if you want to sleep then. I need to put your mattress back in the other room and clear this one," he said.

With my eyes almost closed, I shifted to the bed and curled like a caterpillar underneath the thin blanket. Seeing this, dad picked up another thick comforter, and threw it over me, covering me from my head to the toe.

I was very surprised. I had not seen such a gesture from him when I was younger.

Uncovering my face, I could see him move to the window where he pulled the curtains closed for my comfort. I felt pampered.

Snuggling under the blanket I switched on the tiny blue light on my iridium watch. It was 8:35 AM. We would be leaving home after 9:30 AM, I guessed.

I can sleep till after 9 then, I thought, and closed my eyes.

A sound like thunder woke me, and I opened my eyes inside the comforter. I'd been dozing. This sound was surprisingly quite loud, and seemed to be coming from a far distance. I'd never heard thunder this loud before, and there was something different about it but I couldn't tell what.

The sound was not stopping, but getting louder and louder. In my groggy state I thought that lightning had struck somewhere nearby.

Pulling my head out from under the comforter I looked toward the window covered with curtains. It seemed as if it had gotten cloudy outside, making the room suddenly darker, while the very loud rumbling continued to build.

Maybe it's not thunder. Someone upstairs is moving heavy equipment.

But I realized that was not right either, and the sound became a roar.

Bombs? What if Pakistan has attacked India on the Republic Day? Bhuj was not far from the border.

Was that a crane? Some heavy machinery? No. What was it? Hundreds of thoughts came to my mind within the first few seconds. I had never heard anything like it before. All I could think of was thunder, but I knew that was not it. Before I could take the next breath, the floor began to shake, the bed shook up and down, and the dresser and mirror rattled against the wall.

Earthquake!

The shaking grew more fierce, the intensity mounting exponentially by the second, and the roar was now even louder.

My bed, along with everything else in the room, was now shaking wildly, nearly tossing me out and to the floor. A large and heavy metal cupboard wobbled and tilted and scraped its way across the floor.

RUN TO SAFETY. GET EVERYONE OUT...

Before I could complete that thought, the shaking started to throw everything into the air. I, my bed, the metal cupboard, the dresser—all of it was now slamming against the floor and being thrown back up in the air in an enormously wild and jarring motion. From all around I could hear glass shattering, and the sound of kitchen utensils clattering to the floor.

Now the deafening and ever-growing rumble seemed to be coming from right underneath our building, and just as I thought that it could not get any worse, the shaking became monstrous.

When I looked up, I saw the ceiling fan directly above me swinging crazily in all directions, its metal blades scratching the ceiling. It seemed like it was going to fall any moment. The sound of the ferocious roar seemed like something horrific that wanted to come out of the earth's crust, and as if a series of enormous explosions were going off underneath the ground.

Kicking off the comforter I tried to get out of the wildly heaving bed. But I couldn't. I was being tossed like a rag doll.

Suddenly, plastered cement and concrete pieces started falling off the ceiling. I *had* to get outside the building!

Now the walls started to give way. A six-inch wide crack split the ceiling. Big pieces of plaster started to fall and dust clouds rose.

Unable to move, I knew that the ceiling could fall any second. I had never seen anything more dreadful and terrifying in my life.

What was happening to my family?

Just then I heard my mother's shout from the other room, and felt a surge of anxiety.

Another powerful jolt shook my room and I looked up again—unable to believe what I was seeing. Steel rods inside the ceiling were exposed, twisting and pulling out from the walls, and the whole, huge concrete slab of the floor above me—bigger than a car and weighing tons—cracked before my eyes and started to collapse.

Without thinking I somehow shifted my body, just dodging the slab to avoid being crushed like a bug.

My head struck the headboard of the bed, and before I could think of anything else, the ceiling came down with horrific force.

In an instant, everything became pitch dark and the earth shook with even more fury.

I had no clue exactly what was happening, but there was more rumbling and jolting, as if the whole building—tons of cement and steel—was collapsing on top of me.

Then the shaking was over. Only 15 seconds had passed since I had heard the first thundering sound and opened my eyes.

I shouted as loud as I could.

And in another instant I felt that I was sliding and I knew—*the whole building is tilting!*

I felt myself falling or sliding down from the second-floor apartment to. . .somewhere. . .along with broken pieces of cement, sand and bricks and whatever was left of the room.

In another second I hit the ground very hard, knocking the wind out of me as my back slammed against concrete. The deafening sound hadn't subsided yet, and I knew the upper floors were still falling as the whole structure continued to break apart.

In complete darkness, I felt like I was caught between two massive grinding stones as everything around me was being shifted, pulverized and destroyed. I didn't know what was more deafening, the crashing sound from above me or the sound of churning and explosions coming from underneath the ground.

Now I was flat on my back, and it felt that the vigorous shaking would further break whatever seemed to be two inches above my forehead. Either that or whatever was howling from underneath the ground was about to open its jaws and swallow everything.

As the wild rattling and shaking continued I found myself stuck in a space with cement slabs all around me, and I made my body as stiff as I possibly could to brace for an impact if these slabs should start to press in. By turning just a little to one side I was able to support the slab that was two inches above my head with one shoulder. Pulling out my arms, which were buried under broken bricks and concrete, I instantly realized I didn't even have enough space to support the concrete slab above me with my hands. As that slab continued to shake I applied all my power to hold its weight above me with part of my hands and with my shoulder.

As I pushed up I thought it was the ceiling that had collapsed to about two inches above my forehead. There were six other floors above us, and I did not want the ceiling to settle over my body! With all the energy that I had, I supported the broken ceiling with my right palm and my left shoulder for the next 30 or 40 seconds while the earth continued to shake ferociously without stopping. I had never exerted as much physical power on anything in my life before. My arms trembled and my wrist started to hurt.

When I thought my strength would give out, the intensity of shaking lessened. The roaring sound from underneath the building subsided a little. It was still as loud, but that it was moving away from where I was. Still I used all my waning power to continue to press against the huge slab of ceiling just inches above my body, knowing that if it broke or moved I would be crushed.

In a few more seconds the shaking completely stopped. I could still hear the terrible roaring sound in the distance. And so I remained in the same position for another full minute, until the sound from underneath the ground totally subsided.

Then I tried to listen, but I could not hear anything.

I was engulfed in silence.

I began to shout—for my father, mother, brother. Where were they? Had they gotten out of the building when it started to shake and fall apart? If so they would be worried about me, trying to find me in the rubble.

"Help!" I shouted over and over. *"I'm here. Hello. I'm right here!"*

Lying on my back, pinned under something huge, I shouted as loud as I possibly could.

I did not hear any response.

Very slowly I stopped pressing up on the slab above me with my right arm—carefully, one finger at a time. I needed to be sure that this was not a mistake. What if I stopped holding up whatever was on top of me, and it collapsed suddenly, crushing the life out of me?

As I moved my palm and the fingers one by one I realized that in fact it didn't matter if I supported the ceiling or I did not. It didn't move even a micron.

Very slowly and with extreme caution I disengaged my shoulder from the slab by resting my back on the ground slowly and steadily, as I knew that if there was any part of me supporting the ceiling it was my shoulder.

After I carefully disengaged my shoulder, I now knew that the huge concrete slab did not move anywhere. It seemed to be resting over me, supported by what I did not know.

Now all I was aware of was the pitch-black darkness before my eyes and the rough cement at my back. The smell of dust and crushed cement filled my nostrils.

So. I was alive. But where was my family? They'd all been awake and near to the apartment's door. If they were in the street beside the building they must be frantically looking for me.

"PAPA!" I shouted.

"MOM!"

"BHAI!"

55

"*BACHAO!* (Help!)"

I had to let them know I was okay.

I shouted as loud as I possibly could, lying on my back with dust in my face and mouth. Then I paused to hear if someone answered.

All I experienced was. . .silence. I shouted again. And then again.

I kept shouting. I had to make someone hear me. I imagined my mother standing in the street, wringing her hands and calling for me, my father and brother pulling away slabs of cement, plaster and twisted rebar, searching for me.

Over and over I shouted. But it sounded as if I was in some kind of a closed space that was preventing my voice from going anywhere. It seemed like I was shouting inside a space that was sealed and sound-proof, and as if I was shouting with a pillow on my face.

I continued to shout for help for another minute, staring into the darkness, feeling my words and my breath bouncing back into my face.

I prayed to God, *Please, if my family needs help, save them.* I had no idea where they were and I had no idea where I was either. I had no idea about anything. I thought for a second that maybe I had become blind.

Was the whole building gone?

Was my bedroom the only one that collapsed?

Was I dreaming?

What had just happened?

"No!" I said forcefully. "This is not real. No. It's a nightmare. Wake up, Viral. Wake up."

Then I began coughing, as cement dust clogged my throat and nostrils, assuring me this was very real.

My mind rebelled, and I shouted, "No! This cannot be real!"

I spoke to myself, saying, "I'm sleeping, and I just heard my brother talk about Shalin." I desperately wanted to wake up from this horrible nightmare.

Something in my consciousness did not want to accept that only moments ago I'd been asleep in a comfortable, warm bed. That my family had been chatting happily over breakfast tea and toast. And now I was trapped in what seemed to be a cement coffin.

But I could not be trapped. I'd never been restricted in such severely limiting conditions in my life. I was the guy who was all plans and constant motion.

Suddenly I could not take these thoughts anymore. I wanted to find a way out of this. I wanted to undo what some great force had done to me. *Immediately.*

Closing my eyes I focused hard and tried to hear just something or someone. It seemed as if I was not only in a cement enclosure, but in some kind of a vacuum, as I could not hear anything other than my own voice. It was as if I had gone not only blind but deaf.

I pulled my left arm out from under a bit of rubble and remembered I was wearing my Indiglo (iridium) watch. *Good.* At least the little light would show me where I was, and I carefully slid my arm up my thigh and over my stomach and chest—there was almost no room to do even this—and to pull my wrist up to my chin, so I could glance down at the watch face and check the time. The blue display read 8:49 AM.

Very tightly I clutched both my hands together on my chest and closed my eyes tightly. Once again I thought, this cannot be happening. Such a short time ago, we'd been playing games in the bedroom together as a family. We were going to the beach today...

Once again I prayed. Hard. *Dear God, please! Take care of my father and mother...* I named each one in my family.

Calming a slowly mounting sense of panic, I forced myself to stay still for a few minutes and only prayed. I pressed my eyes closed so tight that my ears had started to make a hollow sound. I only prayed the most sincere prayer of my life.

Please, God, please let my family have escaped the building in time. Please let them be safe out in the street.

These people—my father, mother, brother and sister-in-law and little nephew—they were my whole world. They had to have made it out safely.

They just had to.

6

THE ASSET

*"Do what you can, with what you have,
where you are."*

—THEODORE ROOSEVELT

How much time had passed? I shifted a little, trying to escape the irritation of a sharp piece of rubble that was now digging into my upper back, and listened for the sound of voices, someone—hopefully—moving rubble in search of me. Sounds of anything.

Complete silence.

At least the terrifying rumble and moaning of the shifting earth and toppling building had stopped. But how was I going to get out of this uncomfortable, cramped space. . .wherever this was?

In the pitch-blackness I carefully slipped my arm up over my thigh and stomach, up to my face, took my wristwatch off and pressed the light button. Maybe I could use it like a miniature flashlight to see my tight surroundings.

By now I'd realized that I could barely move anywhere. My body was trapped in what felt like a cement box. If I moved my knees or feet upwards, they touched cement in about three or four inches. My torso and face were likewise just inches from a cement ceiling. I could barely lift my head without bumping my forehead on it. And if I tried to move any of my limbs outward from my body I struck jagged pieces of rubble on either side.

No matter which way I moved I was imprisoned. But maybe there was a way out and I could find it.

Moving the dim blue light of my wristwatch around to examine my enclosure, all I could see was the color gray. In its glow I saw that I was lying on a pile of broken concrete, dust and sand. I was in a space that was barely two feet wide. My left shoulder touched what seemed to be a wall. As I moved the watch toward my right side, I saw that there was a little hollow space toward my right shoulder, which was very narrow and seemed unreachable.

The realization hit me: the space I was in was about a foot in height, and the broken ceiling that was resting above me was only about two inches away from my forehead. This ceiling was at a tilted angle that made a hollow space in the shape of an irregular triangle that was just about 6 or 7 feet in length. There seemed to be a hollow space above the top of my head which, again, seemed unreachable because there was no way I could move an arm up in there to explore it.

My hands could barely pass between my chest and the ceiling above.

Still, I had to explore as best I could.

With my bare feet I began to feel around, feeling little pieces of concrete and broken pieces of bricks. I tried to push the pieces away from me, and as I rubbed the surface with my feet I realized that I was rubbing the bed sheet, which meant that I was still lying on the mattress.

My first thought was, *If I'm still lying in the same position when the ceiling collapsed, then my feet have to be near the cordless phone that was placed on the nightstand.*

Then, *But will the phone work if the whole building has collapsed?*

No matter. *If I can get to it I'll at least have access to the light from its keypad. I have to find the phone. How can I reach it?*

And so I began probing with my feet, hoping the phone might still work and that I might actually find it and get it to my face. . .maybe call someone and let them know I was alive but trapped. With no idea that it was utterly impossible.

In my mind, outside and around me all was well, because, in fact, it was Republic Day for the whole country and all around me—except for whatever had happened to our building—all was well.

The Republic Day in India is the most significant of national holidays, honoring the date on which the Constitution of India came into force on January 26, 1950. Most people were at home in front of their TVs, watching the glorious Republic Day parade as it passed in front of the Rashtrapati Bhavan—the President's residence—and past the India Gate, showcasing the 12 contingents of the paramilitary forces of India. Everyone would be celebrating the military might of India, including thousands of marching soldiers displaying weaponry like tanks and missiles, all passing through the capital city of New Delhi in an extravagant array.

By the light of my watch I could see it was now close to 9:00 AM, the time when the President of India hoisted the national flag. Schools across the nation celebrated this day by conducting a flag-hoisting ceremony, and by distributing sweets to the children.

In short, everyone would be on holiday and at rest. Some relatives would be at home and, if I could just reach them by phone, they could send help.

I was completely unaware, however, of the real situation outside all around me.

Some 16 kilometers under the surface of earth, the Indian tectonic plate that had been pushing against the Eurasian tectonic plates for decades had slipped. "Slipped" being a mild-sounding word, when what had happened was this: When the Indian plate shifted, a major fault-line hundreds of miles long had let go, and a huge area of the Indian subcontinent slid northwards, unleashing megatons of energy, like atom bombs going off in the ground.

The town of Bhuj had been hit by an earthquake of a 7.7 magnitude on the Richter scale, and it was in ruins. There would be no help coming from other places, as big cities in the state of Gujarat, like Ahmedabad, Surat and Vadodara, had also been severely affected. The magnitude of the earthquake was so massive that tremors were felt in various cities across the country. Tremors were reported in Bangalore, which lies some 1,800 kilometers south of Bhuj. Reports of shaking in high-rise buildings were reported as far away as Kolkata, 2,400 kilometers east of Bhuj. Strong tremors were also reported in New Delhi and the financial capital of the country, Mumbai.

Chobari, a village only 70 kilometers away from Bhuj, was the epicenter of the quake. The tremendous shaking had completely flattened Bhachau and Anjar, the two villages that were close to Chobari.

Located this close to the epicenter, Bhuj had been hit by underground blasts and shakings that sent the ground shifting and roiling. Underlayers of rock, dirt and silt were shaken like water, destabilizing everything above them.

Since ours was the tallest building in the town of Bhuj it had collapsed entirely, the floors above pancaking down on the floors below. Two of the wings had fallen to the ground, while part of the building stood broken and tilted, settled over the parking area and ready to crash down to the ground any second.

As I groped with my feet, desperate to find the cordless phone that had been on the nightstand, I had no concept of the reality outside and all around me for many, many kilometers. No thought that I was buried under a complete ruin of cement rubble, tangled steel and shattered plaster and glass.

And certainly no idea that no one would be looking for me for some time. Surely someone was searching for me already—perhaps my family—and I had to let them know where I was.

With singleness of mind I tried to move the broken pieces of cement that I could touch with my toes. Most of the pieces that my toes scraped against were large in size and had sharp edges. While I rubbed my foot against the broken pieces I made sure that I was not disturbing anything that was difficult to move, as it could be supporting the concrete slab resting two inches above my body. Slowly, using my toes, I cleared the small pieces and put them on the side by picking them up carefully. The texture of what I picked up felt like pieces of cement, not bricks. I extended my leg as far as it could reach, and all that my foot touched in the very narrow space were more sharp-edged broken pieces.

Continuing to rub my toes on each of these pieces carefully to see if they moved, it became clear to me that it was going to be difficult to reach where I thought the phone could be. It had only been a few minutes since I'd awakened from my sleep and I still hadn't grasped that what I was experiencing was real.

As I focused on working my way free, the thought constantly played at the back of my mind: *Where was everyone in my family?* I knew that any moment I'd hear them calling for me.

I could not even imagine any of my family members getting hurt, because I thought that it was impossible. I would not even allow such a thought.

"HOW CAN THIS HAPPEN?" I shouted.

My shout bounced off the cement slab inches from my face and blasted me in the ears.

"This can't happen to me!"

"This is NOT real! THIS IS IMPOSSIBLE!" I shouted again.

How could this be real? I wanted to believe this was a nightmare I was going to wake from.

Then we'll go out and have fun at the resort. Yes, that's right, I thought.

Believing in what I thought, I clenched my eyes tightly, and willed myself to fall back into dreamless sleep. Blanketing my psyche with the force of denial I tried not to move. I also tried not to feel the coarse sand and cement shards I was lying on. I was still sleeping on my comfortable bed.

But my mind went back to the loud rumbling sound and the frightening images of wildly shaking objects in the room. I saw the dangling fan and the large metal cupboard wildly tottering and scratching across the floor. Worse, I heard my mother's shout.

No, I thought—*no! I don't want these images in my head.*

But the harder I tried to prevent them, the more I thought about the building shaking, and how I'd been jostled and tossed in the air, and how the ceiling cracked. . .

I had started to sweat, and focused all my energy on directing my mind to one thought only: that when I next opened my eyes, all this was going to be over.

"It is just a bad dream," I said, in a lower tone, thinking that my mother would hear me otherwise and come running from the dining room, wondering why I was shouting in my sleep.

"Nightmares are not real. What I'm experiencing doesn't happen in real life," I said again—and I realized that my voice sounded as if I was speaking in a tight, closed space.

What if this is real? The thought sneaked inside my mind.

So this was going to be a war with my own mind then.

I did not answer that question, and continued to focus on what I was going to do once I woke up to get ready.

On one hand, I was thinking about the shaking building and on the other, I was trying hard to think about what I would do at the resort. This went on for a long, long time, and it became impossible to stop my thoughts from going back and forth. The struggle intensified as I continued to sever undesirable thoughts and focus only on how normal everything would be once I woke up.

A small part of my mind was spent on a sort of "self-defense"—or rather, in defense of the illusion. That part of my mind knew that the smell of cement and dust could shatter my belief, so I took shallow breaths.

As the war waged inside me, it was becoming impossible to have any control over my thoughts. To combat the wild energies of my mind, I tried to relate what I had experienced to my dream life. True, I did not remember any dream from that time, but I tried hard to categorize this as part of a morning dream.

I am going to remember this bad dream—the whole thing—and I will tell some part of it to my mother when I wake up. Still I continued to sweat, as if my emotions and my body were trying to tell my mind to come out of its shock and face the truth. The upper part of my cheeks had started to hurt, too, because I was clenching my eyes shut.

Joining my hands, fingertip to fingertip on my chest, I prayed to God with a mix of nervousness and confidence. Slowly I opened my eyes, hoping to see the little bit of light penetrating through the cotton fabric of the comforter that my father had just covered me with.

All I saw was total darkness.

My mind shouted—*Wake up! Break out of this nightmare.* And I tried to get up by using both my hands as support. My palms landed on broken pieces of bricks and sand, and as I pushed up, my forehead slammed into the concrete slab above.

It was *real*.

With that full understanding, the crushing weight of realization came down on me, like the massive force that brought our building down. It was the most devastating feeling I'd ever faced in my life.

I felt numbness spread from my chest, up my neck, down my torso and out through all my limbs, as the shock took hold.

I was really and truly buried alive. And there was no way out.

My mind went wild.

Where is everyone?

Will they survive?

What happened to the building?

How will I dig my way out?

Along with questions of survival, others blasted through my mind as well.

Where is God?

Why did he allow this to happen?

Did I do something wrong to bring this on myself?

* * *

Thoughts shot through my mind, with great intensity. The strong barrier that was holding these thoughts back could not hold any longer.

I lost control of my mind, very quickly, and felt like my skull was going to break open from the inside.

In a few moments, something deeper inside me managed to seize the reins of thinking. I forced myself to slow my breathing—which had become rapid and shallow—and took a few long, slow, deep breaths.

I remembered then the most basic instruction from my yoga teacher: *Focus your mind on your breath. Keep it there, if it tries to wander—which the mind always does. That's its habit. But your spirit must take charge of your mind.*

And so I forced myself to slow my breathing and keep my mind fixed on keeping it steady—not allowing myself to go into a panic mode. *I have to face this and I have to get out of this.*

In a few more moments—I didn't know how long—I started to feel myself to be in control again.

Hold this steadiness and calm within you. This is base camp.

I shouted at the top of my voice many more times. And this time I paid close attention to what I could hear. All I heard was the eerie, muffled sound of a thick, heavy silence.

Cautiously now, I let myself touch the surface I was lying on with my left hand, which had fallen down next to my thigh. The tips of my fingers and my palm touched the texture of sand granules, and a few broken crumbs of the wall. Then I slid my hand beneath my pelvis and felt what was underneath. I realized that the debris I was lying on were on top of the mattress I had been sleeping on.

From this calm, controlled place I thought: *Don't allow yourself to deal with what happened or why. Deal with what you're going to do to free yourself and find your family.*

And now I knew for sure, neither denial nor panic were options. Staying rational was paramount. I would do nothing without thinking carefully, calmly *first*.

Undergirding my decision was this: I deeply, deeply loved my family. I had to stay alive, either to reunite with them where they were in safety, or to see them through recovery if they'd been injured, or to help rescue them if they were also trapped.

I was not worried about myself, as I somehow felt that I was not in any kind of danger. *Maybe that's denial, too,* I thought.

But even so, I would hold onto that belief. Because, for the sake of my family, I had to survive. I just had to. That was that. The *only* concern I had from that moment on was for my family.

What was I going to do to find them?

So. Survival and escape it would be. That was now determined.

Since I did not know where I was and what had happened to the rest of the building, I started to think about where the bedroom was located in relation to the outside of the building and how close I might be now to the window that did not exist anymore.

In my mind, I started to make a map of our apartment. I had to somehow make my way toward the direction of the window, which, given the direction I was lying in, was toward my feet and about seven to ten feet away.

I'd taken some stock of my enclosure before, but now that calm and determination had set in I needed to do so again. I pressed the red button on my iridium watch and tried to examine it more closely. I held the watch close to the wall that touched my left shoulder.

This was the piece of wall that may have been behind the head-rest of the bed. Barely able to move my arms, I extended my right arm carefully across my chest toward my left shoulder, squeezing it through the narrow space between my chest and the slab a few inches above it. With this uncomfortable maneuver, my right arm barely reached the wall on my left.

Since there was little space to lift my head, I could only turn it to look.

As I moved the watch along the wall, I saw electrical fitting and recognized the white tube-light fixture that had been hanging at least 8 feet above the bed. Broken pieces of the tube light were lying all around me.

My eye landed on a small part of the white aluminum strip

that held the tube light in place. It was mostly buried under the broken pieces of cement.

I switched off the light. This light was the one and only thing that I had, and I wanted to make sure that I did not use up more battery than I needed.

Besides taking stock of my situation, my mind seemed to be in search of something.

What are you looking for? I asked myself.

Assets. Something—anything—that can help me.

I tried to feel the texture of the sand that I was lying on. It was very difficult to raise my back and sweep the particles from underneath my back. Very carefully, I tried to feel what I was lying on. As I suspected, my left elbow and my entire back rested on sharp broken pieces of glass.

Okay, I also need to be careful not to hurt myself as I work to get out of here.

The glass, of course, could slash me if I started to thrash, or even if I moved cautiously.

In the darkness, I tried to feel the texture of every surface that my hands could reach. I then slowly slid my left hand under my back as I started to very cautiously move the small and sharp glass pieces out from under me one by one. If they pierced my skin I would start bleeding.

If a calm mind is an asset, my uninjured body is, too.

Slowly, carefully, I focused on removing the glass pieces.

In this process I began sweating and breathing faster. I started to think about oxygen. How much was there in this space? Was there enough? Would it run out? How quickly would I use it up if I didn't control my intake?

I didn't know for sure, but oxygen itself might be another asset. I had to be careful about using it. . .and not using it up.

My breathing slowed. Again, my mind took charge. *Monitor your breathing. Keep it slow, steady, even.*

And now what?

I thought about the broken tube-light rail that was still stuck to the wall. Maybe that was the tool—the asset I needed. Maybe I could use that piece of metal to dig myself out of this trap.

I had to move pieces of glass and cement to make the tube-light strip accessible. When I could feel it more completely, it was still nailed to the wall. This confirmed that the walls of the room had already broken to pieces and that the ceiling had fallen to the floor.

As I felt along the metal stripe I thought, *If the power is still on I could get electrocuted.*

Still, I had to try to free this piece and try to use it as a tool of my escape. Gripping the metal rail, I gave it a jerk.

Rather than pulling free, it bent. Yanking again, I realized that it was nailed to the wall and had a very strong hold.

As I pulled, my mind kept track of my breathing, making sure I didn't breathe more than necessary.

I began to practice holding my breath for about 30 seconds or so, while I pulled on the metal fixture. . .then stopping and breathing in a relaxed, normal manner for a few seconds.

After a few rounds of this, the rail broke loose.

A small victory.

What I had in my hand now was an eight-inch long and three-inch wide twisted piece of aluminum.

This was the first thing that had worked in my favor since the time I had woken up.

I now knew that I had two assets: a mind that was calm, and a tool that I could use to dig myself out.

7

THE TOTE BAG

*"What one has, one ought to use;
and whatever he does, he should do
with all his might."*

— CICERO.

Buildings in India are constructed in a very different way than, say, in the U.S. No wood is used. Instead, bricks, cement and concrete are the main building materials. The walls in a house are typically made of cement and large heavy bricks. These brick and mortar walls are then plastered with a half-inch thick layer of cement and sand on either side, then covered with a coat of paint. The ceilings and pillars are made of reinforced steel and concrete, which are the heaviest parts of the structure.

All of this—tons and tons of debris—lay directly above me. That was one thought.

Would there be aftershocks? There were always aftershocks in an earthquake. Would one come and unsettle the slab that lay so precariously balanced just inches above my face and body? These thoughts I had to push away.

What I did know was that time was running out. Soon I would need more oxygen.

I tried to feel the edges of the piece of aluminum in my hand. It wasn't sharp or heavy, and I was not sure how this piece was going to help me. I could not imagine being able to break the wall with it. Only time would tell if it was going to be a useful resource.

This is all you have, I thought, knowing that I had to make the best possible use of what was given to me.

Once again I switched on my little wristwatch light, and made sure that all the pieces of glass were cleared from where my left arm rested. I gathered the pieces one by one, putting them as far as possible toward my thigh, or into the small cavities by the wall.

I would have to start digging away with my new tool.

Turning and raising my head again, I tried to see the fallen wall to my left. I could slide my right arm across my chest—barely—and start to dig with the aluminum piece.

My left arm was not going to be of any use, as my shoulder was too close to the wall, and there was no space to bend it toward the wall. In the dim light it was extremely difficult to see, and in only a few minutes I had to drop my head back to the ruined mattress, as my neck had started to hurt.

While I lay there preparing to dig I could not help thinking about my family. Each image that came to mind felt like a sharp needle that pierced my soul.

Where were they? How were they?

"Nothing is going to happen to them. They would have escaped," I said out loud. I had to assure myself of that.

Focus, Viral! the inner voice commanded. *You have to find your way out as quickly as possible.*

The only wall accessible to me was the one touching my left shoulder. It was not one of the outside walls of the building and I thought that there was probably another apartment on the other side of that wall before it collapsed. I had no choice but to start breaking through *that* wall, though, hoping that I would be able to access another hollow space, where there was more oxygen, or maybe access to light.

I moved myself as close as possible to the wall on my left by picking my torso up and making sure that my back didn't scratch against any of the glass pieces underneath that I might have missed. Squeezing my right arm between the ceiling and my chest I touched the wall with some difficulty.

The wall was smooth to the touch. I was trying to find out if there was any spot where the top layer of cement had cracked. The surface of the wall felt smooth all over.

With all my energy and strength, I started scraping the wall near my shoulder with the rough side of the aluminum strip. The scratching made a very unpleasant sound.

Holding my breath, I scraped the wall as hard as I could manage.

My first goal was to make a small hole in the wall to get some fresh air. At the same time I was aware that I was trying to break the only wall that was holding the concrete slab above my body.

And so two forces inside me began to clash. One said, *You could bring tons of cement and steel down on you,* while the other said, *Work harder. You may not have much time.*

And then there was the voice of futility that spoke out of the pitch-darkness. *Do you really think you can get through solid concrete with this flimsy metal?*

Within the next minute I had to lay my head back and stop scratching, as my neck started to hurt. But I could barely touch the wall with the metal piece if I did not hold my head up to get closer to the wall. After I took a break for a few seconds, I pulled my head back up. Only focusing on scraping and scratching the wall helped divert my focus from the hundreds of questions that plagued me, like a dizzying cloud of terrible gnats.

What if someone from my family is hurt?

What if they need your help and here you are, unable to get to them?

No, I shouted silently in response.

What if you're the only one who can help—and here you are, helpless yourself?

I have to get out of here first and save them! But wait—that's not right. They're all fine. They have to be.

Yes, they *had* to be fine. They were my family.

I continued to scratch the wall for the next few minutes, trying hard not to think of anything else. Each time I made a go at the wall I had to touch and examine the surface of the wall to see if it was helping.

So far I had been able to scratch some paint off the wall. How long was this going to take? The wall had to be about six inches thick, and since I could barely even reach it with my right hand, there was no possibility of applying more pressure.

Thoughts about an old movie came to mind, one in which the actor escaped from a coffin after being buried alive. But I also remembered that he was able to escape only because there was a prebuilt passage from the coffin.

I am buried in a concrete coffin and I probably have the whole building resting just two inches above my body. And the wall you're scratching at could collapse at any minute. The thought, which I hadn't entertained until this moment, was instantly unnerving.

The strange thing was that I didn't feel scared. I was angry, and I wanted to get out of this jam.

But I realized something: I could allow certain thoughts to take over my mind—fearful and despairing ones—and then my own mind would become an enemy of my survival. Or I could keep watch over my thoughts, sift and sort them carefully, and choose to focus only on the positive, helpful ones.

This seemed of critical importance.

It was a realization that came none too soon, because right now my mind was starting to serve me a story that I had heard long before. A gruesome tale.

Some people had installed a bell outside the grave of their deceased loved one, and one end of the string connected to that bell was left inside the coffin. They had done this because they had heard an urban legend about an unearthed casket. According to that legend, it was discovered that the inner lid of the casket had scratch marks on the inside. Scraped paint and wood were found in the corpse's nails. Hearing this legend, they had installed a bell so that their deceased relative would have a string to pull to indicate that he was not dead yet, but had revived.

To me, at the time I'd heard the story, it did not make any sense to have a bell above anyone's grave. I had laughed at it and made jokes about it.

Now I realized that I was in the same situation of the man inside the coffin. I had a choice. I could focus on the gruesome details of the story, the terror of a man locked in a buried casket. Or on something else my mind seemed to be presenting to me...

You need a signal, Viral. That's what you need. A sort of "bell." A way to let others know you are alive in case someone is searching for you.

So, there it was. A piece of guidance, tossed up into my consciousness by my memory. I would throw out thoughts of death and coffins and keep the pearl that came out of the darkness.

All right. I'll keep at it.

Almost an hour had passed since the earthquake. I continued to take breaths at 30-second intervals while I scratched and exerted more pressure on the wall, my right elbow and arm scraping the ceiling.

I had to keep scratching the same spot, which was difficult because I couldn't see. With some difficulty I rested my left-hand thumb on a specific spot on the wall. I had to scratch roughly about 3 inches above my thumb now. I made sure I did not move my thumb while I scratched energetically with the other hand. Both my hands now were engaged while I held my breath, and while my forehead touched the ceiling. I wished that I just had enough room to punch the wall with all the energy that I had.

While I scratched, a new set of questions started to swirl in my head and bother me again.

I'd continued to stop and sniff the air, to see if it was growing staler. But in fact I had no idea what carbon dioxide smelled like, and all I could smell was cement dust anyway. But how much time did I have before the oxygen ran out?

How many cubic feet of air does a human inhale in one hour?

How many times could one use the same air?

How many cubic feet of space do I have?

A plague of questions to keep at bay. And no answers. I could guess that I roughly had about 12 to 15 cubic feet of air.

What is the use of calculating? That won't help you. Act.

When I lifted my head back up, this time I felt that my abdominal muscles had just started to hurt a little. I knew it was going to hurt more if I continued to keep my head in the air for a long time.

Dad will get me out of here as soon as he can, I assured myself. Undoubtedly, he was outside the building, clearing away rubble to find me. He and Roshan together.

I would be out of here soon. But I needed to keep signaling where I was.

Once again when I touched the wall, I could feel the loose sand particles on the wall surface. It seemed to be working, and I knew that I needed to apply more power while scraping. The real work was to break the plastered cement, and then to break through the bricks. I knew that I had to do it.

By now, though, I was starting to exhaust myself and I was sweating a little. Stretching my arm, I scratched the wall again without lifting my head up this time. I made sure not to forget about my breathing cycles.

With more power, I scraped the same focused area, and I also scraped other parts of the wall that my arm could reach without taking any more breaks. It was a matter of life and death for me. I would have given anything in exchange for a hammer and chisel. . .but again, I had to push that thought aside.

Another wave of thoughts came at me. If I ran out of oxygen I would go unconscious. And then. . .

No.

Instead of allowing fear to arise from this thought, I would use it as a motivation to work harder.

For the next hour I scraped with as much force I possibly could, and as fast as I could without taking any breaks more than a few seconds long. I sniffed and examined the air during these short breaks. Occasionally I shouted, and then I worked harder every passing minute. I did not even take the time to wipe the moisture off from my forehead.

Any time a thought tried to rise I pushed it aside and continued to work like a machine. . .scratching into a strong cement wall with a tool I thought was worthless.

When I finally stopped I touched the wall and tried to gauge my progress. I was expecting to touch granules of sand and some cement breaking apart.

But as I felt along the wall as far as I could reach, there was not so much as an indentation. Running the dim blue light of the wristwatch an inch away from the wall all I could see were some haphazard scratches.

Mere scratches, where I had been scraping with all my energy for more than an hour.

Scratches that looked like fingernail scratches inside a coffin.

I forced that thought from my mind.

I lay back in the pitch-darkness again. I couldn't believe it. It had been more than two hours since the earthquake, and all I was able to do was to make some scratch marks on one side of the wall. It felt that if should I entertain even one hopeless thought, the breath would be crushed out of me. I could not let this happen. I could not let even a single negative thought grab hold of me. That would surely be the end.

Easier said than done.

At that instant I wanted to shout in frustration, but I couldn't allow myself to do that.

Conserve energy! I commanded myself.

For the first time it occurred to me: *Maybe this is going take much longer than I thought for me to get out of this mess.*

I lay back with my eyes wide open, trying to think fast about what I could do next. How much time did I have, if the oxygen was going to run out? How was my family doing? Were they hurt and needing my help? Or standing outside, anxious about my welfare?

I was starting to feel desperate to get out, or at least to find a way to let someone know that I was alive. I could not waste energy becoming frustrated over the fact that I had not been able to make any progress. It was a difficult task to think with a sharp focus knowing that I had just lost—I now saw by my watch—two crucial hours, and that I had failed to make so much as a mark on a barrier that was more powerful than I'd thought.

I started to touch the surroundings that I had not touched before. I extended my right arm toward my shoulder, and continued to feel the broken pieces for the next few minutes. Once I switched the light on, I saw that there was a deep cavity a few inches away from the top of my scalp.

I remembered that my tote bag was kept in a shelf a few feet away from the bed. I thought that if the entire floor had collapsed and fallen to the ground, the bag would still be at the same distance from me. There was a chance that thrusting an arm up through the cavity could lead me to the tote bag. And I recalled that I had a cellphone in the side compartment of that bag.

I turned toward my right side, and I cleared the small brick and cement pieces blocking the cavity. Reaching my hand up, I could feel that the size of the opening was like a rat hole in the ground. I switched the light on and craned my neck to look up at it.

Pulling my body closer toward the cavity, then, slowly, extending and twisting my arm just right, I was able to thread my hand inside the hole.

As soon as I did my mind recoiled, and instinctively I pulled my hand out.

What if there's a poisonous reptile or snake in there? My mind shouted, making the skin all over my body tingle and crawl. After all, India was famous for its hidden nests of cobras.

Even though I knew that our building was in a town and not a jungle, it seemed as if the darkness and the size of the hole were triggering all my survival instincts.

79

What was I going to do now? Suppose all that lay between me in my cement prison and the cellphone that might summon my rescuers was. . .fear?

I calmed myself again, and returned to the quiet, calm space within my mind. For long minutes I refused all thoughts, and left myself open.

Never fear the unknown.

Out of the silence, the thought struck me. This was something that my father taught us. He would say this when any of his children were resisted a new or unsettling situation.

With that thought I slowly extended my hand inside the small, dark hole again, and I found I could only reach in about 6 to 8 inches in. Stretching, I tried to probe. Snakes be damned.

Now I touched the inside edges of the hole, and felt the edge of a piece that clogged the entryway. I tried to move it with my middle finger and then with my index finger. It was a big piece, and seemed immovable.

Finally pushing it aside, I tried to reach in deeper, which meant stretching my torso more. I tried not to think of broken shards of glass I might have missed beneath me.

After moving aside more broken pieces of brick and cement inside the hole, the realization came.

There was no way to clear enough debris to allow myself to reach any further. All the rest of the pieces, which I could trace with my fingers, were large—*at least a foot long and wide*, I thought, and who knew how thick? I couldn't budge another piece. Still, I stretched as hard as I could—still trying to keep my breathing in check—hoping my hand might touch the nylon texture of my tote bag.

In another minute, however, I knew this effort was fruitless. And my shoulder burned from all the stretching.

Pulling my hand out of the hole, I seized a sharp piece of hard rubble and brought it down to my side.

At least I had one more asset: a harder tool to use in my escape efforts.

The shard felt strong in my hand. Much stronger and more reassuring than the flimsy metal piece, which I'd abandoned.

My determination mounted again.

Closing my eyes tightly, I hit the wall with the shard, using as much force as possible.

The moment the piece of cement collided with the wall, it crumbled into pieces, leaving me with only a few small fragments in my hand. Small pieces splattered on my face, too, into my eyes and mouth, making me blink and spit.

And at that moment, a low sound began. A sound so deep it began with a rumble at my back, and slowly filled my small chamber like mounting thunder.

It was the sound I'd heard at the beginning of the earthquake!

"OH GOD!" I shouted.

Instantly, I tried to turn onto one side and fold my legs up, to draw myself into a fetal position. If one of the huge slabs above me settled down on my unprotected torso it would be fatal.

In seconds, the sound grew louder and the ground once again started to shake. My body was pitched from side to side and I felt a surge of terror.

Any second, I knew, the slabs above me would crack, and it would be over for me.

Then came the most terrifying sound. From deep beneath me, in the earth, a monstrous noise crawled past below me. It felt and sounded as if something huge and malign was churning right underneath me.

Still the shaking continued and, instinctively, I turned and braced my shoulder against the concrete slab above me. —At the same moment my mind said, *Do you really think you can keep tons of cement from crushing you if they let loose and collapse?*

Forcing this terrifying thought from my mind I willed myself to think of a better possibility.

Maybe this aftershock will shake open a hole in the rubble, and I can crawl out of here.

The enclosure continued to shake wildly, and I braced for the inevitable—whatever that would be. There was no sound of things falling to the ground or glass breaking this time, and the unmistakably loud churning sound from underneath the ground continued.

And then the intensity of the aftershock lessened. In a few more seconds the shaking subsided, and then it finally stopped. For a few long moments, I could hear the churning sound moving on beneath me into the distance, sounding very much like a supersonic jet passing by.

Then all was quiet as before.

I relaxed, tentatively, and took stock. It seemed like the aftershock lasted for about 20 seconds. Even though the shaking was not as intense as the earthquake, "aftershock" was an insignificant word for a geological event as big as what I had just experienced.

I lay still, calming my breathing, wondering.

How much time do I have before the next shock comes? And when it comes, will it finish the job?

Somehow I could see father's face again. Think what he would think. *No. Get a hold of your mind and emotions again, Viral.*

Almost mechanically, I picked up the piece of metal and started to scrape at the wall again. I ignored the fact that my mind was shouting at me—that what I was doing was like trying to cut through a sheet of steel with a piece of wood.

No matter. I *would* do what I had to and get out of here.

And I would fend off the forces inside, which were trying to mount again and overwhelm rationality—the ones that were trying to tell me otherwise. Another aftershock was surely on its way. It was just a matter of when, and how intense it would be.

But if I was going to find my family, I would have to keep fighting. . .against this immoveable wall. . .against time.

8

PLAN

*"Recognizing what we have done
in the past is a recognition of ourselves.
By conducting a dialog with our past,
we are searching how to go forward."*

-KIYOKO TAKEDA

What was going to get me out of this trap?

A memory returned, unbidden:

Vasanta was a very thin man. He was short, and he had notice-ably large, gleaming white teeth. That is all I remembered about him from when I was about five years old. Except that he was also a kind man, who made his living by driving the cycle rickshaw, and who pedaled us to school each day.

Vasanta would pick up kids from their homes in the morning, and then pedal us to the school, which was about a half-hour away. He would push hard on the pedals with his very thin legs, and with all his energy and might, sweating, yet always smiling and showing off his gleaming teeth.

I was never happy to see Vasanta in the morning, however, because I never liked school. One morning, in particular, was imprinted in my mind.

It was a pleasant morning in the spring, and Vasanta was waiting outside our home for me and Roshan. He was wearing dark-colored shorts and a yellow shirt, which had a printed design of blue and brown buffalos. He had already picked up several other children, and Roshan had dashed out ahead of me and taken his seat.

Mother had fussed over me, washing my face, smoothing my face, and I was ready in my school uniform: navy blue shorts and a white shirt, with a small backpack full of books and a water bottle hanging around my shoulder.

"I don't want to go to school," I said, frowning as I held the schoolbag in my hand and slumped unwillingly toward the rickshaw.

My mother let out an exasperated huff. "Same thing *every* day! Be quick now. Vasanta is waiting for you!" She seized my other hand and rushed me toward the main gate of our home, where the terrible rickshaw awaited.

"I really *don't want to go*, Mom!"

"I will tell your father if you continue to bother every day!"

Painfully, I dragged my small body onto the rickshaw, joining Roshan, and then waved at my mother with a sad face as Vasanta began to push hard on the pedals. We moved down the driveway, as Mother shook her head and waved.

We picked up speed, and street scenes flowed past. Other children walking to school. Men walking dogs. A local milkman balancing large cans on his bicycle, the newspaper delivery boy returning home, other rickshaws passing full of kids, and people waiting for the bus at the local bus station. I was sad, and I did not talk to anyone. I only continued to think about what I could do to avoid going to school. On one hand, I was scared of my father, who was very strict, and on the other, I had to get out of this going-to-school thing at all costs. I didn't know what to do.

Being a five or so years old, I knew that it was now impossible to go back home. I continued to sit with a sad face. The little heart inside me was in tremendous pain. The thought of Vasanta leaving us at school made me extremely sad, and I pressed my eyes shut to keep the tears from rising. I wanted to stay at home and play.

Within the next few minutes on the rickshaw, almost halfway to our destination, I knew I was indeed going to school despite my heartfelt wish. The pain of going to school grew much larger than the fear of my father and mother scolding me. At that moment, I decided I was most definitely *not* going to school that day.

I wanted to jump out of the rickshaw, but I realized I did not know my way back home. It was a busy road, and we were being passed by all sorts of motorized vehicles. I now had only one choice.

"Vasanta! Take me back," I ordered, with a sad face. "I want to go home!" My lip was trembling, and I was about to cry.

"No, Viral *Bhai*, you have to go to school. Your mother told me to drop you there," he said. Then his eyes got wide, as he looked back and saw me standing.

The other kids in the rickshaw looked at me as if I was committing a horrible crime.

"Be careful, and sit down in your seat or else you will hurt yourself," Vasanta ordered, as he continued to pedal.

"I want to go home! I just want to go *home*, Vasanta!" I cried.

"I cannot take you back to your home Viral *Bhai*. Your mom would shout at me. And fire me! She will get very angry with you, too," Vasanta insisted, pedaling faster.

I stood holding a horizontal metal rod that was part of the rickshaw frame. Standing up on the wobbly and rapidly moving rickshaw felt extremely unstable and dangerous because it was an open carrier. It felt as if I could fall to the ground any moment. My knees shook, and my hands trembled, but all I could think of was the dreaded school.

I knew now that *I* had made up my mind. Vasanta's refusal did not sway me in the least. Besides, he was of lower social stature and most certainly did not make up my mind for me. That was the way things were in India.

Vasanta continued moving the rickshaw forward, and I stood and crept up behind him. Clutching his hair in my little hands, I pulled.

"Take me home! I want to go home!" I shouted.

Vasanta shouted in surprise and pain, and the rickshaw veered wildly.

The gap between the sitting area and the driver was very large for me, and I looked down at the moving ground beneath, almost losing my balance.

"Viral, sit down!" Roshan shouted angrily.

Before Vasanta could react, I leaned over and pulled his shirt with both my hands to stop him from pedaling. The shirt tore, and he shouted in pain and anger as he struggled to stop safely alongside the road.

I pulled his shirt more as I continued to cry and shout. The shirt was now torn, way beyond what I could have imagined. His back was now naked, and the thin cotton cloth hung at his waist in shreds.

"What did you do!" he shouted, parking the rickshaw.

"I want to go home! I don't want to go to school!" I cried.

He looked at his shirt, now in tatters.

I don't have another shirt!" he said, furious and maintaining his distance from me.

Then he approached warily. "I will take you back home! Just sit down back there and don't hit me!" he said, turning the rickshaw around.

Crying, I sat down in the seat, making sure that I was indeed being taken toward the direction of our home.

"Vasanta! What are you doing?" Roshan said, as he saw him making a U-turn to go back.

"Roshan *Bhai*, I have to take him back home, or else he will not let me go on to school," Vasanta replied. "I will drop all of you back to school after I take him home."

None of the other kids said anything. From the angry glares I was receiving I thought they were never going to talk to me again.

As soon as we reached our gate, Vasanta said, "You can get off here. Now let me tell your mother what you have done to me," he added, getting off the rickshaw.

Both of us walked toward the main door of our home, while I heard the other kids laughing at me from behind. Vasanta rang the doorbell of my home while trying to hold the torn pieces of his shirt behind his now naked torso.

When Mother answered his knock, Vasanta explained everything that had taken place in the past half-hour. Her expression went from surprised to shocked. I don't remember what he said or what my mom replied. I only remember that I was very happy to be back at home. All I wanted now was to hear my mom agreeing to let me stay at home.

She did. And Vasanta quickly left after the brief conversation.

From the look on her face I knew that my mother was very angry. She scolded me many times and asked me swear to never do that again.

"You will have to clean other people's homes and do other people's dishes if you don't study! Do you understand that?"

"I don't mind doing dishes, Mom, but I don't want to go to school. I feel very sad without you."

"I am going to tell your father everything tonight. And I know that he is going to be very angry with you."

I was scared of my father. I spent the rest of the day playing, hoping that my mother would not tell him anything.

But when Roshan returned from school that afternoon, he told my mother what I had done to Vasanta, step by step.

"If I had done this, you would have scolded me. But just because he is younger, he gets to do whatever he likes.

"He didn't even come to school today. And I had to go to school because I don't complain."

That evening, once I returned from the playground, my father called for me. While I stood in front of him, he stared deep into my eyes, with a severe look.

"Will you ever repeat this behavior?" he asked.

Whatever my father had said to me—I don't recall exactly— had hit a mark deep inside. I was chastened, meek, and fearful of displeasing him again.

I replied, "No."

Vasanta came the next day to pick me up for school, wearing another shirt. He was a poor man, and buying another shirt was certainly an unwanted expense. My mom called him inside and made me gift a new shirt to him and apologize.

Vasanta smiled, and accepted my apology. All was forgiven and soon forgotten.

But not entirely forgotten—not by me anyway.

This very small incident from my early life had played a big part in the way I interpreted and understood the world around me. It had shaped the way I thought about myself, which was this:

If I wanted something and if I had the courage to follow through, I had the ability to find a way. I also had learnt another important lesson that day. If I believed in myself, impossible was possible.

It had also taught me that I was more effective when I was desperate.

These beliefs had become a big part of the foundation of my being. And that time on, the more experience I gathered, the stronger I became and I started to believe in myself much more. Deep down I had learned to believe, respect and trust my own actions.

And now. . .

Lying flat on my back, in utter darkness, trapped, I had no control over the situation. Nonetheless, I truly believed I would be able to find a way out. I knew it was possible. I also knew the situation would not have control over me for much longer, that I would soon be in control. I knew all of this as if it was a *fact*.

What I didn't know was *how* I was going to gain control and *make it* happen.

There is something inside us that tells us things, sends us signals, and guides us. This sense, which lies inside all of us, is always at work, giving us the cues. I think that each one of us experiences a time when you say to yourself, "I knew that!" and you couldn't explain how you knew that.

I was getting a very clear signal that nothing was going to happen to me. The signal to me was so strong that I did not even question it. Even though there was no one to put their hand on my head and say that I was going to survive. I knew that I was going to be okay, I didn't know how.

And yet I knew that on a practical level, in order to do my *karma*, I had to find a source of oxygen.

The *feeling* of being trapped was not helping. My infrequent breaths that bounced off from the ceiling continued to remind me of the limitation I faced. I was desperate to break free, and could feel again the energy of that little boy who'd felt trapped in a rickshaw wanting to cut loose.

But losing control in here would be the worst thing. I had to keep my mind from going wild with anxiety and overtaking my body. I had to somehow keep my rebellious side tamed, because something told me that the escape was going to take some time.

It was now close to noon – three hours into my ordeal. It had been some time since I had started to feel a burning sensation in my stomach. My mouth had also started to become dry. I was not sure how I was going to handle hunger and thirst.

While I continued to scratch at the wall with a shard of rubble, my thoughts now kept going back to the growing discomfort the burning sensation was causing. I could easily bear hunger for a long time, and it never bothered me before. But now, I could not think of anything that would make the burning sensation go away. Every few minutes the growling sound in my stomach reminded me that it had been more than 14 hours since I'd had anything to eat or drink. The growling was beyond my control.

I called on that gut determination I had learned in the course of my life. I'd find *something* to eat and drink to get me through this.

Sliding my hand beneath my back I took a pinch of cement and dust in my fingers. I touched it carefully to make sure there were no glass pieces in it. Then I put that little pinch of grit in my mouth.

I had eaten soil during my childhood and I knew how it tasted, but I had never tried eating cement before. I wasn't thinking that it had any nutritional value, just that ingesting a tiny bit might stop the discomfort in my stomach.

The pinch of sand crystals and cement that was now in my mouth felt much worse than what I had expected. It was tasteless and inedible.

I can chew it, I thought while I did not want to give up.

As I tried to chew slowly, the sound and feel of crushing the sand crystals between my teeth was very unpleasant, and I realized this was going to chip my teeth if I tried to chew any harder. So I tried biting down with my molars on the granules in my mouth.

That did not help either.

Even if it works, you'll end up clogging your intestines. Give it up.

I wiped the mess off my tongue with part of my T-shirt.

Still, I would have to deal with the hunger and thirst somehow—and soon. The rumbling in my stomach was becoming a dull ache.

The thought that now came to mind was about the *Guinness Book of World Records*. I had watched the *Guinness Book* series a few years ago on television. I remembered a record holder who could eat pieces of glass and scrap metal, and who held the record of consuming a real truck in a few months' time. How could someone consume all parts of a truck, made of metal, glass, rubber and everything else?

I knew that I was wearing clothes that were mostly made of cotton fabric, a watch made of metal, plastic and rubber, a silver bracelet, a golden ring, and a gold chain. I also had the aluminum strip that I was using to scratch the wall.

I was aware that none of it was edible, but I knew that someone had successfully eaten such things in the past.

I should have trained myself to eat everything like those record holders, I thought in desperation.

At the back of my mind there was guilt. I knew that someone from my family could be in trouble, just like I was. Maybe someone was struggling between life and death, and I was thinking about hunger?

How could I? How could I even think about food in such a situation? I felt ashamed.

"I am not hungry. It is just a burning sensation in the stomach. And I don't care about it," I told myself.

How was I going to get out of this?

At this time, it was not just a matter of deciding to take action, like tearing Vasanta's shirt. None of my physical actions were helping. I needed to focus all my energy into how I was going to find my family, or let them know that I was alive.

There was one thing that seemed to be working for me, though. I was getting more convinced that the air around me was not getting diminished. Even though I did not know what used air smelled like I knew that I was not feeling suffocated in any way. Yet, at least. I knew that I had used up all the air in this enclosure many times over in the past few hours.

The burning sensation in my stomach had gone down some by itself during the next few minutes. I tried not give it too much attention. I shouted a few more times, and I continued to scratch with even more energy. I also prayed for the wellbeing of my family.

As time passed, it was becoming more and more difficult to control the rebellious mind inside me. Contradictions within me were starting to mount. I was fighting with my own self every single second. One part of my mind wanted to break everything apart, and the other part of my mind knew that it was not physically possible, and thus stopped me from repeatedly exerting pressure and wasting energy by trying to push the slab above me.

In desperation, I picked up big pieces of mortar out of the debris and started hitting the side of the concrete wall with all of my energy to make some noise. Most of it broke to pieces and fell all over my face and body. It was not helping.

What should I do? *What if I die of suffocation*, I thought, even though I did not truly believe that thought.

Before I could kill this thought, very quickly a chain reaction of negative thoughts started inside my mind. Instantly, dozens of thoughts rushed inside my mind, about my life, my family, and about my relatives and my friends. The only possessions I had.

My mother would die of pain. My father would break down. How would they handle it? Would anyone be able to find my body? My friends would be shocked. How would my grandmother handle this? And the thoughts continued.

The chain of negative thought lasted only for a few seconds before I stopped myself, but it seemed as if my body loosened up, and it had suddenly become vulnerable to the negative feelings. I felt as if the energy inside me was squeezed out in an instant. It took just one negative thought to cause all this.

I wiggled my toes just to make sure I had control over my whole body. I touched my head and ran my palm around my hair.

The last few seconds had made me realize the potential of a single negative thought. Negative thoughts were like mud swamps that had the ability to drown me if I tried to test them. Negative thought were dangerous. I had to be extremely cautious about my thoughts, which meant killing every single negative thought before it could enter my mind.

It wasn't going to be easy. The only freedom I had was to be able to think; I now had to control that, too.

Ever since the earthquake struck, so many things were running in my mind that I was unable to clearly focus on anything. I was now starting to understand that I needed to have a clear focus, and I needed a plan in place. That is how I always functioned.

If you don't have a clear plan in place, you will have no control over your thoughts or the situation, I told myself.

I had no clue how or what I was going to plan. All I knew was that this was the time to put a plan in place.

All I needed now was a clear focus. A sharp focus, just like what I had seen in my father.

9

FOCUS

"Who touched the nail clipper?" my father called.

I ran upstairs to his bedroom and saw that he was standing in front of the dresser.

"I used it," I said meekly. How on earth had he known? It wasn't like I'd dropped it carelessly on the floor.

"You should put something back in place exactly the way it was kept before."

I was amazed. It wasn't that my father was a tyrannical perfectionist. It was that I'd set the clippers down maybe a millimeter from where he'd laid them. And because of his incredible powers of focus and observation he knew someone had used them.

Many times I was awed by this gift in my father—the ability to be super-focused and highly aware.

Sitting miles away, and while on phone, if my father had to give directions about finding something he needed, his directions would go something like this:

"Go into the basement, walk toward the area where there are various shelves. Look to your left, on the second shelf from the top, you will see a cardboard box. Open that box, pull the fourth file out from the stack on the right. Now read out the number that is printed at the bottom of the second page in the file. Then make sure that you put everything back *exactly* where you found it."

That was my father. Sharp, focused and acutely aware that things worked smoothly *if* you observed order and you were sharp in the way you handled yourself. Chaotic thinking meant disarray and quite possibly disaster.

Why was this image of my father coming to me right now, though? What was it trying to tell me?

At the moment, my muscles were cramping a bit, I was possibly running out of oxygen and my hunger pains were increasing. My thoughts were going in all directions. Thinking of my dad I knew that what I needed at this time was a sharp focus and the kind of clear mind that I had seen in him all through my life.

Who knew what might happen next? I had to get out of here, quickly.

During the next five to six hours I anticipated another aftershock, and the more time passed, the more I was tempted to lose focus and become anxious.

Over and over I tried all the things I'd tried before. What else was there to do but keep trying? I scratched the wall with all the power that I had. I continued to control my breathing. I once again examined the surroundings. I had searched for the cordless phone, my tote bag and the cellphone many more times. I frequently smelled the air to check if it felt any more stale and diminished. I shouted dozens of times. And whenever I took a break from scratching the wall I tried to push the ceiling above me with all my might.

With each failed attempt I grew more frustrated and edgy.

At some point an image of my whole family arose. And with it the thought: *They may be struggling for life at this time. . .or maybe everyone is outside moving concrete pieces and desperately trying to find me.*

My breath stopped. The thought about my family made me freeze once again. Anxiety twisting in my stomach, I joined my hands together above my chest and I prayed fervently for their safety and wellbeing. I prayed to God, even though I was furious at what he had allowed to happen.

And while I prayed I was frustrated, not because I was trapped but because I couldn't do anything more than pray for my family. I felt torn: it felt so futile and yet I also felt it was important to do it.

While I prayed, with my eyes tightly closed, I once again secretly wished that when I reopened them everything would return to normal, and I would find myself lying in my comfortable bed. Maybe it was still possible that all this was just a bad dream.

When I opened them, of course, I found myself lying in the rubble, exactly where I was before. Even though I had expected this outcome, it was heartbreaking. I felt as if I was repeatedly pleading to God to take me back to a normal life, while he did not want to listen.

Now an irritable voice sounded inside. "How many times do you want to be assured that it is real?" I whispered to myself in frustration.

More time passed, and I was tired. It was difficult to understand why I was unable to make even a dent on the wall in the past so many hours. All of my physical efforts were going to waste.

I had spent a lot of time and energy thinking, but every thought ended due to the limitations that I faced. None of the ideas or thoughts were further pursued after realizing that I lacked something. The cramped space, zero visibility, hunger, thirst, and the limited air to breathe stopped me from thinking further. All I had was darkness, my own self and my thoughts. And the harder I tried and the more my mind jumped from idea to idea, the more wretched I felt that I could not come up with anything that would help me in any way—other than controlling my breaths.

Unbelievably—even to me, in a way—as my sense of helplessness continued to mount, I continued to look for the tiniest bit of success and my confidence remained unshaken. I only concentrated on thinking how I could resolve the situation.

As I continued to focus on my escape, my mind started to present stories from the movies I'd seen. A thought from the movie *Superman* passed through my head: In one rescue scene Superman effortlessly saves a young woman who is falling from a tall building, and then saves a helicopter from falling off the same skyscraper by catching it in one hand, and the woman in another. He then safely parks the helicopter on the building terrace, and leaves after saving her life.

I wanted to lift the tons of rubble that lay above me.

But the truth was dawning, however slowly: I had tried everything, several times, and all my puny efforts only made me feel like an ant trying to move a mountain.

I sank back helplessly in the dirt and rubble. I was not going to exert myself in wild, futile attempts anymore. It was becoming clear that what I really needed was to start conserving my energy.

What have I learned that I can use here? I thought, closing my eyes.

There *had* to be something I had learned in the past. *Something* I had experienced or something I knew that could help me.

The first thing that came to mind, again, was the thought of my father and his steady, patient, intense laser focus. *Wait.* Maybe that's why the memory of the nail clippers had come unbidden hours and hours before. I'd thought it was random, but now it seemed to contain a message.

What you need to do, Viral, is to use your mind not your body. Your physical strength is useless here. But your mind has the knowledge and memories of things important—the way your father's mind knew exactly where to find the number he needed, on the file buried among a pile of other files in a folder on a certain shelf in the basement at home.

It hit me like a revelation. I somehow knew, deep in my being, this was right. Yes, I needed to let my mind take over from my powerless body. Of course I didn't know what my mind would produce to help me, but. . .frankly, there really was nothing else I could do. Except panic or give in to anger or despair, which I refused to do.

With a long, slow breath I settled back to see where this would take me. . .

First came random thoughts about my childhood days, my school days, and then my college days, and then about my family, my friends and about my relatives. I thought about my environment, gymnasium, sports, tools, physics classes, yoga and many more things in the next few minutes.

As I allowed the events of my life to just flow by, a part of my mind continued to look for something that I could get help from. But the thoughts were vague. It was as if I was browsing through my life fast and looking for something useful. So many stray and disconnected images floated by—my family, school, teachers, a hammer, my toolbox, movies, a crowbar, laser, a magic kit, cellphone, cricket bat, Star Trek, knife, oxygen supply, drill machine, police siren, axe, rescue workers, God. . .and the list went on and on. . .

All the while I was sort of quickly handling each thought or image and just let it slip away. It was not as if I'd think about my school, for instance, and reflect deeper into memories of my childhood. I wanted to fetch something useful and then continue to look for more. It was a 1000-foot view of my life.

As I continued to think and concentrate hard, my eyebrows got close, and I tried to immerse myself into the thoughts about what I had learned in school, through my parents, and in my life. I tried to think about places where I had lived, the problems I had faced before, and the problems that I had solved. I thought about anything that was reminiscent of my current situation. I was willing to do anything, but I didn't know what to do.

After a time I felt exhausted and mentally squeezed out. My mind needed a break, but I was not going to allow that. I felt the earlier intensity coming back.

"Humans created breaks! No other being gets breaks," I said out loud.

No break. I was going to push myself.

I was finding it hard, for some unknown reason, to think clearly in absolute darkness, and yet at times the darkness helped me stay focussed. And there was something else.

The darkness around me had slowly started to become uncomfortable. The discomfort of being in pitch-blackness, and the wanting to break free thing now reminded me of the yoga classes that I used to attend back at school. I could not push that thought away because that thought kept coming back to me, as if it, too, wanted to tell me something.

I took hold of myself again. How close had I come to giving in to frustration again? I would have to stay on guard against that.

Anger would waste energy, so it was an enemy.

With a few more calming breaths I returned to the platform inside my mind from which I had been observing thoughts and memories from my life. There had to be something helpful. . .

At about 12 years of age I was one of the 42 students in the yoga class at school. No one was allowed to talk during the two-hour yoga class. It was boring and none of us liked it.

Our yoga teacher was a young man in his 20s with a thick black beard, and a ponytail. He had a great personality as well.

During the yoga session, after performing various *asanas* for neck, shoulder, back and for the posture, various breathing exercises—*pranayama*—came next. And finally, it was time to perform meditation.

The yoga teacher would sit in front of the class on a raised platform, while all pupils would sit in the classroom on the thin carpet and follow his instructions.

Sitting in cross-legged position, called *padmasana*, and while resting our wrists on our knees, with our eyes closed, we were given this instruction:

"Concentrate only on your breaths, while you focus only on a single point in the darkness."

None of us were allowed to open our eyes during this time, and there would be pin-drop silence in the yoga room.

"Let go of all the other thoughts in your mind, and focus *only on your breaths*," he would repeat.

It was strenuous for all of us to stay focused and not get diverted by other thoughts that ran in our young and easily distracted minds. To focus on an imaginary point in the darkness and to concentrate only on our breaths for an hour seemed impossible.

Most of the pupils only focused and waited for the bell to ring, so that they could go back to their classrooms. None in our class liked the quiet and dark environment, or the silence of the yoga room.

At the current moment, more than a decade after completing high school, it felt as if I was back in the quiet yoga room.

Now my mind had settled into a distinct focus, and started to examine every piece of the memory—the "file on the shelf in my head." I remembered the things I had learned about yoga from the books that I had read, and I suddenly, vividly remembered the words of the yoga instructor.

"You can see through water only when it is clear."

"When you see clearly, only then you can focus."

"Calm your mind, and let go all the thoughts fogging your mind."

I had never paid attention to these words before. At this moment, they rang like a bell in my inner being.

This is what the earlier memory of my father had also been trying to tell me.

In sheer darkness, I wished that I could focus on one thing alone, and stop my mind from thinking about other things that created disturbing noises in my mind. It was crucial. I knew that it was going to be difficult for me, and I also knew that it was the only way.

I did not want to think about anything that was bothering me, I did not want to focus on my helplessness or my inability, and so I only focused on how I was going to escape. I tried very hard to only think about how I was going to find my way out.

It was not as if I could simply flip the switch for all the other thoughts running in my mind. I had to consistently bring my mind back to focusing on the problem and try and stop thinking about everything else. I had never done this before, and as time passed, it became very wearying. It was intense. While I tried to focus hard, I didn't realize that my energy was draining rapidly, and that I was getting tired much faster.

I exhausted myself so much that I did not even realize when I fell asleep.

When I woke—I was not sure how long I'd slept—I realized I was taking normal breaths and was using up breathable air inside the enclosure rapidly.

My heart began to pound.

10

HUNGER

There was darkness all around me. I had no clue about what happened, and that I'd slept. My heart was pounding, and I looked at the dim, blue display of my wristwatch: 5:30 PM. I felt utterly disoriented and lost. Darkness made me think it was late night, and I didn't know if I'd slept for a few minutes or the whole 24 hours, though my watch showed 26 JAN.

I couldn't believe that I'd gone to sleep. Failing to stay alert in such chaos was beyond my understanding. How could I do that? I hit my forehead on the concrete ceiling a few times in frustration, and sand crystal on the broken ceiling scraped my skin.

Even when I knew that my family was possibly trapped the way I was, I allowed myself to sleep. Shameful.

I forced all images of my family trapped under rubble from my head. Then I glanced at my watch again to make sure that I had not slept through the whole day. What time was it when I'd closed my eyes? I was still confused, and could only guess that I'd slept for maybe just 30 minutes.

Just as frustrating, I knew I had been using up all the air during the time I'd slept, with no control over my breaths. What if I had used up all the oxygen and had fallen unconscious? What if I didn't survive to help rescue or reunite with my family?

The anger I felt at myself surged again.

And in another moment I realized: If I was going to get out of here I would need to tame the energy of my frustration at myself. But how? I was so used to being able to do anything I wanted to do. . .to solve almost any problem that life threw at me.

A thought occurred: *You've never had to tame yourself before— not in a situation anything like this.*

Closing my eyes I took a slow and deep breath. Tame myself. I wasn't sure exactly what that would mean, much less how to do it. But I did know I'd have to be alive to do anything. And fortunately, I didn't feel anything different about the air I'd just inhaled.

Yes, angry outbursts and hitting my head in frustration were not just foolish, they worked against me. I needed calmness and clarity.

I recalled reading somewhere that if eyes were deprived of oxygen for a long time, the vision could get blurry, or one might experience a burning sensation. I could not see anything in the darkness anyway, so I switched on the light on my watch, and tried to look at it from an arm's length. The display looked clear and there was no burning sensation in my eyes. In pitch-darkness, this was the only vision test I could do.

So my anxious thinking that I'd use up all the oxygen had been for nothing. I thought, *Instead of using mental energy killing myself with worry about my own wellbeing I need to focus on getting out of here for the sake of my family.*

Even so, it took me some time to stop attacking myself. Eventually, I was able to stop allowing words to arise in my mind, like "stupid" and "selfish." It was as if some new voice and energy were starting to take control, assuring me these words would do me no good at all and harmed my efforts to survive and escape.

I realized a shift was occurring somewhere deep in my being. Almost anyone in my place would normally lose some level of control by now or would have panicked after waking in the dark. But I wasn't in such a state. I knew I was fine.

What was definitely occurring, though, once I calmed the surging thoughts and angry energy, was that some deep strata of calm and confidence was being allowed to emerge.

I didn't think of myself as someone who was "born confident," if such a thing was even possible. Confidence was something that had been gradually building inside me through the years of my life. My parents never "taught" me to be calm and confident. I'd just looked at them and somehow absorbed the traits.

I realized then that who I was as a person wasn't influenced so much by the experiences of my life alone, but more by who was holding my finger at that time.

What about this moment though? I had never experienced an earthquake before, but I had seen my father go through seriously adverse times—like the time I thought that I was going to lose him. Lying there, and while I once again started to scratch the wall with the piece of metal, I had another memory return—of the time when we'd eagerly awaited my father's return from a long work trip during the monsoon season, but the days passed and he did not return.

Dad worked as a Class-I officer with the Indian government, and his job demanded rigorous travel. The extent to which I knew his work was that he had to visit various remote geographical locations to measure and record the level of water flowing underneath the ground. This helped the government develop groundwater policies, programs and practices to effectively use of the country's resources in a sustainable manner.

During his touring season, he would drive through remote towns and villages in the state, and visit pinpointed locations along with a team of surveyors. These rural areas that he visited were days away from our home, and days away from one another. His typical tour would last for about 15 to 20 days.

This was in the 1980s, when the rural areas in India had extremely limited access and facilities. Telephone and communication facilities were difficult to find in the villages. Cellphones were unheard of.

"If there are problems on the highway, I may be a few days late," my father would usually say, before leaving for the tour. "Do not worry for me."

The length and arduousness of his tour would depend on weather, traffic, vehicle breakdowns, highway traffic jams and all the rest of the uncertainty that came with travelling by road to the most unconnected villages in the state.

"Leave this job! It involves so much travelling," my mother would often say to him, to which he would not respond.

My father's open-door office—a Jeep—arrived during the wee hours to pick him up, and off he went for the next few weeks. He waved at us from a distance, and we all waved back until the Jeep faded away in the distance. This was during monsoon season, that long, rainy period when about 90 percent of the annual rainfall is expected in India. It was considered normal when it poured heavily for weeks, nonstop.

Each time Dad was gone I watched my mother becoming sad as weeks passed. She would often sit by the window and look at the oncoming vehicles driving through rain during evenings.

Usually dad would return from his tour on time, but this time in particular we had not heard from him since he had left. It had been more than four weeks since we'd seen him. My mother had contacted my dad's colleagues and the main office several times to find out if they had any information about him or where he was. The office had no information about anyone, since the communication lines everywhere in the state had crashed due to record-breaking rainfall.

My mother had become unusually tense, and she cried often while she sat by the window every single day waiting for my father. She only got more worried after hearing about the devastation caused by the rain in our state and about the accidents on the highway. She could not do anything but wait for my father and only wish for his safe return home.

And so there was an uncomfortable silence at home. An underlying tension. Roshan did not talk to anyone. I did not tell anyone that I was worried, and I knew that he was worried, too. Days felt like months.

Often when I woke up in the middle of the night, I would see my mom silhouetted at the window in our living room, looking at the long stretch of road in front of our home while the nonstop, heavy pounding of the rain continued.

More and more days passed. We did not ask anything about our father, because we knew that my mother did not have any information.

One night the sound of tires passing over loose gravel woke me up. Immediately I knew it was my dad's Jeep. Then I heard the rear door of the Jeep slam shut, and I leapt out of bed and hurried out to see if my mother was awake. She was already rushing to open our main door. Roshan came bolting from the room in a sleepy state as well.

Flying to the door I peered out to see the driver unloading bags. The dark canvas over the Jeep was wet and shone like silk under the streetlight. I could hear the loud pattering sound of raindrops from a distance as they hit the canvas top.

And then I saw Dad. Totally drenched, he waved toward the driver, who saluted him and drove off into the darkness.

As he neared the front door, water pouring from the brim of his hat, he paused a half-moment. "Why are you all awake?"

He looked like a warrior who had just returned home.

In that instant, Mom broke down and cried. "I was so worried for you!"

The next day when all of us sat in the living room, Dad told us about the experiences he'd had when he was out on the tour.

"If it was anyone else on this tour, they would have not have returned yet," he said, calmly. "I saw at least a hundred lorries turned over or vehicles that had fallen into ditches. There were countless accidents." He was giving us the live version of the havoc that the record rain had caused across the state, which we'd been watching on TV since the day he left.

"I saw several bridges where the water was flowing over the bridge itself," he said, gesturing with both hands. "There was devastation everywhere, and several major bridges were unsafe to cross. For that reason, all the traffic stood still waiting for the water level to drop. And after waiting for about a day in heavy rain, we turned back to find different internal routes.

"We were able to navigate successfully, since the driver and I had a driven through the local connecting roads in the area.

"We had a lot of things to consider because of the extreme rainfall. Gas stations were closed, some of the circuit houses were unreachable and the government guest houses were inaccessible.

"Finally on the third day, when we were able to bypass most of the bridges by taking long and unpredictable internal routes, we got stuck at one bridge that was unavoidable. People had been waiting near that bridge for two or three days for the water level to drop. No one even knew if the bridge still existed!" he exclaimed.

We looked at him in awe, and I tried to imagine what he must have witnessed. And what it felt like to be stuck and thwarted on every side.

"Some of these bridges that are old get washed away by the flooding waters. No one can determine that the bridge is destroyed until after the water level drops.

"But," he continued—and his tone changed—"I had travelled over this bridge several times, and I knew that this was one of the strongest bridges in the state, and the depth of the river passing under it was not very much, even though at that particular moment it was being pounded by a ferocious current.

"After waiting for half a day in stalled traffic, I asked the lorry drivers to drive over the bridge, as I knew that the water current had become weaker, but none would dare to move forward. After some time, they finally had to make way for our Jeep so that we could go at our own risk. I asked the driver if he felt confident to drive through the bridge. He told me that he would simply rely on my judgment. So I had to make a decision.

"Looking at the velocity of the gushing water, I knew that we would have to keep the Jeep moving forward, and make sure that we did not stop midway during our crossing."

"Why did you have to cross the bridge!" my mother suddenly interrupted in anger. "Couldn't you just wait like others?"

Roshan and I looked at each other and said nothing, as we both knew how tense Mom had been before my dad arrived, so desperately wanting him home safe.

Father paused only a moment before continuing. "So I went to survey the flowing river and tried to gauge the height of the flowing water above it. It seemed about two feet high, which was high. The water flowing over the bridge was dirty, but it didn't look like it had any debris flowing.

"We securely covered the electrical components under the hood of the jeep using plastic bags and tape. We used a long pipe to connect it to the exhaust tail pipe of the Jeep and made sure that its opening was more than 4 feet above ground."

"Oh god! What if the bridge was not there!" Mom interrupted again.

Father lifted his chin slightly, with that confident air that he always had. "I knew—I *knew*—that this bridge was strong enough to withstand this kind of rain and gushing water.

"We then got the Jeep loaded with several bags of sand to add some ballast weight to the vehicle. It took a few hours to thoroughly inspect and prepare the vehicle for driving it through the gushing water. The driver revved the engine for a few minutes, so that the engine was heated enough. All the villagers and nearby lorry drivers had gathered to see if we could make it to the other end. No one wanted to stop us, and none wanted to be responsible, but everyone around was ready to offer help.

"I told the driver not to panic and to just keep driving straight toward the direction where the other end of the bridge could be seen. I instructed him multiple times to make sure that the Jeep was always moving and did not stall, and to make sure that he drove slowly to keep the water from splashing up onto the engine and drowning it out. He understood that it was crucial.

"Everyone stood by the side to watch us drive the Jeep toward the water where the asphalt road slowly disappeared into murky brown flowing current. The water started hitting the vehicle from all sides as soon as the vehicle started to pass through the current. It was not deep yet. And it seemed like we were moving ahead fine. But the water hitting the wheels started to create ripples and shake the Jeep and we'd barely driven a few feet."

"You are never going on a tour again!" Mom interrupted. "Leave this job! How can you take these risks?" My father continued in his calm manner.

"Luckily, there were no obstacles on the bridge, so we kept moving forward. The level of water only got deeper as we progressed, and then some water started making its way inside the Jeep, making it heavier. I told the driver to keep his foot on gas firmly and keep moving, and not to worry about the water. This was expected.

"Soon, we were halfway across the bridge and I knew that the water level would not get any higher. The engine seemed to be working as expected."

I listened to my father in awe. As he spoke casually, he stroked his dark beard. How I admired his strength.

"Within the next minute or so, we were in the safe zone where the water was less than a foot deep. We could see the faces of the people on the other side of the bridge looking at us in disbelief as we continued to move toward them. People on this side of the bridge clapped, cheered and hugged us once we were out of the Jeep, while people on the other side waved and whistled from a distance."

"While it continued to rain heavily, we stopped and had a hot cup of tea, then we continued our journey. This happened three days back."

"*Bhagwan! Bhagwan!* (Oh my god! Oh my god!)," Mom exclaimed. "You *have* to leave this job. The government is not going to give you an award for any of this," she insisted.

Looking at Roshan I could see he was deeply impressed, as I was. My father had probably known how much agony my mother was going through while waiting for him, and in his deep love for her he'd done what he'd had to do to make it home as soon as he possibly could.

"Fear is inevitable," I'd often heard him say. "You only develop strength by facing fear, not running from it."

My father's colleagues, the drivers, his friends, our neighbors, and everyone else who had heard about this were amazed to hear about his experience.

At nine or ten years old, I'd been scared of losing my father. But when he came back, his spirit of confidence had made my fear seem so insignificant. The confidence and the determination I'd seen in him continued to impress me through the years. I only hoped that one day I could become as strong as he was.

While lying in the dark, I thought about him, and realized I could give in to frustrated impulses and lose it. Or I could tame those impulses by engaging the calm, confident spirit I'd witnessed in my dad my whole life.

What will it be—fear or confidence?

I allowed myself to relax then. Not just in body, but at a much deeper level, down in my spirit.

From this new place I made my mind go over the facts: I knew that the oxygen in the enclosure would not have lasted beyond a few hours after the earthquake if it was not being replenished from somewhere. With that, I silenced the anxious thought that I was going to run out of air, and stopped forcing myself to breathe shallowly or at infrequent intervals.

Just like my father, who knew that the bridge *had* to be there, I started to believe that the oxygen was there, and it was getting replenished...somehow.

I took a deep breath. No matter what, with the same confidence my father had had—the confidence that was a gift from him—I felt courage and determination replace the anger that I had.

Something else was happening every time thoughts of my family returned, though focused on my surroundings I was not aware of it at the time. With each memory, each truth or lesson about life, it was as if a light came on inside me there in the dark. And with that came a renewed sense of energy and determination.

I resumed scratching at the wall, with even more energy—working and resting and working again for the next several hours.

It was about 9:00 PM when I took a long break—more than 22 hours since I had eaten anything and about 12 hours since the earthquake. My stomach was growling and begging for food once again.

I hadn't been able to make much of a dent in the wall, but I would not allow thoughts of defeat. As I lay there I tried to think how to subdue the feeling of extreme hunger. It was becoming hard to think of anything else with my stomach acid burning me from the inside.

Like my father taking stock of the submerged bridge, I took stock.

Saliva, came to mind. And the thought, *Reduce the space for stomach acid.*

I started to think about food. I thought about food that was spicy, food that was tasty. I thought about the food that my mother made. I thought about the meal that I'd had at the Prince Hotel the night before the earthquake. I thought about chilies, and a jar full of pickles. Breathing in, I imagined the smell of delicious food.

These thoughts made me salivate.

I tried to gulp down the saliva and pulled the walls of my stomach inside. I then applied pressure on my stomach with my palms and pressed hard. It helped. In a few minutes, the burning sensation gradually subsided.

But then it was back. And so were hints of the frustration.

I had to get the reins on this. Fast.

Reaching inside myself I found the calm and confidence again. And a voice with the sound of authority.

You can live for many days without food. Thinking you need food the minute your stomach growls is a mental addiction.

But I also knew, pragmatically, that I would have to do something about the hunger issue. I knew that as time passed I'd get hungrier and I'd start to lose energy. I'd also become more thirsty, and I'd need to use the bathroom. There was a high possibility of facing *all* these problems at the same time, and many more that I wasn't even aware of.

Again, there came a surge of energy, as physically trapped, a part of my mind wanted to run away from the situation. I could have just closed my eyes and pretended that the problem in front of me didn't exist, and stopped thinking about a solution. But I decided not to run away from it. Shifting my thoughts to calm ones, I declared:

I cannot solve the big problem of getting out—not yet. But I can solve the smaller problems.

A strategy came to me: The need for food, water, and finding a cellphone seemed to be bothering me every few minutes. I knew that I would be able to control my hunger for a very long time. But my focus could not be merely to *control* hunger. My focus had to be to not *feel* hungry.

In that moment, I knew exactly what I was going to do next, and I was confident that it would work.

11

BRINJAL

"Not being able to govern events, I govern myself."
— MICHEL DE MONTAIGNE

I wanted to feel rested before I tried something new, so I took a break for a few minutes by covering my eyes with my palms.

As I lay there, I had no clue about what was happening outside my cement coffin—which was utter devastation.

The entire district of Kutch had been flattened. The town of Bhuj had turned into a wrecked ghost town. No structure had been spared. Any of the structures still standing were badly damaged and uninhabitable.

It was the first day after the new moon. With no electricity in town, the broken structures now stood in the cold dark night that engulfed every street and alley in utter darkness.

Government offices, hospitals, local shops and the emergency service buildings were destroyed. Major highways in the state, bridges and roads were severely damaged, and several local streets across the town were blocked due to structures that had toppled in heaps of rubble onto the streets. Telephone lines were down and all the cellphone towers had been severely damaged.

Besides the devastation, there were groans from the injured caught in the tangles of cement and twisted rebar and the cries of the living who had already found loved ones, dead. Bhuj looked and sounded like a war zone.

As for the citizenry—thousands were dead and thousands more were unaccounted for. No one wanted to go back into their homes due to unstable structures and the ongoing strong aftershocks. Hordes of people hovered around their broken homes. . .helpless, crying and trying everything that they could to find their loved ones from underneath tons and tons of steel and concrete.

There were miles and miles of devastation. Tragedy was everywhere. School buildings had collapsed, trapping hundreds of little children who had gone to school for the Republic Day flag-hoisting ceremony. The search and rescue efforts to find or evacuate them had not even begun.

From under the rubble of some of the collapsed buildings, shouts and screams for help could be heard. The town was not equipped with heavy machinery to handle such a catastrophic event, however, and even though people were desperately trying everything that they could, they could not reach some victims. Helpless, they had to wait for the heavy machines to start the rescue work. To make matters worse, there wasn't enough food or water supply for the tens of thousands of people who had become homeless in an instant of time.

Ahmedabad, our own home city 400 kilometers away, was shaken up as well. Never having experienced an earthquake before, the people of Ahmedabad were in a state of shock and dismay. Would the devastation that destroyed Bhuj and other western coastal cities strike here, too, with a second quake?

Our next-door neighbor Mona aunty, Rajen uncle, and their son Jaishal had run outside the house when the earthquake struck.

Standing on the street, they had seen their entire house shaking and they thought that it was going to break apart. The earth had shaken so violently that they'd almost been thrown to the ground.

In the city of Ahmedabad, many high-rise buildings had come crashing to the ground, trapping hundreds of people underneath the ruins. Most of the tall structures had significant damage.

My maternal aunt Panna and uncle Mahendra lived in a high-rise building in Ahmedabad along with Hiral, their daughter. It had been a typical holiday morning for them. When the earth started to shake ferociously, Mahendra uncle ran toward the balcony, and he gripped the metal railing with all his might. He shouted at the top of his lungs as the building shook violently without stopping and he thought he might be pitched off the balcony to his death.

"The shaking was so violent that I thought that the entire building was going to collapse any moment. If I would not have shouted so loud, I think I would have had a heart attack," he would say later.

Hundreds of people from both wings of their building had rushed toward the ground as fast as they could. Most of them were still in their nightwear.

"Mansi complex collapsed!" was the first thing my uncle and aunt heard as they ran down the stairs, along with others. Mansi Tower was the building right next to theirs.

Within minutes Raghu, my cousin's husband, along with my cousin had reached their building to make sure that they were safe. Everywhere, people rushed to locate their families.

Later, they rushed toward Mansi Tower along with a huge crowd of people, and discovered that part of A-wing of the 12-storied complex had crumbled to the ground—with people, and everything else inside—crushing the strip of shops on the ground floor. The stairwell that ran toward the center of the building was mangled, fragmented and exposed. Each flight of the collapsed stairwell dangled from a height, as if it was going to break loose at any moment, making search efforts perilous. It was a horrific scene.

Within the next few minutes, news started flashing on all the TV stations around the country, and before long it was determined that Bhuj was the town closest to the epicenter of the earthquake.

Panna aunty drew in a sharp breath. She knew that we were in Bhuj, and also knew that we had plans to leave for the resort early that very morning. Knowing my father, she knew that we all were going to be safe—that we probably had left for the resort town and were safe there. She relaxed a little. But just a little.

For their family, it wasn't easy to stay outside their building for a long time. But looking at the chaos in the city, and fearing another earthquake they thought of going to our home in Ahmedabad, which was on ground level. They later decided to go to my grandmother's home instead, where we all had spent time together during the kite festival.

Once at my grandma's home, each one of our relatives including my grandma, my maternal uncle Dinesh, my aunts and cousins, all voiced the belief that our family was going to be fine. Everyone convinced each other and thought that as soon as the phone lines were back up we would call. Everyone continued to leave messages on Roshan's cellphone.

Savita *Baa* (Grandmother) was a very positive and strong woman, but after a few hours of no news she had started to lose patience. She went inside the *Pooja* room (worship room) that was located in the center of her home and prayed for our wellbeing. When she came out, she continued to hold her *mala* (string of prayer and meditation beads) that she used every day while praying. She became more and more restless after she continued to watch news on TV that evening with everyone else in the family. This was one of the biggest earthquakes in India's history, the news channels reported. Being very close to our family, Dinesh uncle continued to convince my grandmother that everything was going to be all right as hours passed.

All of the family members were aware that this was not the first time our family had encountered a near death situation, and remembered the time in 1984, when we were in Bhopal, in central India. Everyone remembered the day when the world's worst industrial disaster had taken place in Bhopal, when over 500,000 people were exposed to a poisonous gas.

Thousands of people, animals, and cattle died overnight, in their sleep when about 30 tons of mithyle isocyanate, a heavy gas, leaked into the atmosphere from a tank of a pesticide plant. Thousands more died over time or were blinded, or suffered other lifelong health problems.

The location where the poisonous gas had leaked in the city was not too far away from where we lived. In fact only a hill that divided the city of Bhopal had prevented the gas from reaching us.

At first, the seriousness of the Bhopal disaster wasn't known because there were only bits and pieces of news about the world's worst industrial disaster. Then radio and TV channels started to report about another possible leak during the day, emphasizing the importance of keeping the doors and windows sealed, and to breathe through a wet cloth if there was a burning sensation in the eyes.

Without wasting any time, Father got all of us in the Jeep and we all travelled southwards where one of his colleagues lived. The rest of the day was spent at their home. We returned to our home only after it was determined that the air was safe to breathe.

Each one of our relatives remembered that day clearly, and assured each other that we were safe somewhere and that one of us would call soon. But my grandmother had had enough. She called for my cousin Punal and Raghu.

Sitting with them by the swing where she spent most of her day, still holding the *mala* in her hands, she said, "It is crucial that if the need arises, someone is ready to go to Bhuj."

Being the closest to my grandmother, Punal took her hand and assured her that everything was going to be okay.

Punal and Raghu were the only younger males in our family who were in Ahmedabad at that time. Punal had always been very close to our family, and had utmost respect for my parents. He was a street-smart and an energetic man who had been the go-to guy for my father.

Raghu was my closest cousin's husband. We had known him as a very hard-working individual and a truly genuine guy. He was still new to our family though, and we had only started to get to know him. I had left for the U.S. not too long after he'd married into the family.

"I believe that my daughter's family is safe in Bhuj, but I am starting to lose patience," my grandma had said.

My cousin Biren *Bhai*, a quick thinker, and who happened to be very close to my father, continued trying to contact us after what he saw on TV. Once that did not work, he called Surendra uncle—my father's younger brother in Hyderabad. Surendra uncle hadn't heard anything about us either. And so, Biren took the first flight from Mumbai toward Ahmedabad, leaving home his wife Namrata, who was then 7 months pregnant with twins. He wanted to get to Bhuj as soon as possible.

Initially, Namrata had forced Biren to stay back because of her condition and because of what the doctors had advised then.

"I am going to Bhuj. You figure it out," Biren had told her, leaving her with his parents, and before leaving for Ahmedabad.

I had no idea about these things, of course, as I lay with my palms covering my eyes, that my family members were planning to start a search for us.

The very short break I'd just taken from my efforts was long enough. I was still hungry, and again my stomach made sounds every few seconds. It was now time for me to try out my plan to vanquish hunger. And the reason I was confident my idea would work was this:

My mother loved to cook and she loved to try new recipes all the time. I loved her food. But not every dish. As a child I ate most of my vegetables—but I had a problem with eggplant. Whenever my mother cooked eggplant, I would not eat that day. Everyone would sing praises for the *Bagara baingan* that she made, but I wouldn't even touch it. I don't know why. I had never even tasted eggplant, but for some reason I had it in my head that it tasted awful. To think about it shut off my appetite.

Lying in darkness, hungry, I'd been thinking about food constantly for hours. I thought about the food that my mother prepared. I thought about our last night's meal at the Prince Hotel again. I thought about how far the collapsed kitchen and the dining area were from where I was lying. I thought about everything related to food, and I only hoped that I could get something to eat so that I could make the burning sensation in my stomach go away. Every thought about food had made me more and more hungry, and every single thought made me feel more helpless.

But now I thought about. . .*eggplant.*

No, I wasn't so hungry and desperate that I was going to even try eggplant. For me, the distaste of imagining eating eggplant was far greater than my hunger. Over the years, I had developed so much dislike toward this vegetable that I just couldn't ever think of eating it. So whereas I'd been desperate to make hunger go away, now I felt my hunger subsiding. I disliked eggplant *that* much.

Yes. It was working.

The only thing available to eat is eggplant, I told myself.

Whenever you feel like eating, the only thing you'll get is eggplant. That's it.

I could feel my stomach responding with a firm, *No.*

I chuckled, and continued my new mantra.

If you feel hungry, you will only get one thing to eat—brinjal—*Mom's best eggplant dish. You will have to eat the dirty, squishy* brinjal, *Viral. Do you want to eat that?*

From that calm, confident place I'd discovered in my mind, I knew of course that I was playing a trick with my mind. But it was working. The more I thought about eggplant the more I felt better staying hungry.

For a long time I continued relating every single feeling of hunger with being fed eggplant. I repeated the same things to myself many more times to make the feeling of disgust more intense. Since I had not tasted eggplant yet, it was easy for me to imagine any taste and any texture that my tongue would find revolting.

More time passed—hours maybe—and I had stopped feeling uncomfortably hungry. If the feeling returned I focused on telling myself the different ways that I was going to be fed eggplant, and let my imagination run wild with it.

I thought that if I became too hungry, I would be thrown into a dirty bathtub filled with weeks-old, rotten, brown-colored pulp of thousands of eggplants. I imagined an old and rusty clawfoot bathtub filled with dark, slimy eggplant paste that was dripping all over the dirty bathroom floor.

I imagined dirty and sick rodents going in and out of the tunnels in the pulp. I imagined creepy bugs crawling out from the same holes. I imagined hordes of flies sitting on the rim of the dirty bathtub over the rotting paste. I imagined a dead rat lying next to one clawfoot of the tub.

It started to work too well.

As I continued to imagine things that were disgusting, and as I tried to associate that with food, it didn't take much longer for me to feel as if I was going to throw up.

But at least it was working to eradicate the feeling of hunger. My mind was taking charge of my body.

I imagined the gross bathtub part a few more times, and every time that I thought about it, I added different details. I imagined a dirty spoon next to the tub, so I could use it to serve myself. I could see the green-and-white-colored fungus growing all over the eggplant glop. I could see a greasy porcelain plate lying next to the tub. I also imagined a stinking dump truck filled with rotten food. I imagined larva infestation.

All I'd been trying to do was to disassociate pleasure from food and associate happiness with hunger. The hunger pangs seemed to be losing their power.

To stay hungry and *not* have to eat was almost bliss.

I wasn't sure if this was because of my imagination or just a phase of hunger, but my stomach had stopped making the growling sound and, after some more time had passed, I thought that I was not feeling hungry anymore.

I felt triumphant, and thought, *I can stay hungry forever but I can never eat that disgusting stuff in those terrible conditions.*

I had so much aversion and feeling of disgust for food at the moment that if I had been offered food I wasn't sure I could even look at it.

In fact, the feeling had become so real in my mind that when I swallowed a small bit of saliva, it made me think that I was gulping down something disgusting—and I had to wipe my tongue with my T-shirt.

I don't want food.

Apart from the aluminum strip, I now had found another tool that I could use. Though intangible, it turned out to be a useful one. It was my imagination. Just like the aluminum strip, it could help me get out of this mess. I was going to keep this tool aside, and use it when I need it. Meanwhile. . .

Time continued to pass slowly, and in the decimated streets outside searchers were just starting to pick through rubble. When someone was pulled from inside a collapsed structure there was cheering.

In my confined space, I celebrated my small victory. I thought that in a small way I was successful. I didn't know for how long this feeling was going to last. I didn't want to feel too happy about this because my end goal was to get out, and I had only been able to jump one little hurdle. . .for the time being.

Was this tool in my arsenal going to work for much longer? I was going to find out. All I knew was that—at the moment—the burning sensation in my stomach had subsided.

But before I could focus on anything else, I heard the familiar churning sound from the bottom of the building, and the earth once again started to shake.

I made my body as stiff as possible, thinking I might be able to shield myself if the massive slab above me slipped and pressed its weight down on me.

Oh god. How was this nightmare going to end?

12

THIRST

"The best way out of a problem is through it."

— A N O N Y M O U S

The sound of churning underneath the building was noticeably louder than before, but the shaking did not have a jarring motion. It was like riding in a slow-moving train, and then there was some up and down motion. I wasn't scared this time, but I stayed cautious and remained in the same position until the shaking finally subsided.

After exhausting myself by thinking about ways to free myself for about an hour, I slept. I was unaware of the problems that the next day would bring.

I woke up around 2:00 AM. I was lost, still exhausted and very sleepy. This time when I woke, I did not expect to be back to a normal life. I think my mind had started to accept what was really happening around me. I now knew that these things were real and that it was not a nightmare.

In my sleepy state, I thought that the entire city was dead, and I was the only survivor. But I also knew that it was not possible because my father was somewhere outside, and most definitely my family was safe somewhere. After shouting for help a few more times, I went back to sleep.

I woke up once again past 4:00 AM, and there was darkness around me like before. For some reason it felt darker, I wasn't sure why. I kept gazing into darkness for the next few minutes with no thoughts in my mind. The air that I was breathing did not feel any different, and I did not feel suffocated in any way. I did not know how that was possible, but I now knew for certain that the air around me would last longer since it was somehow getting circulated. I felt trapped, more than I felt before, probably because I was not used to being in the same position for such a long time. A big part of me was expecting to hear the sound of bulldozers and cranes, and the voice of my father, but I quickly stopped myself from relying on it.

I did not want to sleep since I had gotten some needed rest, but I was tired of repeating what I had tried before. I wanted to try to approach the problems differently, but I had no energy to think of anything new.

I rested my palms against the concrete slab above me and with all the power and strength that I had I pushed!

"AAAARGHHH!"

I tried to exert as much pressure as I could while I shouted in anger and in pain. I continued pushing with every ounce of energy that I had in my body, shouting aloud, while my wrists started to hurt and shake.

A few more seconds passed, after which I stopped exerting pressure. I was breathless and I had started to sweat a little. I then very slowly and carefully withdrew my hands from the concrete slab, expecting to see the slab move back to its original position. It didn't move. I knew this. I had done this before.

"I will move it! I will break it to pieces!" I said aloud in the darkness.

After one more failed attempt I had no energy left, even though I had just woken up and gotten some rest. I decided to get some more sleep so that I could start with a fresh mind.

I couldn't turn on the side, so I just closed my eyes and thought about waking up within a few minutes when I would be evacuated by my father. With my eyes closed, I tried to keep my mind calm and tried not to think about anything. Once I tried hard not to think, more thoughts started cluttering my mind.

"Where is everyone?"

"Does anyone know I am stuck?"

"Is anyone trying?"

"Does anyone know that this building has collapsed?"

"Why is dad taking so long?"

"What can I try tomorrow?"

"How will I get out?"

"What will I do about thirst?"

"When will I get out?

Drained of energy and looking for answers, I slept after some time.

I woke up a few more times during the next few hours, and then I finally woke up around 8:00 AM. I had done everything that I could, what else was I going to do after opening my eyes?

I reluctantly yawned and then smelled the air around me. The air once again did not feel any different. It was usual to hear birds chirping in the morning or hear sound of traffic around the house after waking up, but it was pitch dark and there was no sound of any sort around me.

I remembered waking up half a dozen times during the night and gazing in the darkness and checking the date and the time. I had slept because a part of me did not want to wake up and face the reality.

"You have to get out today, Viral!" I said to myself.

As I said that, I could smell bad breath from my mouth. Once

I ran my tongue over my front teeth, I realized that there was bacteria buildup over my teeth. It wasn't surprising. It had been more than 36 hours since I had brushed my teeth. I pulled up my T-shirt from the waist and carefully only wiped the front teeth with my index finger covered in it. I made sure that I didn't wipe any of the precious moisture from my mouth.

I knew that there was a long day ahead of me. It was going to be a day full of unsolved problems, a day full of struggle, and yet a day full of hope. Maybe I would be able to solve some of the problems that I was facing, or maybe I would face more problems than I did the previous day. I didn't know. It did not worry me, but it did make me feel demotivated when I thought about what I had been able to achieve yesterday. The one growing concern that was bothering me the most was that I was still not hearing any sounds from outside and that there were no sounds of bulldozers or cranes or heavy machinery. There had only been absolute silence.

Until last night, I was secretly hoping that I would hear the sounds of bulldozers in the morning, and then I would walk out and see my family. That had not happened. . .yet.

"Not now, Viral! It takes time. He will get you out! Do what you have to do!" I said to myself.

I started to feel the surface of the wall with my hands to find the spot where I had been scratching. When I switched the wristwatch light on, while raising my neck in the air, I could see the scratches clearly. There were a lot of scratches, whereas the surface of the wall still seemed intact. It was extremely demoralizing.

I found the piece of aluminum next to my thigh where I had kept it last night.

"It's time to start working!" I said to myself.

I did not need to brush my teeth, take a shower, get ready or have something to eat or drink. I was ready to start.

"This is not going to work."

"You have tried it before."

"This is a waste of time."

These were the instant thoughts that came to my mind.

Sometimes you have to stop yourself from stopping you. And I did just that. I did not care about what my mind told me. I started to scratch the wall. I did not want to be driven by the previous day's results.

I remembered a verse from the *Bhagavad Gita* (a Hindu religious scripture) and its meaning.

Karmanye vadhikaraste Ma Phaleshu Kadachana,
Ma Karmaphalaheturbhurma Te Sangostvakarmani

This verse was about *karma* (deeds). This is what the verse meant:

You only have the right to perform your karma. You do not have any rights to the fruits of your karma. Neither let the fruits of your karma be your motivation, nor let your attachment be to inaction.

I remembered this verse, and I knew and understood its meaning, but at this time it wasn't easy for me not to think about the fruits of the work I was doing. I tried very hard only to think about what I had to do, and I tried even harder to not worry myself about its outcome. Most times I failed in doing so, and my mind kept going to the end result of being able to escape from a two-feet by two-feet hole in the wall.

Like before, I had to hold my neck up in the air when I scratched the wall. It was now more exhausting. My neck muscles felt sore after the previous day's work. My abdominal muscles were hurting even more.

I tried not to learn anything negative from yesterday and I wasn't afraid of facing the same problem again. All I kept trying to find were different ways to solve the same problem. I didn't want to stop looking for a solution.

Ten hours passed. During these ten hours I shouted, scratched, talked to myself and prayed hard.

My family was a part of me, and not knowing where and how my family was, and not being able to do anything about it felt excruciatingly painful. It felt as if my legs and my arms were cut off, while I was still conscious. I had not experienced such pain in my life before.

During these ten hours, my equation with God had changed. I was not on good terms with God anymore.

"I don't care what you do to me. Please, God, save my family. Please. God, please..." I prayed desperately, and with a lot of anger.

How could he do this!

Questions that had no answers were pulling me down and making me weaker. I would then wallow in the sea of questions and thoughts, and use all that anger and frustration to break the wall, and then fail once again.

There were a few bouts of hunger during the past few hours, but before I did anything about it, the burning sensation had subsided.

At this time it had been about 36 hours since the earthquake, and about 42 hours since I had used the bathroom.

I also knew now that losing even a microscopic bit of precious fluid from the body could mean the difference between life and death, but I had to go, and I could not wait any longer. I wasn't able to think about anything but was trying to control the overwhelming urge to urinate.

I started digging into the area near my thigh and by the wall, where I had kept all the broken pieces of glass, and where part of the tube-light strip was still attached to the wall. I carelessly started to move the pieces of broken wall and glass aside, and tried to look for the strip that was attached to the wall.

I then switched on the wristwatch light to see what I was touching. I could see the part of the wire that was covered with rubble, and a lot of dust, and some sharp pieces of glass.

And as I continued to run my hand over each piece and continued to move the rubble around, I thought I touched what I was looking for. I touched the little plastic piece that works like a cover for the electrical wires. This piece of electrical fitting is made of plastic. It is called a ceiling rose and is typically found in various residential buildings in India. It is a circular plastic mount that typically is used for covering the wires coming out of the wall.

The plastic cover looks like a small cup and has a hole in the middle for the electrical wires to run through. I unscrewed the plastic cover, which seemed intact to the touch. I cleaned it a little.

During the next few minutes, I did something that I had never imagined or done before.

I drank three small cups of my own urine.

13

THE TEAMS

"All human wisdom is summed up in two words: wait and hope."

—ALEXANDRE DUMAS

Failure.

That's what all my attempts to escape had been so far. Still, the battle for my mind continued. I would not let my consciousness settle on that word.

I had always looked away when someone even used that word. I always replaced it with other words in my mind, and it had always worked to this point. Sure, I had been unsuccessful many times in life, and yet I didn't think that anything like failure existed, unless someone desperately wanted to feel that way. For me, failure was not an occurrence, it was a feeling. Failure was nothing by itself.

But the feeling that was trying to take over was a different matter. And so the wrestling match between my feelings and my mind became more intense.

As time passed, I tried hard to replace this negative feeling with something else. It was becoming more and more difficult to do so, especially when my efforts fetched no positive results every single time. Every passing second made me think that it was going to take much longer for me to get out, and that I was in a place that was not easy to escape. And so by this time I was starting to realize the gravity of the situation.

It was now night of day two. During the next few hours, various thoughts came to my mind while I worked. I started to think about things like, what would I do if I could not break the wall? What if there was no help coming? And what if someone from my family had passed away?

It seemed as if some darker part of my mind wanted to take over, and I now found myself fighting off images of life without my family. The thought of losing even one of my family members was dreadful, and the pain that came with it was beyond what I could bear. I had no answers to any of the questions that continued to hurt me, which caused more agony. I couldn't do anything about it. All I could do was to try and push those thoughts away each time they tried to return. If I allowed such thoughts to enter my mind, my mind would try to find answers. Each question would pull me down and try to make me weaker, and these same questions also made me work harder. Even though I knew that breaking the wall did not seem achievable, I continued doing what I thought was the right thing to do. *Persist.*

But the enemy thoughts continued to rise, like ranks of an invading army appearing on an inner horizon. And all the while I continued to work, the questions continued to batter me. And now, since I was thinking more seriously, it had started to make things worse. I could not even think about what I would do next. Every single negative thought that I could think filled my mind with only more questions. I would stop working, and then I would think, and then again I'd work, and then throw the metal piece away, and think. For the next hour or so I was paralyzed, and I remained in my thoughts, not knowing what to do next. Not knowing what was going to happen next.

Every question that I thought about was important and was a link to freeing myself, but there were no answers. I had started to slide deep into my own thoughts, only to find questions that would bother me even more.

Then came a new realization: For the first time in my life I recognized that my mind was actually capable of destroying me—completely, if I allowed it.

That brought me to stark attention. While I was struggling to escape on one level, I knew now I would have to wage war on another level as well.

But could I do both? Was I strong enough?

So began a battle for full control of my mind, much more pitted than before. I was alone and trapped with my thoughts, which were starting to run wild.

Still, the tiny space I'd created in my mind by stepping back, as it were, and observing the ranks of negative thoughts marching through my head was just enough. I had to replace them with something else.

What is good about my situation? I thought, quickly forcing myself to focus on something positive.

No answers came to my mind for a few seconds.

And then:

- *What if my arm or my leg was crushed under massive weight while I was still conscious?*

- *What if I was still in the U.S., and my family was trapped under this collapsed building?*

- *What if half of my body was buried in concrete, and I couldn't even move?*

- *What if my skull had cracked, and I was still alive?*

- *What if I was paralyzed?*

- *What if I had already run out of oxygen?*

- *What if the dangling ceiling fan had fallen onto my head?*

I ran my palm over my forehead, and then over my hair. I was alive and I could breathe.

A slight change in perspective had made me think that I was okay, and that in fact I was in a much better shape than my mind had been trying to tell me just a few moments before.

"Do you even know what Mom, Dad and *Bhai* may be going through right now? Stop acting like a child!" I shouted at myself.

Another entire day had gone by, while I continued trying to free myself. I looked at my watch again. It was 2:00 AM. The analog display showed the U.S. Eastern Standard Time. It was 3:30 PM in New York City.

Times Square in New York City, the place that I visited every single day after work, was probably buzzing with energy at this exact moment.

Thousands of people might be having a wonderful time around the city. So many people might be taking pictures and posing for the cameras around the massive electronic billboards. People must be so happy right at this very moment.

Nobody in the entire world knew that I was alive and that I was here alone in the dark, struggling. Out of the billions of humans all around the world, there wasn't a single way I could reach out to even one soul for help. I was totally disconnected from every other being on the planet. Even an insect didn't know about my existence.

I compared my state to a patient lying on a bed inside a hospital, struggling between life and death. This was the only thing I could relate my situation to. It wasn't much different. I thought about what a seriously ill patient might have to go through on a daily basis, when he sees that no one from the outside world even knows about his daily physical and mental struggles.

Someone inside a hospital may have been struggling to have one more breath, or may only have a few days to live, while people just outside the building are busy with their normal lives.

What would a person who only has a few days to live think about people getting furious over something petty like hot weather, or bad food?

No one outside our collapsed building knew what I was fighting with. Everything was probably going on as a normal day. And even if there were people aware of our collapsed building, there was no one who knew that I was alive and struggling.

Unrealistic thoughts tried to enter now. I wanted desperately to go back to the time a few minutes before the earthquake, even though it was not possible. A part of me was still under shock, and it was still hard to even imagine what was happening with me.

I joined my hands above my chest and closed my eyes tightly. I then thought about the time a few minutes before the earthquake. I saw my father coming inside the room and throwing a comforter over me. I spent time thinking about the time before the earthquake again and again. I wanted to make myself feel as if I indeed was going back in the past. I thought about the time we spent with Shalin at the kids' park that evening, and about the songs I was watching on MTV the night before the earthquake. I thought about how Shalin was playing peek-a-boo with me just a few minutes before he went to bed.

I saw him duck down and look at me from underneath the bed from the other side.

"*Chachu!*" He called again as he came running toward my side and hugged me with his open arms. And then I saw him run back toward the other side of the bed and calling me from under the bed.

"*Chachu!*" he shouted. And when I saw him looking at me. He once again ran toward me and hugged me.

I saw Roshan and Jaishree standing near the door waiting for Shalin. I saw every single thing in the room. I saw my mother who was tired and wanted to get some sleep before we headed out for the resort the next day.

I spent a lot of time thinking only about the things that surrounded me 24 hours before the earthquake. That is where I wanted to go.

For me traveling back in the past was believable, but what had taken place still seemed unthinkable and beyond possibility.

I thought about the Prince Hotel where we had had our dinner that night. I thought about the food that we had ordered and the conversation that I'd had with Bhai during dinner.

After spending a lot of energy repeatedly thinking about the same things over and over again I finally opened my eyes.

Without realizing what I was doing, I had allowed wishful thinking and fantasies to parade through my mind.

How clever the mind is, I thought. *It is always trying to find escapes from reality.*

But of course escapist fantasies had not worked. I could not go back in the past. I knew that it was not even humanly possible, but I was driven by my desperation to find a solution.

Why can't we live life backwards?

Why is the past always inaccessible even though it's mine?

Why can't I go and mend my past?

Why can't we travel both ways?

The questions about not being able to go back in time bothered me for some time, and then I decided it was time to win this war going on inside my mind.

I determined I would be more vigilant and guard my thoughts, and not spend any energy over something that was not possible. A big part of me genuinely believed that it was possible, and that I didn't have enough knowledge about how to do it. I believed it because I genuinely thought that anything was possible and that there was always a way.

Since I had not eaten anything, part of me thought that my mind was not under my control anymore, and that I was starting to think about the things that didn't make any sense.

More time passed.

It was some time after 3:00 AM when I lay in total darkness looking in the void. I wondered how no one in the world cared about what had happened here. I desperately wanted to reach out to just one person in the world and tell that person that I was alive.

All the while that I thought I was alone and abandoned I wasn't aware of the efforts taking place outside the building, even on an international scale.

Thousands of miles away in Scotland, the International Rescue Corps, a volunteer organization, had mobilized a self-contained search and rescue team to help with the rescue efforts in India. A strong team of 17 members had arrived in Ahmedabad just a few hours ago. The IRC team was one of the first ones to arrive in India. This also was the first time in history when a British military aircraft had landed in Ahmedabad.

At that very moment, this volunteer team of engineers, rescuers and medics were ready in their blue jumpsuits, and were on their way toward the disaster zone. They had just started their journey toward Bhuj, where about 120,000 people were reportedly missing.

It had been about 45 hours since the earthquake, and the death toll was assumed to be about 10,000, and rising quickly. For the IRC team, getting to Bhuj wasn't easy. Two of the crew members were on one truck along with the equipment, and three on another, while the rest of the crew was on a bus that travelled through the unsafe roads and highways that had significant damage. For the IRC team, the race against time had just begun.

Back at Ahmedabad when none of my family had called back after so much time had passed, my grandmother and all our other relatives started to lose patience.

Punal and Raghu packed some food, a few snacks, and an additional pair of clothes, and, hoping to meet us all soon, they had left for the bus station. Before leaving, Punal and Raghu reassured my grandmother that everything was going to be fine.

Both of them were now at the bus station in Ahmedabad, waiting to catch a bus to Bhuj while no bus operator was ready to send a bus to the disaster zone.

"The highways are unsafe!" the bus operator shouted in frustration to the passengers who wanted to travel to Bhuj or to the towns nearby the disaster zone.

Punal and Raghu were determined to reach Bhuj, though. They were not going to return home. As time passed, they gathered all the passengers who wanted to go to Bhuj and planned to forcefully convince the bus operator to ready a bus that would take them to Bhuj. During the next few hours, they continued to argue with the local bus operators, aided by the other passengers. And after hours of heated arguments, the operator finally agreed to send a bus to Bhuj.

Biren, who had left his pregnant wife home, was now only a few hours away from Bhuj. He had left from Ahmedabad during the day with my father's brother-in-law, my uncle Bharat. They had packed some snacks and a pair of clothes, and were headed toward Bhuj in a rented cab.

Unaware of any of these efforts, lying in darkness, I continued to think about the colorful and dazzling lights at Times Square, its electric atmosphere and the people.

For the moment, the battle with my mind was over. I had managed to calm the wild thoughts.

I will go there again, I promised myself.

14

WHERE IS BHAI?

"When the past has taught us that we have more within us than we have ever used, our prayer is a cry to the divine to come to us and fill us with its power."

— RUDOLPH STEINER

Though I felt myself winning the battle for control of my mind—at least I hoped I was—I still needed to occupy my thoughts and not let them run wild. At all. Definitely not allow words like failure or defeat to return.

I searched my memory again, in hopes of finding one to use as another of those "tools" from my past to help me through this ordeal.

Very soon, one emerged. I wasn't sure why, but I sensed that this one contained something special that would help me.

Being an earth scientist, my father occasionally would bring rock specimens home. Every rock that he had brought home had something unusual or unique that I had never seen before. I had seen some truly exceptional rock specimens over the years. I was about 12 years old then and seeing these rocks used to be very exciting. I had developed a hobby of collecting various types of stones of my own. I cleaned them with an old toothbrush and proudly displayed hundreds of them on our terrace.

I had seen rocks that had impeccable crystal formations, rocks that looked like a piece of molten metal, beautiful coral rocks that looked as if the stems of the plant were frozen in time, rocks that had glittering slices of mica. Some of these rocks that Dad brought weighed more than 10 pounds.

Whenever Dad brought a rock home, I hoped that he would let me keep it, but he would bring them only to study them, and then he would always take them back.

Once I saw him bring a big rock home that looked like a big piece of trap rock to me.

"What is so special about this one, Papa?"

He looked me straight in the eyes. "You should worry about your exams, not this rock."

I didn't ask any further questions and went inside my room. I was curious though, about this rock that looked like it was picked up from a construction site.

The next day after I came back from school, I picked up the rock and started examining it. I realized that it was the ugliest rock that my father had brought. When I asked my mother about it, she told me that she didn't know enough. Roshan didn't know anything about the rock either, and so I left it back where I had found it.

A few days later I asked my father again, "What is so special about this rock?"

He hesitated only a moment, then said, "Bring it here, I'll show you."

I picked up the dark shapeless slab and looked at it closely one more time before handing it over to him. He took it in his hands, turned it around and showed me one of its sides.

"Do you see this? Do you know what this is?"

"Yeah, it's a small hole."

He then passed it over to Roshan. Roshan looked at it disinterestedly for a second and passed it back to me, since my mother didn't even want to look.

"The special thing about this rock is *what* caused that hole," Dad said. "This two-inch deep hole was caused by consistent drops of water falling on the same spot for more than 10 years," he replied, with a look of amazement on his face.

"Just a drop of water, falling on the same spot for more than a decade made a hole in one of the toughest rocks known to man!" he added.

Roshan was quite impressed, and he kept feeling the rock. I was a little surprised, but I wasn't as impressed. I would have preferred to see something colorful and beautiful. I looked at the rock closely and saw that indeed the dent on the rock was about two inches deep, and that the rock was softer to the touch around that hole.

A few days later, Dad took the rock back to work and I never saw it again.

It had been a few hours since I had woken up, and I had been scratching the wall in darkness since then. I had never thought about that rock until now, when making a two inch hole in the wall was the difference between life and death. I knew that I did not have 10 years, but I knew that with persistence, impossible was possible.

I continued to think about that rock, and then about the drops of water. It made me think that the consistent drops of water had more power than I had exerted since the time I was trapped.

That was the message of the memory—the "tool" it had surfaced from my subconscious to give me.

Keep chipping away. Every single scratch is accomplishing something, however little. And every single bit of effort counts.

It only made me work harder.

I was feeling very thirsty since the time I had woken up. During the night I had had two more cups of the usual drink, but it didn't seem to have helped much. My tongue was a little moist but my throat was extremely dry. I kept trying to gulp down some saliva even though there wasn't any saliva in my mouth. I wished that I could moisten my throat with my tongue. My nostrils were dry too, and for some reason, I couldn't breathe well, and so, I was now mostly breathing through my mouth, which started to make my throat drier. Nothing seemed to be helping.

In my mind, breaking the wall was now secondary. All I thought about was water.

Now I knew what I needed to do. It was time to use my mind to wage war against thirst. And I returned to my earlier tactic, using thoughts to make water undesirable, the way I'd made myself think of food as disgusting and unnecessary.

Water is not going to save you, I told myself.

What if you were in a flood?

Myriad thoughts rushed through my mind, which were against water. It was as if my mind was pushing me to play a trick once again, same as the one I played when I was hungry. My mind had started making up things so that I could start linking pain to water. I didn't think that this time it was going to work, though. I was thirsty, and my throat was dry, how was that even going to change? But with all my heart, I followed where my mind wanted to take me.

The first thought that came was of people drowning in water. I forced myself to think about people who would have drowned and who couldn't be rescued in time.

How difficult it must have been for those people, I thought.

I thought about hurricanes taking away lives of fishermen in an instant. I thought about the amount of time anyone would have, when they were in the middle of the ocean, and when there's no help coming. To stay afloat in an ocean wasn't easy. How long would anyone last in such a horrifying situation?

I thought again and again about people stranded in such situations and who ultimately drowned. I tried to recall scenes of floods that I had seen on TV. I thought about one of my friends at the local swimming pool who drowned during the summer of 1990. I compared my situation with someone struggling to be found and rescued from the middle of the ocean.

My imagination then yanked scenes from the movie *Titanic*. I thought about the people who drowned. They probably didn't even live beyond a few minutes in the freezing cold water. I also thought about the days when I was learning to swim underwater, and how difficult it was to hold my breath when I was underwater. How desperately I wanted to take just one breath.

I was trying very hard to build a belief that I didn't need water and that water was bad for me. Again, the thoughts about water were like the ranks of an invading army, and with each rank I brought up a countering thought.

It's just hydrogen and oxygen. It's nothing. All you need is oxygen.

My situation was nothing in comparison to someone fighting for life while being swept away in the water. I could talk and breathe, and I had the time to think or to wait for someone to find me. How ridiculous it was to think about nothing but water. I felt a genuine sense of sympathy for the people who died in floods. It would have been so horrific for them.

"I know that I don't want water!" I said again.

My throat was still dry, but I did not care to drink water.

I continued to think about contaminated water, infected water, and so on.

Even though I tried hard, this time the little tricks did not work as well as they did the previous day. It did help me to remain thirsty longer, and made me not give much importance to water, but my throat continued to remain dry. During the next few hours, I had to have another small cup of the usual drink.

It was now January 28th, the third day of being trapped. In my mind, even though I thought that I knew about the seriousness of the situation, I didn't. I thought that it was going to be over in an instant, any moment.

I shouted a few times in frustration.

As before, no one answered.

Dad has big plans for Bhai's 30th birthday at the Taj Ummed Palace Hotel. We all have to be in Ahmedabad in two days!

Roshan didn't know that I had brought a gift for him for his birthday—a wristwatch. It was safely kept in my suitcase in Ahmedabad. Only Mom and Dad knew about it.

I knew that he would show it to his colleagues and friends, the same way he proudly flashed the other gifts that I had brought for him.

Thinking of him brought another twinge of sadness—which I fought off. I headed off this enemy—sad thoughts—very quickly and would only allow good thoughts. Fortifying my mind again, I brought up the best memories and images of him.

We fought a lot when we were kids, but one time in particular had left a very strong impression on me.

He was studying engineering. During the college summer vacation, he had returned home. I had a vacation at school, too, and so the time was spent playing carom or chess, having ice cream, going for long walks with our dog Rocky, and spending leisurely time together at home in the very hot summer.

I had seen pictures of his friends group in the college, and there were some girls in his group too, which was new for him, something I used to often tease him about.

It was about 44°C (110°F) outside when the postman dropped

off the mail. I ran outside without slippers and grabbed the mail quickly so that I could run back inside. But, even before I stepped back in, I saw that there was a letter for Roshan. It was from the girl I was teasing him about. I wanted to read the letter first, but since Roshan was in front of me asking for the mail, I had no option but to run.

With no footwear on, I ran with the letter outside the gate of our house, on the scorching asphalt road. The road was so hot that I had to tiptoe as fast as I could. The little sharp pieces of gravel were piercing the bottom of my feet as I ran, while I tightly gripped the letter in my hand. Oh, I was so desperate to read that letter. It didn't even hurt.

"BHAI! I HAVE YOUR GIRLFRIEND'S LETTER!" I shouted with joy, teasing him from a distance, while trying to open the envelope.

When he heard that, he ran behind me. He was wearing his slippers, and armed with one of my slippers to throw at me, he chased. I had run quite far, so he wasn't going to catch me, but I had nowhere to go! My feet felt ignited, and I kept jumping, and I kept trying to step on the soil and the dead grass that I could find, to avoid the burning hot lava-like asphalt.

I then heard my mother calling for me from inside the home while Roshan tried to catch me. She was the one who finally convinced me to come back and return the letter to Roshan, and told me that it was personal. With charred and hurt feet I returned under the shadow of our cool veranda. What a huge relief it was to step back inside on the cool mosaic tiles.

Before I could look up I got a sharp slap. I didn't even know where it came from. The letter was now in Roshan's hand. He then walked away with the letter without uttering a word. My mom hadn't anticipated any of this, so she quickly took steps to calm the situation down, and told me that it was my fault. Roshan did not speak to me for a few days, which was not a big concern to me. All I wanted was to find the letter and read it.

I knew as a matter of fact that however happy and calm Roshan was for everyone else in the world, he did have a very strong mind, and even stronger control. Only I knew it. He was like a volcano. He wouldn't hurt anyone, and would have tremendous control over his emotions. He was always smiling, always doing everything that he could for others. He would let you mess with him, too, and just laugh it off. But, if someone crossed the line, the volcano inside him would explode. And this anger inside him would not care about what came in its way.

I had had many fights with him when I was younger, and I had gotten beaten to a pulp many times, and so, I knew my limits, and I knew when to stop.

"Where was *Bhai*?"

I had heard his voice the morning of the quake, and before I could even think, the building had started to shudder and then fall.

But this was my brother. My strong, determined brother. I knew that he would have made it outside for sure, because he was awake.

And so, while I continued to win the battle for control of my emotions and my mind, questions did continue to rise.

If he was okay, then why was he not doing anything to find me? Where was he?

15

INTERNATIONAL RESCUE CORPS

"They who lose today may win tomorrow."
— MIGUEL DE CERVANTES

Meanwhile, the previous night, while I was struggling with thirst. . .Punal and Raghu were on their way toward the disaster zone.

Their bus had started from Ahmedabad after midnight, carrying about 40 passengers. It traveled through the broken highways and through the towns that didn't look like towns anymore. Collapsed structures, broken homes, broken highways and homeless people were all that anyone could see from the moving bus. When the bus passed through the small villages like Bhachau and Anjar, the passengers began to realize the degree of devastation. All they witnessed was misery. There was no going back.

After taking various alternate routes and going through various traffic deadlocks, the bus finally reached Jubilee Ground bus station in Bhuj. It had taken the bus more than 11 hours to reach Bhuj instead of the usual 8 hours.

There were no auto rickshaws or taxis available due to the emergency situation in town, and so, after asking for directions, Punal and Raghu started walking toward the direction of our building, Sahjanand Tower. Once they saw what had happened to the town of Bhuj, they went numb. They were surrounded by utter devastation in every direction that they could see. Homes, shops, apartments, small buildings—everything was broken. Most of the buildings or homes they saw were now tilted, or they had collapsed and fallen to the ground. Hundreds of people were in the streets. And before Punal and Raghu could even react to what they were witnessing, "OH GOD!" Punal exclaimed, when he saw our building from about a kilometer away.

Being the tallest building in town, our building was visible from a far distance.

Neither of them had seen anything like this in their life before. They were looking at the disintegrated 8-storey Sahjanand Tower. From a distance it looked like a big part of the building had collapsed. The remaining structure was tilted and still standing, leaning on the other sections of the building, and it looked like rest of the building that was standing could crash to the ground at any time.

Punal and Raghu had come just to make sure that we were okay. Not even in their wildest nightmares had they imagined the horror they were witnessing. They rushed toward the building, with no idea what they were going see or hear next.

The IRC team had arrived in Bhuj at around the same time, and had set up their base camp only a few kilometers away from our building. For them, the immediate and most critical task at hand was to rescue as many people as they possibly could. After coordinating with the local authorities to set up a base camp, they split up into two different teams. The teams started visiting the locations where there had been reports about missing people, and where the locals had reported hearing voices from inside the collapsed structures.

Ray Gray, who was leading the team, had been with the IRC since 1988. He had seen several disasters in his lifetime worldwide. He had seen different faces of tragedies, and he was someone who had previously rescued people and saved lives.

Along with John Anderson, who was the team coordinator, he was supported by Rab Barrie and Paul Wooster, who were the section leaders, and Jimmy Livingston, who was the team medic. There were 11 other team members who worked closely with Ray:

Mark Baker

Brian Davison

Davy Dawson

Simon Drayton

Dave Egan

Stuart Kinsey

Dave Maddock

Sheena McCabe

Jim McElwee

Alan Turner, and

Mark Wilson-North.

All of the IRC team members were now in the disaster zone, which was still experiencing aftershocks every few hours. They were half the world away from their families and loved ones, only to save lives.

Once Punal and Raghu reached the site they were at a loss for words, and they were terrified. Two of the wings of the Sahjanand Tower had fallen to the ground. Slab after slab after slab were piled up on one another, and all they could see was a mountain of heavy cement, concrete and twisted rebar.

The elevator shaft in the center of the building was broken, and was leaning on the other wings of the structure. These wings leaned against each other, and looked as if the entire building would fall if there was a slight aftershock. The collapsed structure had flattened the parking level that was under the building. The pillars that supported the building were obliterated completely, or had pierced through the ground due to the massive crashing force of the building.

Hordes of people had gathered outside the building as this was a known building in town. Locals recognized this building as the one where the movie star Aamir Khan had stayed recently. People were working hard and moving the debris with their bare hands and the tools available to them. They were looking for survivors, calling names of their family members and shouting into the hollow spaces of the broken structure.

After asking around, Punal and Raghu met one of the residents from the building. His entire family was inside the broken structure, and he was desperately trying to find them. He had no information about the whereabouts of our family.

"Yes, I know Dalal *Sahib!* He lives in number 208," the old watchman said, when he heard them enquiring.

Once Punal and Raghu told the watchman about how they were related to our family and that they had come from Ahmedabad in search of us, the watchman gave them all the information that he had.

"I am absolutely certain that the entire family is inside the collapsed structure."

"Dalal *Sahib* came downstairs in the morning to clean the car, and then he went back upstairs. It seemed like the family was about to go out somewhere."

"I also saw his two-year-old grandson the day they arrived. Their entire family is here.

"I am absolutely certain that they are inside the building," he insisted.

Then he described for them how horrific the shaking was and how lucky he was to be alive. He had gone out for a few-minute walk, and when he came back running, he saw that the building had collapsed.

"I haven't found my daughter yet. She had gone to Dalal *Sahib's* home, to help take care of his grandson."

Punal's heart dropped. Raghu was listening to the unthinkable. Both of them were in shock. None of them had faced a situation in life that was even remotely comparable to this.

Punal and Raghu then saw Biren, who had reached Bhuj earlier along with Bharat uncle. They had rented a cab from Ahmedabad and travelled to Bhuj in search of our family. Biren had the same information that Punal and Raghu just heard.

Punal and Raghu now had to let everyone in Ahmedabad know what had happened as soon as possible. The cellphone networks were still down, and there was still no electricity in town. They were told that there was an emergency phone that people were using in town to make long-distance calls. The one and only phone booth that worked was a few kilometers away.

No heavy equipment existed at the site, everyone was hoping that the government would mobilize workforce and heavy equipment as soon as possible. Bhuj wasn't equipped with an army of heavy machinery ready to be deployed. The government had to make efforts to get heavy equipment from various other locations outside the town to help with the relief operations. The majority of the excavators, bulldozers and other heavy machinery were currently on transportation trucks that were stuck in major traffic jams due to highway damages and closures.

After getting enough information, Punal and Raghu started walking toward where the telephone booth was, which took them more than an hour. The queue leading into the phone booth extended beyond the length of a football field, the longest line that they had ever seen. They stood in the line for more than two hours. Each individual in that line was only granted one minute of talk or less.

At Ahmedabad the situation had been such that no one knew what to do. No one wanted to even think that our family was in any sort of danger. It had been two days since anyone had heard anything about us.

"Girdhari uncle's building has collapsed," Raghu told Dinesh uncle in Ahmedabad over the phone. Then he offered more details about what he had seen:

"We need strong young people here. No one else should come here. There is only devastation all around. Please send enough food, water, and clothes for everyone who is planning to travel. There is nothing available here. Money will not help. We need manpower."

"We will call back again tomorrow. There is only one phone working here, and so we won't be able to call again today."

Everyone's worst fears had come true. The news about our family spread like wildfire.

My grandmother was not told everything about what was discussed over the phone. She was told that all of us were inside the building, and that people were trying to find us. She wasn't told that there was nothing left of our wing other than piles of slabs.

My maternal and paternal side of relatives got in touch and discussed what had happened. After a few calls back and forth, a team of individuals was formed who were going to leave for Bhuj within the next few hours. My aunts started preparing home cooked food in quantities that could last for days. A large SUV was rented to accommodate everyone who was ready to go to Bhuj. Additional food packets and tanks of water were loaded in the vehicle. As soon as Surendra uncle from Hyderabad arrived, the loaded SUV with a driver and seven members of the family started toward Bhuj.

In the SUV there was Surendra Dalal, Dinesh Kothari, Kiran Desai, Bijal Shah, Viraj Shah, Jatin Desai and Rupesh Dalal.

"Jai Shree Krishna (Praise Lord Krishna)," everyone said unanimously, as their journey began.

In their hearts they could only hope and pray to find us.

16

THE CLINKS

*"Everybody lives for something
better to come."*

—ANONYMOUS

Was there another tremor? I couldn't tell. My mind had gone beyond arguing with itself and begun to play tricks on me. I shifted my attention to my body.

My muscles were cramping and my lower back was sore. When my breath bounced off the cement slab inches from my face it smelled stale. I tried not to lick my dry lips, as the sticky saliva in my mouth only made them feel drier.

Over the past 55 hours I had told myself many times that I was in true danger and that I would die if I didn't work hard enough. I said that to myself repeatedly, to push myself to work harder.

My thought was that if I could scare myself, then the adrenaline rush "to save my life" would help me break the wall, or it would help me raise the broken ceiling in desperation.

The problem was that I didn't really believe what I said to myself. There was nothing that indicated that I was safe, and yet

I thought that there was nothing that told me that I was in any kind of danger. However odd it may sound, I wasn't seriously thinking about my survival, and I wasn't scared in any way. I thought that I was being too dramatic by even thinking that my life was in danger.

On one hand I was trying to scare myself to death, and on the other I told God that I didn't need any of his help, and that I wasn't scared of anything.

If my spinning thoughts had only been diamond bits, I would have drilled my way out in no time.

As for my physical condition, I wasn't hungry or thirsty, and I realized that if I thought about my hunger or thirst, it grew. Similarly, if I thought about problems, they grew, and if I thought about pain, that grew, too.

Again—*one more time*—I had to come to terms with the fact that I had no control over anything, other than my body to some extent. Outside of this concrete coffin, I had never been in a situation where I couldn't do what I wanted to do.

This was getting harder. Much harder.

Why is nothing working for me?

What am I doing wrong?

What are my enemies?

What did I do wrong in life that God is doing this to me?

How do I keep moving forward?

No answers came.

I believed that most of the ideas and breakthroughs in the world occurred only when the right question and the right answers aligned. I had all the questions, and I continued to look for the answers.

It was getting harder to believe there were any.

It was now January 28, near 9:00 PM IST—some 60 hours, or nearly two-and-a-half days after the earthquake.

Was that right? Was it possible? Had all that time passed?

Even though I had a functioning wristwatch I started to lose track of time. It seemed to me as if the earthquake had occurred an hour back. It felt as if it was still the morning of the earthquake. I was becoming more and more disoriented.

Without the presence of the sun, moon or any shadows, the definition of time for me was my state of mind and a mere digital display on my wristwatch.

A part of me had started getting used to the situation. The darkness, the enclosure, the wristwatch, the environment, the discomfort caused by all the feelings, and even the routine of trying to break the wall.

It was starting to take supreme effort to stay focused. To do so I thought about the problems I had faced during the past two days: darkness, hunger, thirst, lack of oxygen, lack of movement, enclosure, and things that were hurting me physically. The emotions and thoughts like anger, frustration, worry, helplessness, discomfort, shock, unsuccessful attempts, disconnection from the world and sadness came to my mind, as I continued to go over all that I'd faced and dealt with. I did not know if physical problems were causing more pain or the emotions I faced caused more agony. It did not take too long to realize that none of these were the real problems. Concern about my family was the only thing truly bothering me, though. All other problems seemed like nothing to me. These were immaterial hurdles that were preventing me from getting to my family. I thought that I could manage hunger and thirst forever if I knew that my family was safe somewhere.

Again, I took on the battle to keep my mind under control.

I closed my eyes and I pictured myself as a soldier who was out in the jungle. A jungle surrounded with wild animals, poisonous plants, and a dangerous landscape. I thought of it as a dark jungle full of dangers and uncertainty. I had to find a way out of this dangerous place. And even though I had to deal with its dangers and its wilderness every passing moment, I had to make sure that I was not fighting *with* the jungle, but only making my way through the challenges it threw at me. My goal was not to worry about these challenges, but to reach out to my family members who were somewhere nearby and needed my help. I was desperate to find them, and wanted to tell them that I was alive. I didn't want to fight the feeling of hunger or thirst or discomfort. Those were not the real problems. They were just hurdles that were preventing me from getting to the bigger problem. Getting to my family was the problem that was eating me up from the inside.

Even though I hadn't located the cordless phone or my tote bag carrying the cellphone, I started thinking about who I would call once I got out. I was positive that I'd be able to locate the phones then. Maybe I didn't have to call anyone since my father would have it all taken care of, or he would have his contacts take care of all that.

I still thought of calling everyone that I could from Ahmedabad and making sure that I had enough help. I memorized everyone's telephone numbers. I knew that it would take at least half a day for anyone to get here to Bhuj.

I knew that I did not have any cash on me. It was going to be tough to make a long-distance call without any money. I was hoping that someone would lend me money for the calls. I had a gold chain, a diamond ring, and a silver bracelet. I thought of using them if I needed to, to get some money. I wasn't willing to let my watch go.

In my mind's eye, I suddenly became one of the rescue workers. I could see it vividly in part of my mind: I was busy evacuating everyone right away and making sure that none in my family was hurt. I wanted to show everyone else working among the ruins and rubble how rescue work is done.

At the same time, another part of my mind knew that all of this was not needed, because my whole family would be outside, waiting for me.

They are going to be so relieved to see me.

What was going on with my mind? I was the rescued and the rescuer. I was saving my family from the ruins—and I was seeing them waiting for me. And all the while, I was planning more things than needed. Here in the dark, I had to hold it together.

I shook my head. I had to keep my consciousness from fragmenting like this. Keep my mind steady. Focus sharply again.

I tried to imagine how the building would look from outside. As per my imagination, some of the ceilings and walls might have broken and fallen down, but the overall skeletal structure of the building including pillars must be intact. I imagined hollow gaps between the broken pieces of the structure where I would be able to go and search first. I thought that if the building had tilted and fallen sideways, then maybe I would need ropes to climb inside the fallen and tilted rooms.

Since I had fallen two storeys down along with all the floors above me, I wasn't sure if the floors had crashed on top of each other or the entire building fell to the ground sideways. I was confused and did not even know where I was. It was very difficult to even imagine where I was because I had never seen a building collapse before.

I'll find the people responsible for not working, and beat them up if they don't help, I thought in frustration.

For some reason my mind was jumping around again, and I was imagining what my mother would say and how she would react to what had happened. Instantly, though, I killed the thought that came to my mind about the wellbeing and survival of my mother.

It brought such a twinge of anxiety in my gut. I never went back to that thought.

"She would be so happy to see me!" I shouted aloud this time—burying the thought that fought for attention: that maybe she was no longer alive.

For the next few hours I fought with the returning hunger pains, I fought with God, and I fought with the feeling of thirst.

I was extremely exhausted and very sleepy. I felt that I was between the time when you fall asleep and when you are awake, when I realized that the comforter that was tucked under the settled ceiling smelled odd. I tried to bend my neck toward my shoulder to smell it, but the smell did not get any stronger. I did not know what smell that was. I then tried to smell my T-shirt and all I could smell was some sweat, but not the other smell that seemed to be coming from the comforter. A few minutes later, the smell subsided. I slept sometime after that.

A clinking sound woke me up in the middle of the night. I thought that I was dreaming. After a mentally exhausting day, I was in a deep sleep and did not want to open my eyes.

The sound came again. No, I wasn't dreaming.

Shocked, I opened my eyes and immediately looked at my watch. It was close to 3:00 AM. All was quiet as before. I knew that I heard the sound, but I was still not sure if it was a dream or if it was real. While wide awake, I partially closed my eyes and waited for the sound. I had heard it very clearly. I *knew* I wasn't dreaming.

About a minute passed.

The clinking noise was the only sound from outside that I had heard in the last 3 days.

Now awake, I shouted as loud as I possibly could.

"BACHAO! (HELP!)"

"HELLO!"

"AYE!"

Clink.

Clink.

Clink.

I heard the sound again—like two thin metal bars were struck against each other. It was sharp and clear, and it was coming from right above where I was lying. Was someone trying to communicate with me? Or was someone trying to break the ceiling?

I shouted a few more times.

I shouted more, and then I once again heard the sound.

Clink.

Clink.

Clink.

Was this my father or my brother?

The clinking sounds occurred at one- or two-second intervals. There were three distinct clinks, and then it would stop for about a minute. Then again there would be three clinks. Was this someone stuck on a different floor in the building?

I picked up a sharp-edged piece of brick. I closed my eyes, and hit the pieces on the ceiling above my head. Some sand and cement disintegrated and fell into my face and over my body. The ceiling and the wall on the side were the only places where I could hit the wall with all of my energy. I continued trying to make some sound with other stronger pieces of bricks or cement that I could find, while I shouted aloud.

Clink.

Clink.

Clink.

I was now sure that there was someone stuck on another floor, someone who was trying to communicate with me.

Again I hit the piece of cement on the side wall and then on the ceiling exactly three times.

There was no response.

I could not generate a metallic sound, but I hoped that someone was able to hear it.

I heard three again.

Next, I hit the wall four times, to see if someone could hear me and respond accordingly.

Only three clinks came back.

Was it my father? It had to be. Had he been successful in breaking part of the structure in the last three days? Of course he was. That was my dad. Always strong and victorious. Even though I could not be certain this was true, I was ecstatic.

Once more I hit the wall three times and waited for the response.

And so it continued—with me hitting the cement four times, and three clinks coming back.

But only three, not four.

Gradually, the sound became subdued, like it was coming from a greater distance.

With eyes still closed, I tried to make a stronger sound by hitting the cement piece with more energy.

I again heard three distinct clinks in the distance. Now, this time I could not make out where the sound was coming from. It seemed like it was right above me but it also felt as if it were coming from my right side.

I once again heard the three clinks, and responded, and shouted a few more times.

And then, I waited for the clinking sound to return, while holding my breath and focusing every ounce of my attention.

A few minutes passed while I cleaned my face and tried to

brush the sand off from my hair.

Who was it?

Why did no one hear me?

I waited for a long time. I could not think of anything that made that sharp clinking sound. What could it possibly be?

I didn't know. But as the noise faded I fought the sense that maybe someone had come close to finding me but had moved on.

17

PRAYERS

"I am the master of my fate;
I am the captain of my soul."
—WILLIAM ERNEST HENLEY

A *voice* inside said, Should I even bother waking up?

My body felt heavy and drained. I did not want to open my eyes. I didn't know what I was supposed to do. I also thought that I had overslept, and I was feeling very guilty.

Quickly, I shut that voice down and forced myself to open my eyes.

Nothing had changed. It was as dark as it had been before. Nervously, I checked the time on my watch, and realized that I had slept for about 6 hours, and not 9 hours as I'd thought.

Even before I was fully awake I felt upset. I was hungry, I was tired, and I was still in the same situation. I was even more upset because I had another day in front of me and I did not know what I was going to do with it.

Then I remembered the sounds from previous night, and it occurred to me that I had fallen asleep while waiting for the sound to return. Picking up a piece of brick, I hit the wall a few more times to see if the clinking sound from above me returned. Again I shouted.

There was no response.

I'd tried everything to break the wall—and nothing.

I'd tried shouting and banging in hopes someone would hear me—and nothing.

The effort to control my thoughts was getting tougher as I got weaker. All I could do was sincerely hope and pray that the sound had been made by someone from my family trying to look for me.

As the day progressed I was struggling to find ways to keep moving forward, and so instead of just trying to break the wall I decided to write my name on it.

What was I going to write anyway?

Viral Dalal—29 Jan? Maybe.

Even though I didn't think that I was going to die, and that it was pointless, I decided to write my name. I knew that it was going to be difficult.

Writing my name on the wall was not important, but it was crucial to divert my mind from the unsuccessful attempts of breaking the wall.

I started to scratch the wall about 3 centimeters higher than where I was trying to break it. I started with the letter V. I continued to do this for what felt like a very exhausting hour or so.

Suddenly, I heard a sound.

I stopped breathing and froze, trying to listen carefully.

The sound seemed to be coming from a very far distance, and it was not the sound of the churning underneath the ground, but it sounded like a machine.

I couldn't believe my ears. The first thought that came to my mind was that the sound was coming from the highway, which was about a kilometer away. It sounded like a truck. The pitch of the sound was so low that if I wasn't lying in absolute silence I wouldn't have been able to hear it. I had to concentrate really hard to hear the barely audible sound. It made noise like a broken-down lorry in the far distance.

How could I communicate with the driver of that truck and tell him that I was here, not too far away from him?

No answers came. While I scratched the wall, at the back of my mind I was thinking about the number of days I should be prepared to stay without food or water. I did not want to keep my hopes high just because of the sound of a truck in far distance.

Time was moving with glacial slowness. When would I be found? *Would* I be found?

I shook that last question from my head.

"I will be fine for 7 or 8 days," I said to myself without thinking.

I don't know how or why I came up with that number in my mind, but I thought I would be able to bear the pain for that long.

From somewhere deeper than I'd had to reach before, I drew on my determination. "So I have four more days to go!" I whispered.

Once I heard those words, my breath stopped. It was the beginning of the fourth day, which meant that I was not even halfway. I knew that things could get exponentially difficult in the coming days.

The previous night, while I was trying to get some sleep, my cousin Biren, Bharat uncle, and their driver had spent their first night in Bhuj inside the car. They had never experienced hardships in their life even remotely close to what they experienced the first night in Bhuj. All they wanted was to find us, and they were going to try whatever was humanly possible.

For Punal and for Raghu, the previous night had been one of the worst nights that they had experienced in their lives. They had nowhere to stay and nowhere to go. They had spent the entire day doing everything that they possibly could, to get things moving at the site. They had reached out to the town collector's office multiple times to see if they could get heavy equipment working. While trying everything that they could to locate our family, they also had to make several rounds back and forth to the government offices during the day to get help. When they were at the site, both of them would climb the top of the broken structure from different sides, and shout in the hollow spaces wherever they could find one. They had done this many times all through the day. They called our names, they shouted aloud, and they eagerly waited to hear a voice.

After spending the entire day going from office to office to get the heavy equipment to the site, they learned that the town was not well equipped with machines at such a large scale.

There was chaos everywhere. The government officials, local policemen, rescue workers, doctors, firefighters, and everyone who was duty-bound to work operated from outside their office buildings. None of the buildings had been spared. Most of the buildings that were still standing were unsafe to enter because of the strong and infrequent aftershocks.

Files, papers, and everything else that was needed was placed outside on desks and tables that were on the dusty sidewalks and open grounds, or under the shadows of nearby trees. The doctors were trying to help as much as they possibly could, and operated out of tents and makeshift clinics out in the open. With no electricity or an operational telephone line and without an active cellphone network, it only made the situation much worse.

In a situation with a dire need for around-the-clock rescue efforts, everything had to be shut down after 6:30 PM due to the lack of daylight, when the entire town would be engulfed under the shadow of darkness.

That night Punal and Raghu sat a few minutes away from our building, tired, not knowing what the next day would bring.

A large Jeep drove past them, and then it stopped. Someone from the Jeep got out and came closer.

"*Sahib*, have you gotten something to eat?" the man asked.

"Yes we had something that we had brought from our home in Ahmedabad. Who are you?"

"We are the locals from the nearby town, *Sahib*. We loaded our Jeep with homemade food, and we are looking for people who haven't had anything to eat."

Punal and Raghu told them about what had happened, and that with what they were going through emotionally, they had no inclination to eat.

"You need to eat, because you need energy for tomorrow, *Sahib*," the man told them.

The other man waiting in the Jeep joined the conversation. A few minutes later they served a warm homemade meal from large metal containers, making sure that Punal and Raghu ate.

These were locals from the nearby town who probably had lost their own dwellings. They were there to help the other humans in need. They were there to share the pain of others and lend a helping hand.

These men left only after making sure that Punal and Raghu were not going to sleep on an empty stomach. Looking for other people in need, they drove slowly into the cold dark night.

Punal and Raghu slept on a cement platform around a tree that was nearby the building. It wasn't easy to sleep. The temperature was close to 7°C (44°F), and the wind was making it seem much colder.

Raghu, who had spent some time playing with the few-months-old puppies nearby where our building had collapsed, was now sleeping, trying to get some warmth from the puppies who cuddled near his legs.

And as if all of this wasn't bad enough for them, they were awakened and shaken up by strong tremors. They ran, away from the tree they were sleeping under, not knowing where to go and how to run away from the ground that they were standing on.

I had experienced the same tremor that same night, but I did not even wake up since I had experienced plenty of them.

Back in my cement trap. . .

A lot was going through my mind after one more unsuccessful attempt at writing my name on the wall. I was thinking about why I was going through all this. I did not even know how I could gauge this level of pain. To be cut off from the family and the rest of the world without food, water or light and not even know if my family was still alive and have no clue about how many days I would have to spend inside. Was there any more pain than this? Was this the ultimate pain? My mind had started to ask such questions.

I once again noticed that there was an odd smell coming from the comforter. I pulled the comforter near my face and smelled it once again. The smell again subsided after a few moments.

As more time passed, I could no longer hold back worry about my family. It had been tough for me to deal with hunger, thirst and the confinement in the past few days, and I did not know how any of my family members would have coped with that if they also were stuck inside the broken building.

I knew that my father was strong enough to handle such a situation, but I wasn't sure if anyone else in my family could manage without food or water for such a long time.

The level of frustration and agony inside me was such that I felt as if I was going to explode. I wanted to break and crush the walls and the ceiling that were keeping me from doing what I wanted to do. As my anger grew, I started to breathe hard and I could feel my blood boil. I shouted aloud with anger, and I once again tried to raise the ceiling above me. It was yet another unsuccessful attempt.

"I will not give up on this!"

During the next few hours I kept hearing the sound of the truck in far distance. I would hear it for a few minutes and then again I would not hear anything for about an hour.

Here was the strangest thing of all that occurred during this time, when time seemed to stop.

The fact was I had never come across anything like this before. And even though this phase was not coming to an end, I was preparing myself for what could be days of more captivity. I had full control over what I hoped for and I had infinite hope for the future, and I truly believed in myself at this moment. I knew that it was going to be difficult— but that it was possible.

Where was this strength coming from? So many challenges were mounting.

Not the least of which was the fact that I was suppressing my thirst by drinking my own urine, but I wasn't sure if I would be able to do that for four more days. There was nothing else that was going in my body other than the urine and recycled urine. As a result the taste of my urine had intensified ten-fold in bitterness on the fourth day. I wasn't sure how I was going to handle this for four more days.

"You can do anything if you decide. You can move mountains if you have the faith." I remembered my father say.

Did I? Did I have faith that was *that* strong?

Outside. . .

An SUV full of my relatives that had started from Ahmedabad the previous night had reached the town of Bhuj during the day.

Surendra uncle and the driver took turns, since they had to drive through the night. The situation of the town was much worse than what anyone had imagined or had ever seen in their lives before. All of them were speechless once they saw our building. After meeting other relatives, they learned that there was no information available about anyone from our family yet, and that the building watchman was positive that our whole family was inside.

Punal, Raghu and Biren explained the situation that the town was facing and how many times they had tried to get the rescue work moving. They gave everyone a brief idea about how they had spent the night, and what to expect.

No one had anything to report back to Ahmedabad, where my grandmother spent hours in the *Pooja* room, praying to god for the wellbeing of our family. Holding the *mala* in her hands, she eagerly awaited news about our family. She wasn't yet told about the condition of our building.

It was well into the fourth day after the earthquake now. There was a very depressing atmosphere at my grandmother's home where everyone waited for some news about us, while the news channels continued to report the mounting death toll and the devastation across the state.

Mahendra uncle, who had experienced the shaking from the third floor of his building, and had seen the neighboring Mansi Tower fall to the ground, was now staying at my grandmother's home along with his family. All the relatives who lived in the city now stayed at grandmother's home, to give moral support to each other.

Waiting for news from our family for days, Uncle couldn't bare the pain anymore. While everyone in the family gathered together and prayed in the evening, he broke down. He cried aloud like never before.

His daughter Hiral had never seen her father cry like this. She saw the pain that he was going through while waiting for news about our family. She cried with him, and so did everyone else in the family.

Everyone wished the best for our family, but everyone knew that it was now the fourth day after the earthquake. Everyone hoped that we all were inside an intact enclosure, trapped and ready to be rescued, but seeing what was being shown on TV, everyone had started to question their beliefs.

Whenever all the relatives discussed our family, they all agreed that there were only two individuals in our family who could face a situation like this and still come out unscathed. There was no doubt that one of them was my father. Everyone was confident that my father would be safe. Everyone knew about him and his life experiences, and all of them knew that he had always managed to win against all odds. The other person that everyone could think of who could face something like this was me.

All of these relatives were very close to us, and they knew each of our family member's personalities. They knew where everyone's strengths lay.

Everyone who had just arrived in Bhuj saw things that were tragic and demoralizing. They were standing in front of a broken wing of a building that had pancaked beyond recognition. It was difficult for any of them to even comprehend how the building had fallen to the ground.

Looking at the mountain of concrete, all they could do was hope for a miracle.

18

DUMB DOGS

"Experience cold or heat, pleasure or pain.
These experiences are fleeting;
They come and go. Bear them patiently."
—BHAGAVAD GITA, LORD KRISHNA

Other than the dim, blue display on my wristwatch and an occasional glance at the wall, all I had seen in the past four days was darkness. It had been more than 80 hours since the earthquake. I had been lying in the same position since the night before the quake.

For the first three days I had not paid much attention to my body other than for needs like hunger, thirst and the infrequent urinating. Now, well into the fourth day I was starting to observe what was happening with my body.

My back was starting to feel like a slab of stone. Whenever I got a chance, I had tried to remove the sharp bits of gravel that continued to prick and irritate my back every time I tried to move. I was sure that there still were broken pieces of glass from the tube light under me. I could feel them scratch any time I moved. Lying down all this time, my body had become so stiff that I wasn't sure I would be able to bend my back or stand up when the concrete slab above me was removed.

Unlike my back, I could move my feet and legs a little. But since my toes had been facing upwards all this time, the big toe on my left foot had started to feel numb. I tried scratching it against the pieces of gravel and bricks around it. There was still sensation, but it was starting to go numb.

Every half hour or so, warmth would build up underneath my pelvis, which was making me very uncomfortable. I had been moving my pelvis a few inches on either side every few hours to feel comfortable. The temperature inside wasn't uncomfortable, but it was just the heat of my body building in this small chamber that was causing the discomfort.

When I moved my pelvis, I noticed now that my abdominal muscles hurt. They had been hurting a lot during the last few hours. Since this was the fourth day and I was repeatedly lifting my head to reach the wall beside me to scratch, I had been placing a lot of stress on my abdominal muscles. Now the pain was such that I wasn't sure if my stomach was hurting due to the muscular pain or because I was so hungry.

I was experiencing some pain in my shoulders as well, but this was minor. It was the same low level of pain that I used to have when I would work out in the gym.

I seized on that thought. I would think of this pain as something good since it seemed like I was building up strength and muscles in my shoulders.

Then there was pain in my neck; that was a different story. It had become so excruciating that I couldn't raise my head above ground more than three times in a minute. The sides of my neck were hurting and it felt as if my neck would explode if I held my head in the air much longer. I hoped that I could support my head with a large pillow while I tried to break the wall.

I had to do something about the pain that was slowly taking over.

To get some relief I stretched my back a little, then other parts of my body one after another, since I didn't have enough space to stretch my whole body at once. I stretched my legs first. I then folded them a little and tried to stretch my back again. Then my arms.

Immediately, I felt a little better.

My body wasn't getting the required fuel that it needed, but I thought that I was fit physically.

Mentally—well, that was a different matter.

The battle for my mind was starting all over again and becoming more and more difficult. I had to continue to believe what I believed. I had to keep telling myself that everything was going to be all right. I had to keep telling myself that it would be over soon. I had to keep telling myself that four more days stuck in here was easily doable.

But there was one major battlefront where I was not doing so well.

To this point, I had repeatedly told myself that everyone in the family was going to be okay.

Now. . .While I believed in everything else I was telling myself, believing that everyone in my family had escaped unhurt was becoming difficult.

I tried to fight back. I continued to imagine how everyone could have escaped the falling building. But now every time I thought about it I had to force myself to think that everyone was fine.

What was taking so long for someone—anyone—to find me?

As I lay there with my palms on my stomach I could still hear the sound of the truck in the distance. I remembered my school days when I would be awake late in the night studying. During the quiet night I could hear the sound of a moving train ten kilometers away. The sound of the truck sounded similar. I was sure that the sound was coming from a far distance.

I stretched and shrugged my shoulders. It was becoming increasingly difficult for me to just pass time lying and doing nothing. I was not interested in scratching the wall, for now, as I had done enough of that.

I shouted many more times in anger during the next few long, slow hours. Then I would catch myself, and remind myself not to lose my cool.

I had to win mental control again.

"Think of this as a game, damn it! You are hiding. If you are caught, you lose. No one can catch you here. No one in the entire world knows where you are. You can do or say whatever you want. Shout as loud as you like for as long as you want and no one will ever know."

Even as I told myself these things, though, they sounded lame. I knew that I couldn't do even a single thing that I really wanted to do.

The battle was starting to tip in a bad direction.

I realized I was too tired mentally to make up many more stories and put energy and time into believing in them. Every single cell inside my body was screaming at me and telling me that I had to get out, even as I fought to keep telling myself that I had four more days to go.

I was desperate to see even a thread of daylight through a pinhole.

No. Don't give in. Nothing good can come of giving in to desperation.

I tried to locate my lost tote bag once again, and I also tried to locate the cordless phone that could be near my feet. I did everything that I could during this time. I did this with a fresh mind and with all my heart. Nothing brought good results. It was heartbreaking.

Tired and frustrated, I continued to think about what else I could do. I went to sleep between 9:00 and 10:00 PM, tired of thinking.

Apart from a mild aftershock that had occurred during the night, there was another sound that woke me, at around 4:00 AM.

Dogs were barking.

I could hear them clearly. I was in shock, and now wide awake.

How was that even possible?

The barking seemed to be just a few feet right above me. I was in total disbelief. Hundreds of thoughts flooded my mind.

I am going to be out soon.

I will see my family!

Everything is going to be back to normal.

We are going back to Ahmedabad.

This nightmare is going to be over.

My heart started to pound with excitement. Everything was going to be normal once again.

Hearing the dogs, I made sounds like a little dog yapping, so that they could hear me. I then made loud barking sounds. Then the smooching sound you make when you try to get a dog to come. So energized to be found, I kept making that sound thinking that the dogs would hear me and they would bark and bring that to someone's attention.

They had to find me now.

Didn't they?

I could hear the barking so clearly. I could not understand why I wasn't able to hear any other noises all through the day. I thought that probably there were no humans nearby our broken building, as no one responded to my shouts.

I continued to make the sounds of barking like a big dog, and then made all sorts of sounds that a dog would get attracted to.

The barking stopped for some time.

I listened, my mind and soul on edge. Had anyone heard me? My mind was tempted to begin its round of questions, doubts and recitation of beliefs again. I forced myself not to think about my body, how it was stiffening, cramping and aching again.

And then the barking resumed. Along with that noise, I heard the squeaking sound that dogs make when they play. It seemed like maybe these were some small pups.

If I can hear them, then they can hear me, too.

But why were they not responding by trying to dig or bark? Maybe these were just stray dogs roaming around freely on the streets.

But I was desperate.

While I tried to attract the dogs' attention I did not want to lose my main focus. Because, after all, hoping that the sound of barking somehow signaled my immanent rescue was unrealistic. I had not yet heard even a single human voice, and how were dogs going to get me out from under tons of rubble anyway?

I pushed such a foolish hope aside. It was only going to make it difficult for me to stay prepared for the next four days inside here.

"Stop expecting to be out soon!" I shouted at myself, trying to control my groundless elation.

But another part of my mind, and my whole being, was screaming for release.

I began to shout at the top of my voice, many times. It was late, and maybe it was possible for someone to hear my shout, the same way I was able to hear the sound of a passing train a few kilometers away.

No response.

Now I could even hear the sound of wobbly pieces broken concrete pieces the dogs must be climbing all over. But it didn't sound like any of the dogs were trying to dig or raise an alarm by barking.

"DUMB DOGS! BARK! GET SOMEONE!" I shouted in frustration.

"BARK, YOU FOOLS!"

For the next few minutes I kept shouting and making different sounds, my parched dry throat getting rawer and my voice more raspy. In my mind I kept praying that the dogs would do something. Anything.

But again, they stopped barking.

In the silence I fought to keep my spirits high. It seemed like the whole pack had gone somewhere else.

"HELLO!"

"AYE!"

"HELLO!"

No use.

They were gone, and I did not hear them again.

Later that night I slept fitfully, and in between waking and sleeping I thought about why I did not hear any other sound from outside. Why I did not hear Dad's or Bhai's voice during the last few days.

The thought that wanted to break through got me worried—so I would not allow it.

"Once I'm free I will get everyone out!" I reassured myself.

At this moment I thought that I was going to be out soon, and yet I had to keep my furor subdued. I repeatedly told myself that I had to be prepared for four more days. I knew that false hope could cause serious damage to my plan of staying on track.

As time passed I was finally able to focus on how I was going to spend my time instead of thinking about what dogs were going to do for me.

I thought about the number of times I should consume urine during the upcoming days, the number of hours I should sleep, and the number of hours I should spend trying to break the wall.

It took a long time to plan all of this.

Even though I was planning all of this, from inside, I knew that there was a high chance of getting out much sooner.

Or so I needed to believe.

19

I AM ALIVE!

"Of Lights, I am the radiant sun."
—BHAGAVAD GITA 10.21, LORD KRISHNA

Viral, you have to do something be*cause you know that she cannot wait any longer!*

The thought of my mother being trapped somewhere between life and death made me enraged. I started breathing heavily in anger as I thought about her waiting for me to rescue her.

If I did not get out of this cement coffin soon, it felt like some inner spring that had coiled to the breaking point would give.

My body felt like it was on fire with the titanic rage that now surged inside me. My breath came in heated bursts from an inner inferno that felt as if it could vaporize anything around me. Even my skin felt tight and tense.

The biggest core of this monstrous anger was my frustration at not being able to do anything for my family. The other raging core of this fire was not knowing where my entire family was. There were other numerous cores of this hot inferno. Helplessness, thirst, hunger, feeling of entrapment, the lack of movement, the constant disappointments, the inability to do anything, the inability to see anything, and the lack of every single human need.

It was the start of the fifth day after the earthquake, and I had awakened from a fitful sleep around 7:00 AM, hungry and tired after a very disturbing night. I could fight negative thoughts entering my head when I was awake, but while half-sleeping and half-waking, worry about my family flooded my mind.

Lying awake now, I remembered hearing dogs bark during the night and I shouted several times—to no avail. Then I slipped back into fitful sleep.

What was happening outside? Was anyone searching for me? For my family?

Mahendra Uncle, who was in Ahmedabad with all my other relatives, had had a difficult night himself. He didn't know what to say or what to do. All he knew was that our building had collapsed, and that everyone who had reached Bhuj was now looking for us. Later during the day, he went to Lord Hanuman's temple that he used to visit often. He stood in front of Lord Hanuman's statue, and with true heart he prayed.

"Please, my dear God," he cried, clutching a garland of flowers in his hand. "Please. . .please save at least one family member out of the whole family."

He left the temple with tears in his eyes, not knowing what to do. So close was his relationship with our family that he felt he was about to lose everything.

The sound of the truck woke me up after a few hours, this time clearer than before. And now it occurred to me it wasn't a truck but some kind of heavy equipment, like a bulldozer or a crane. Its noise also seemed to be much nearer than before.

People know that our building has fallen.

This was the first thought that came to my mind.

Were they just a block away? Nearer?

How could Bhuj have this kind of a machine?

Then it occurred to me there was a possibility that I would get out today. I was going to be reunited with my family today—because surely if rescue efforts were going on Dad was helping.

My heart pounded inside my chest, and I smiled a little.

I could hear the diesel engine pulsing. . .and then I could hear a louder rumble. Then the sound would go down. To me it seemed as if there was more than one machine working. I was sure that the machine was brought to work on our building, because ours was the only big building in the area. But I had yet to hear a human voice.

Fervently, I prayed for my family over and over. God had to save them. He just had to.

For the next few hours, the intensity of the sound did not change, and I felt more and more certain that I might be found and freed today.

Still questions came: *How are they going to know where to look for me? What if they come close, but never find me?*

With that thought—no one knew exactly where I was—came the daunting realization: A wrong move by the machines outside could crush me at any moment.

In time I began to hear a very low-pitched murmuring sound of what seemed like people shouting. These sounds were extremely difficult to hear because they seemed to be coming from a far distance, and there was intermittent background noise—engines revving, the beeping noise of backing up—coming from the machines. Whenever I heard the voices I could not make out what anyone was saying.

Whenever I heard these voices, I shouted at the top of my lungs. Knowing I was buried under tons of rubble, I was doubtful anyone would be able to hear me even when the machines were shut down.

And then I heard a loud rumble from above—I thought that it was another aftershock.

But the earth did not shake this time, and then I heard a loud crashing thud, followed by what sounded like a heap of bricks and rocks just broke loose and crumbled to the ground from a height. It was a heavy and clear sound that continued for a few long seconds. This sound did not come from underneath the ground, but it sounded like it came from only a few feet away from where my feet were.

I am going to be free soon.

But I had stopped breathing, and my heart started to pound heavily. I could hear beating in my ears.

Breathe...

I dug deeper into my soul, wanting to find that calm place inside of me. *I had to find that place and stay there!*

Now I could hear the outside noises more clearly, and make out the direction where the sound was coming from—somewhere near my feet where I had been looking for the landline phone. I could hear the beeping sound...then the engine revving up...then the sound of metal hitting concrete.

"BACHAO! KOI HAI!" (Help! Anybody there?)

No response.

I shouted again, paused to hear if someone had shouted back and then I shouted again.

No one answered. My voice seemed to be going nowhere, as if I was shouting in vacuum, still.

I now knew that it was only a matter of time before someone would hear my shouts.

Even though I was anxious to get out, another feeling was becoming more acute—and I felt in conflict: I was deeply worried about what I might have to face once I got out.

Brushing dust and sand from my hair and face, I wanted people to recognize me once I got out. And I anxiously waited for the machine to shut down.

All at once it became quiet, except for some voices nearby and the sound of birds—and I let loose with a blast.

"BACHHHAOOO!"

"BACHAAOO!"

"KOI HAI! HELLO!"

"QUIET! QUIET!" I heard from outside. "Someone's shouting. Over there!"

"HELLO! BACHAAO!" I shouted again.

"*HA, KAUN CHE*? (WHO IS THIS?)" Someone shouted back.

It sounded like the person outside shouted for help and called a few more people. Then I heard the sound of bricks and concrete being moved.

"HELLO! WHAT IS YOUR NAME?" he called.

It seemed that he had walked closer to where I was, as I could now hear this man's voice more clearly.

At the top of my voice I shouted, "VIRAL DALAL!"

"I CAN HEAR YOU! I CAN HEAR YOU, VIRA DALA!" He shouted back. Then he shouted to others, "VIRA DALA! VIRA DALA!"

Now I heard others shouting my name.

"SOMEONE IS ALIVE HERE! SOMEONE IS ALIVE!" voices were calling.

Then I heard another voice.

"VIRAL! VIRAL! ARE YOU OKAY?

"VIRAL. ARE YOU THERE?"

This voice sounded familiar to me, but I could not quite make out who it was.

"YES, I AM HERE! WHO ARE YOU?"

"I AM RAGHU!"

With the sound of Raghu's voice, lights turned on inside me. Was my time in the prison of darkness really almost over?

I could not understand how and why Raghu was here in Bhuj. Why didn't I hear Roshan's voice? Or my father's?

"RAGHU, WHERE IS EVERYONE?"

"VIRAL, YOU FIRST COME OUT!"

I tried not to think what this meant. I knew that if my father was outside I would have heard his voice.

"ARE YOU HURT?" someone asked.

"NO!"

"IS ANYONE WITH YOU?"

"NO!"

"DON'T WORRY! WE WILL GET YOU OUT!" Raghu shouted back.

"WHERE IS EVERYONE ELSE!" I shouted.

"WE DON'T KNOW! BUT YOU DON'T WORRY! YOU FIRST COME OUT!"

Why were they asking me about my family? Wasn't someone from my family outside?

The bright sensation I'd felt moments before wavered.

More immediate questions landed on me. How were they going to get me out without hurting me? I knew that even after surviving through more than 100 hours, one small mistake while evacuating me could crush me underneath the concrete slab. I had no clue what it was like from the outside, but all I could tell was that it probably wasn't easy. Someone with a crane carefully had to pick up the broken pieces above me without disturbing what was underneath, and keep doing that until everything was cleared.

"IS ANYONE NEAR YOU?" Raghu asked.

"NO. NOBODY IS HERE."

By now, Bijal, my other cousin-in-law, had rushed to the open ground where the IRC had set up their camp. He told them that he had just heard a voice coming out of the rubble at our building. As the sound of concrete being removed continued I was expecting that people who were outside would know everything, but they kept asking me questions from outside. It was becoming clear they did not know where everyone else in my family was.

I felt a shock of dismay.

"YOU HAVEN'T FOUND ANYONE?" I shouted.

"VIRAL, WE ARE LOOKING. YOU FIRST COME OUT!" Raghu responded.

"CAN YOU HEAR ANYONE ELSE?"

"NO. HANG ON, WE ARE GOING TO HELP YOU TO GET OUT OF THERE."

Maybe my family was in a hospital and Raghu wasn't telling me. Or maybe they were waiting at some rescue station. That had to be it, or they'd be standing right beside him, helping with the rescue effort.

After a few minutes I could hear Raghu talking to someone in English. He told them my name and that I could speak English.

In another moment I heard a voice with a British accent, and then one or two more people talking in the same accent. Were these people called from abroad for help? Why was an international team in Bhuj? Was the earthquake that massive? Having watched rescue operations on TV I knew how methodical and well trained the international rescue teams were and that there were now much higher chances of my getting out without getting hurt.

I closed my eyes and prayed hard, for the first time asking God for *my* life. This was the time when I realized that all things were now in his hands, not mine. "Mr. Dalal, talk to me. Talk to me for a few minutes so that we can pinpoint where you are."

I once again began to ask Raghu about my family—feeling a new sense of excitement to be reunited with them, *finally*—while the British team tried to locate where the voice was coming from.

The team told me that they were now going to dig, and I had to help them pinpoint my exact location.

"Please shout and let us know if you start feeling any pressure anywhere. Okay?"

The first time they started digging, the sound seemed to be coming from above my feet. I told them that they needed to try a little lower, while I was worried that at any time the slab above could crush me.

The next time they started digging, I told them that the sound still seemed to be coming from a higher point. And then when they started digging one more time, it felt as if the sound was coming from where my feet were.

"YES. THAT IS NEAR MY FEET."

The team somewhat knew where I was located, but they were only going based on what I told them. They did not know what cavity my sound was coming from and what position I was in.

While the rescue team dug, using the power tools to cut rebar, steel and concrete, I continued to pray. Very hard.

Images passed through my mind as the loud power tools cut through the concrete and twisted metal rods…closer and closer. I saw myself walking out of the rubble and giving a hug to my mother, a firm handshake to my dad as soon as I saw him. *Bhai* and *Bhabhi* had to be outside with him—of course. I could see all of us playing a game of Scrabble one of the nights before I left for the U.S. I envisioned my mother sitting with Shalin in the lawn of our home in Ahmedabad, in her favorite lawn chair. I saw all of us sitting around the glass-top, cane coffee table, chatting over tea. I saw my dad sitting in his chosen seat on the cane sofa sipping his cup of tea and reading the newspaper.

I could see my mom hugging Roshan and me, with tears of joy in her eyes. I knew that she would take us to the *Pooja* room in our home, and make us bow down to God. I could see myself with everyone in the family, travelling back to Ahmedabad in a bus, and talking about the experience all through the night.

And then I also saw one more image. I saw myself wearing a white Indian long *kurta* and pajamas, sitting in a chair on the lawn.

I was alone.

I didn't know why that thought came to me. I did not return to it.

I knew that once we reunited, we were going to talk about this earthquake for many years. My mom and dad were going to be so grateful to see both their sons.

And then I heard another loud sound, like a hammer hitting the wall. I heard some rubble breaking lose, and I then heard another loud thud. . .

And this was the moment I would never forget.

I saw a tiny ray of light enter the enclosure—this concrete coffin—down near my feet.

"I CAN SEE THE LIGHT! IT'S NEAR MY FEET."

"Light is the most beautiful thing
your eyes will ever see."

— V I R A L   D A L A L

The tiny amount of light lit up the inside of the enclosure, for the first time.

For the next few minutes, the team worked cautiously and meticulously to make the opening bigger. This meant cutting through piles of concrete slabs and the disintegrated walls and pillars that were now a heap of rubble—one that could crash at any time. It took some time because they had to put supports in place so that the whole cavity didn't collapse into the hollow space below. . .where I was lying.

More and more light entered through the hole as minutes passed. And then, I saw a hand.

"I CAN SEE YOUR HAND! I CAN SEE YOUR HAND!"

"YOU CAN SEE MY HAND? CONTACT!" the voice shouted.

So close! And yet I knew it would take only one slip and a split second for the slab above to come down on my body, so I continued to pray.

"DO YOU NEED ANY WATER?"

"NOT RIGHT NOW, I WANT TO FIRST KNOW IF ANYONE IS ALIVE IN MY FAMILY."

"VIRAL, YOU DON'T WORRY ABOUT THEM. YOU FIRST COME OUT!" Raghu shouted back.

I knew that the rescue team still did not know my exact position, they only knew that I was somewhere in the cavity, and the hole was near my feet.

Once I saw that a big hole was made near my feet, I told them that I could try to move myself near them if they cleared the debris and the rubble blocking the hole.

"CAN YOU TURN AROUND?"

"NO, I CAN'T."

As more light fell into the cavity, I could see my surroundings more clearly. I was lying between pieces of mortar and concrete. I now also could clearly see the broken tube-light rail stuck on the wall, the broken pieces of glass all around me, the heaps of broken bricks and mortar, and the haphazard scratches on the wall.

The scratches on the wall seemed so insignificant.

"ARE YOU ABLE TO MOVE YOURSELF FORWARD?"

Now I could see the face of the rescue worker who was bending down and looking at me from the hole.

I picked up my torso, and tried to slide forward, moving inch by inch, as my body brushed against the ceiling.

Then someone grabbed hold of my feet and started to pull me, and I tried to slide my pelvis more toward the opening—praying that at this last moment some disaster would not strike.

Looking up through the hole I could see the faces of three members of the rescue team. All of them were wearing helmets and blue-colored jumpsuits.

"Nice and steady."

"That's it. Take your time."

While they were pulling me out I saw sharp steel rods that were poking out toward me from the concrete slab that was cut.

Two or three people pulled on my legs, while the others grabbed for me as well.

And then my whole body was outside of the hole, my lungs filling for the first time in days with fresh air, and sun beaming down on my skin!

I saw Raghu. He reached out and grasped my hand, while one of the team members quickly covered my eyes with his palms before I could blink. There was so much light I felt blinded by it.

"Okay," one of the workers was saying, "I just want you to lie there. There is all rubble out here and we are going to take you straight into the ambulance, and then you can. . ."

"Actually, let me explain," I interjected. "I am perfectly fine. I just need a little bit of water and a little bit of food. That's it. I just want to be here, that's it. I don't need any ambulance."

"You are going to be checked out. . ."

But I was adamant. "I am fine!"

"Did you hear anyone?"

"There was something going on about two days back, above me."

The rescue team had put me on a stretcher. I didn't want a stretcher. I wanted to find my family and did not want to leave the site. I thought that going to the hospital would mean that I'd have to stay there for days.

"I just want to sit here for a few minutes."

"Take him!" someone ordered.

Before I could argue any further, my stretcher was moved down the slope. As soon as the stretcher was moved toward the waiting ambulance, the crowd erupted. I heard claps, whistles and shouting in the background. People were hugging each other. I saw their utter joy.

What were hundreds of people doing here? And as they moved me away from the rubble I'd been trapped in, I got a momentary glimpse of the bigger picture.

Everything lay in ruins.

What had happened here?

The international rescue team members were in tears. They hugged each other, while I was being taken to the waiting ambulance.

Glucose water was brought into the waiting ambulance for me, but I didn't want to leave the site. I saw more international team members, I saw soldiers from Indian Army, I saw news crews, and I saw hundreds of people who had gathered.

Then I spotted Punal, Biren, Bijal, Dinesh uncle, and then Surendra uncle and Bharat uncle. All of these relatives lived far away from Bhuj. I could not understand why all these people were here.

The more people I saw, the more curious and scared I became. All these faces were familiar, but I was searching for at least one face from my family.

Where were they?

20

THE SEARCH

"This too, shall pass."
— WILLIAM SHAKESPEARE

As soon as my stretcher was lowered inside the ambulance, I wanted to roll off it and dash out through the open back door.

"Please try to relax and remain calm," an attendant said, touching my arm.

I was not going to the hospital. I needed to help move rubble. Now.

"Viral—please!" Punal begged. "We're with you! We'll come back as soon as we can."

IRC team medic Jimmy Livingston came to offer help. He advised me to stay inside the ambulance and told me that I should take small sips of glucose water all through the day, and then he told me that I needed to go to the hospital for a checkup. A few minutes later Punal, Raghu and Jimmy were finally able to convince me to go to the hospital for a checkup. They told me that they wanted the doctor to make the decision about my current state. They assured me that it was going to be a quick checkup.

No one understood how crucial time was to me. Having been trapped myself, I knew that time had to be running out for anyone else buried in the collapsed building. The only thing running in my mind was to get back to the site as soon as possible.

As we began to move slowly through the streets of Bhuj, the ambulance honked at the people milling about. I looked outside the window, and was in shock. I was looking at a town in shambles, one that resembled the aftermath of a war. All I could see were collapsed and disintegrated structures in every direction. I saw roads blocked due to fallen residential apartments, fallen walls, broken shops and unstable buildings, and I saw large heaps of cement and rubble everywhere.

Multi-storied buildings that offered parking underneath were now leaning dangerously to one side, and I could see crushed cars underneath them. Many other structures had

five - to ten-inch wide cracks gaping in their walls.

I saw makeshift beds on the sidewalks and along the roadsides, away from the buildings, and there were people everywhere, clearing and hauling debris. There were excavators at many of the sites and the presence of the Indian Army in the area. The whole town looked as if it had been crushed.

Images of my family ran through my mind, and I felt a sickening twist in my stomach.

The ambulance pulled up to the "hospital"— a makeshift clinic, really, put up in an open area away from the tottering buildings.

The doctor checked my eyes, throat, stomach, blood pressure, reflexes and strength. Only after a five minute checkup did he tell everyone around me that I was perfectly fine, and that there were no abnormalities. It convinced everyone that I was perfectly normal and okay to be released. And before we left he told me that I needed to have small sips of water every few minutes.

When asked by the media about my wellbeing, the doctor said, "Yes, it is a miracle."

As we returned to the site, Punal, Raghu and Bijal gave me as much information as they knew. They told me how massive the earthquake was, and that it was now a national emergency. I learned that Biren, Bharat uncle, Punal and Raghu had come to Bhuj three days back and that some of the other relatives had arrived the next day to provide help.

Biren, who was eagerly waiting for me at the site, looked at me in amazement, his eyes fairly sparkling with joy and relief.

"He is fine! He is fine!" Then he pulled off his footwear and gave them to me, so I could walk near the disintegrated structure.

As soon as I picked my way over broken glass and concrete I saw Dinesh uncle, and Surendra uncle waiting for me, and then I saw all my other relatives who had come from far distances. I saw Kiran uncle, my mother's cousin, and then I also saw Viraj *Bhai*, who was my cousin-in-law's brother, and I saw Jatin *Bhai*, who was my second cousin. . . These were distant relatives whom I hadn't met in years.

It shocked and amazed me that they were here. I felt a small surge of relief and comfort—but I was not in a state to meet and greet anyone.

"Does anyone know anything about my family?"

Eyes looked away. No one did.

None of my relatives seemed to know *what* to say to me—or whether it was a happy moment that I'd been found or a sad moment that my family was still missing.

I was churning inside with the same mix of feelings. Mostly an anxiety and inner pressure were growing by the minute to tear away at the rubble and find my family.

One member of the rescue team approached me and asked if I was feeling better. I was still disoriented, and did not really understand where I was. I had only seen the building from the front, and I did not know how it looked from any other direction. It seemed like I was evacuated from the other, far side of the building where the bedrooms faced, and because of that it took me some time to understand where I was.

Now I walked closer to the broken structure and felt my throat tighten. A huge section of the building had crashed to the ground in a mountain of cement and twisted steel that was about 40 or 50 feet high. I was told that was our collapsed wing. Parts of the building stood tilted, and everything else had crashed to the earth.

My hands and feet felt numb. My lips felt numb. This was not what I had imagined when I was inside the rubble. It was a terrifying scene.

As I got close to the mountain, I was looking at heaps of broken wood, metal, steel and pieces of things crushed beyond recognition. I could also make out some dusty clothes lying on one side of the debris, flattened kitchen appliances, and then some kitchen utensils. The rest was cement, sand, concrete and dust, everywhere. I maneuvered my way toward the debris. Rescuers from the IRC team were working near the rubble. Punal *Bhai* and Raghu walked after me and so did two of the men from the rescue team.

Where had the rooms gone? I kept looking at the ground trying to find something that I could recognize. There were eight floors, flattened, and lying in the form of debris where I was standing.

When I finally was able to reach the spot from where I'd been evacuated, I could not believe my eyes. It was a tiny hole a few feet above the ground level, almost hidden and sandwiched between piles of concrete slabs. It was about a foot-and-a-half wide and less than a foot in height. When I looked inside, nothing was visible. It was dark, and it seemed as if there wasn't enough space even for a small animal to live inside. I couldn't believe that I had spent almost five days in that wormhole.

"Did you hear any noises, Mr. Dalal?" one of the rescuers asked.

I told them about the sound that I had heard two days back, late in the night. "I did not hear anything else."

Then I pointed out where I thought the other rooms were located based on the spot where I'd been evacuated.

By this time hundreds of people had now gathered near the building. More media personnel, news reporters, and many other locals who had heard about my rescue gathered near the building to make the situation more chaotic.

The sense of urgency I felt was now beginning to run up against another feeling. My hands were sweating. But I could not allow the feelings or the thoughts that came with them to push through into my mind.

I shouted many times in the hollow spaces that I could find, while the rescue team members continued to look inside the hollow spaces with their flashlights.

I tried to pick up a large block of concrete and realized it was far too heavy. It was not possible to move anything with bare hands, because concrete was tangled in rebar, which made it difficult to break, even for the heavy machines.

Then I recognized the sound of the excavator that was left running on the ground. This was the same sound that I'd been hearing for the last two days.

"Why is nobody working here? Where is the driver?" I asked Raghu.

"It looks like the driver may have gone somewhere."

"There are a few Indian Army men who are helping out. Other than that there are local people who are making all the efforts that they can," Punal said.

A surge of rage flooded over me. I rushed back toward where all my relatives were gathered.

"Why can't we all work and clear the debris?"

"*Béta* (Dear Son), we cannot do anything without the heavy equipment. The concrete is too heavy and it's a very big building," Dinesh uncle replied.

I could see his point, but the frustration was eating at me.

One of the IRC team rescuers wanted me to draw a map of our apartment for him, so I drew a map on the dusty ground and showed the team where I was when the earthquake occurred, and where I thought the rest of the family might be.

My relatives had as much information about my family as I had. I told everyone about what had happened—that I was sleeping when the earthquake occurred, that everyone else was awake, and that all of them were probably in the breakfast area at the time of the disaster.

"I heard Mom shout just before the building collapsed," I told everyone.

"Your father is a very strong man, Viral. He will come out just like you did," Dinesh uncle said. "Yes! We will find everyone, Viral," Raghu assured me, holding my shoulder.

I took a slow, deep breath. I *had* to steady myself by holding onto this belief.

One of the IRC team members told me that they had been at our building site two days earlier, during the night, to perform a search.

"So was that your team making the clinking sound in the middle of the night?" I asked.

"Yes! Did you hear that when you were inside?"

"Yes! I heard that and I kept hitting the wall and then I kept shouting, but no one responded."

He told me they were performing a TPL search that night, meaning Trapped Person Locator. The device that they use to perform a TPL search is a highly sensitive instrument that can detect noises, cries, knocking, scratching and many other nearly inaudible sounds made by trapped persons as they struggle to be rescued.

"We didn't pick up any signal at your site, though, and so we moved on."

For half a moment, it occurred to me again how extremely lucky I was to have been found at all.

And my next thought was how difficult it was going to be to locate anyone else buried in the mountain that had been our building. I felt my stomach knotting.

While we were talking, I saw the hydraulic arm of the excavator move. I saw that the driver was now inside the glass cabin, and was getting ready for work. He recognized me by looking at my dirty clothes and a dusty face, and his face broke into a big smile.

"Where are the rest of the workers?" I called out to him.

"They are there," he shouted back, pointing somewhere at the crowd.

I saw a few laborers with big wrought-iron *taslas*, large, bowl-shaped containers that workmen carried on their heads to haul away dirt. They were lugging the *taslas* at their sides at the moment, getting ready for work.

"I don't have good shoes, but I can help you to clear the debris."

He then told me that the concrete had to be broken down into smaller pieces first, so that it could then be carried away. I was desperate.

And I was *angry*.

"My entire family is in there. I desperately need your help. Please."

The smile left his face, and he nodded somberly. "Yes, *Sahib*. I will help you. The other driver ran away yesterday, because he couldn't handle the pain anymore. I will stay."

For the next few minutes, I tried my best to point out to him where the other rooms were, and where I thought the adjoining bedroom was. I then moved away and watched. All through this time, Punal, Raghu and Biren were around me, trying to help in every way they could.

It was then that I spotted comforters and bedsheets over at the side, in a heap of debris adjacent to where I'd been evacuated. Raghu told me that it was an air-conditioning unit that our neighbor wanted to preserve and thus it was kept covered. It made me more furious. How could people think of preserving an air-conditioning unit in such a situation?

Within the next hour, more searches were performed by the IRC team, and now other international rescue teams had joined the search operation. Some came with search dogs and more equipment. Different teams in different-colored jumpsuits were now walking around the building, looking for signs of survivors.

Looking at the crowd standing at the distance, it seemed as if there were more media people than locals. Someone told me that they were waiting to talk to me. I did not want to talk to anybody.

All I could do was continue to watch the steel arm of the excavator, while taking small sips of glucose water. As I watched, it became very clear how difficult it was to break through the concrete and carefully move the debris. The steel teeth of the excavator bucket would scratch the surface of a concrete slab—then it would slip. It would take about 20 minutes to break one steel bucket full of rubble. All of this reminded me of. . .me, scratching the wall with the piece of aluminum in futility.

Other power tools were being used to cut through steel and to drill holes in the concrete, but the progress was extremely slow.

The picture of a destroyed building that I'd entertained in my mind before was totally different than what was in front of my eyes. When I was stuck inside, I had thought that even if the structure had broken apart and the walls, ceilings, pillars and everything else from the building had broken to pieces, a crane could still pick up the pieces one at a time to clear the debris. In my mind, I thought that it was as easy as picking up each piece and putting it aside, just like a game of Mikado pick-up sticks—the children's game in which sticks are removed from a pile without disturbing all the others.

What I'd never pictured was this mountain of rubble more than 40 feet high—so high that the arms of the heavy machinery could not reach the top, and so the tons of rubble could only be cleared from the bottom, one scratch at a time.

Looking at the massive mountain of rubble, I couldn't even think of the number of days it would take to clear the whole area at this pace.

Punal, Raghu and Bijal watched the excavator, while I now tuned in to what my relatives had to say.

"We did not hear from anyone from your family after the earthquake. Knowing your father's nature, we thought that your father would return the call as soon as he can. We waited for some time, but then our patience ran out. We then planned to send Raghu and Punal first, and then we came to know that Biren and Bharat uncle had also reached Bhuj.

"And then when we learned about your building, we formed a team of a few men who were ready to stay in Bhuj in these conditions."

There were many other people from the same building who were waiting to find their loved ones who were still missing. I met them and answered their questions. I told them about the noises that I had heard. Unfortunately I only had that tiny bit of information for them.

Dinesh uncle then called Raghu, who was watching the excavator. He and Raghu went on the side and talked to each other for a few seconds, then came toward me. Raghu took a white handkerchief out of his pocket which had a few knots. He undid the knots and then gave it to Dinesh uncle. Dinesh uncle uncovered what was in the handkerchief—a diamond ring, a gold bracelet and a gold chain.

I recognized them immediately.

"These are *Bhai's*! Where did you find them?"

My heart had started racing. Was he in the hospital? Was he somewhere around here? Was he deceased?

My uncle looked at me carefully. "Are you sure?"

"I *know* these are Bhai's belongings. Where did you find all this? Where is he?" I pressed him.

"No, no Viral, we haven't found him. We have only found this in the debris."

A bolt of anger shot through me. "There is no way you could find this in the debris. *Bhai* never would take his ring or bracelet off. Never. Tell me, where you found it?"

"Your brother may have taken them off while taking a shower and probably set them on the bathroom window."

"No! Bhai never would take his ring and bracelet off before taking a shower!"

"We found this in the debris, Viral. We have been looking for everyone in the family for days. We just wanted to confirm that these were Roshan's, because none of us knew what gold ornaments he was wearing. We guessed these were Roshan's, but we were still not quite sure."

My head throbbed. I did not know what this meant. Had some-one else found Roshan, and he was in the hospital? I kept trying to get answers to the questions about where the jewelry came from and I got the same answer from everyone. Everyone told me that this jewelry was found lying in the debris and that none had claimed it yet and so they were carrying it.

I could not think of a reason why anyone would hide anything from me.

And even though I was asking everyone questions, somewhere deep down inside me I knew. I did not want to hear the words from anyone, though. So I kept asking questions and wished that everyone would give me the same answer as before. "We found these in the debris." Secretly, I hoped that Bhai was in the hospital, being treated for a minor injury. But my heart told me otherwise.

Bhai is no more.

21

THE TENT

"And if not now, When?"

—HILLEL THE ELDER

Biren and Bijal stood next to me, watching the excavator.

A dark feeling was tugging at me. Our building had crashed so quickly and come down with such force. I thought about Dad's meticulously kept car, which had been parked on the lowest level. It had to be crushed completely now.

I shook that image out of my head.

Biren told me about the devastation all over the state, and that the earthquake was felt even in Mumbai, where he lived.

"No food or water is available anywhere. Cash in your pocket is worthless. We had to stand among the flocks of people waiting for the government-assigned relief trucks distributing bread and snacks."

He told me about how massive this event had been, and that it was now termed as one of the biggest earthquakes in India's history. He also told me that there were thousands of people dead in Bhuj alone.

"I didn't even know that it was an earthquake until the first few seconds, Biren *Bhai.*"

I told him about the shaking, and the dangling ceiling fan, and then the ceiling cracking and falling on me, and then the fall of the building.

Punal watched the excavator while he sat on the mound of red soil that was about 20 feet away from where the operator was digging. There were several big and small mounds all around the machine.

Raghu told me about how difficult it had been for Punal and him to get an excavator to the site.

"After demanding an excavator for two days, we finally got one for this building. Nobody knew what to do. There was only chaos everywhere."

"People came here to have a look at how the tallest building in town had fallen. They would look and then stand there and talk. And then more people would join and look."

He told me about the heavy machinery that was stuck on the broken highways and that some of the machinery operators had not shown up for a second day of rescue work, because they couldn't handle the job of retrieving dead bodies.

"So this machine sat here, and half a day got wasted going back and forth to the government offices requesting another operator."

As I listened, I could hear that Raghu was angry and extremely frustrated. He had seen and helped evacuate many dead bodies from the rubble in the last two days, and helped to take them to the cremation ground for their last rites. More than 30 bodies had already been evacuated from the building.

"It's a pathetic situation. . .I have no other words," he concluded, and fell silent.

"We are really glad that we found you, Viral. We had given up hope of finding any of you alive," Punal said.

I was now slowly beginning to understand things that were happening while I was struggling inside.

"So where did you all sleep?" I asked.

"We slept where all the relatives are sitting right now," Punal pointed. "Right under that tree."

Some of the relatives, I learned, were sleeping in the car and the SUV, while others were sleeping in the large tent that was erected by my dad's colleague for the purpose of a house-warming ceremony on the January 25th, a day before the earthquake. The tent wasn't removed after the earthquake, and was kept for people to get shelter during the nights.

"There are no hotels available. Most of the hotels here have been damaged or have totally collapsed. None of the structures in Bhuj is intact or safe anymore. Each and every house, big or small has been damaged. We will be sleeping in that tent tonight."

Two of the other IRC team members came toward me and looked me in the eyes and with heartfelt smiles shook my hand.

"You are a very lucky man, Mr. Dalal, a very lucky man," one said, as he clapped me on the back.

Did I feel lucky? Even though my life had been spared—there was still my family to consider. Those who still stood the chance of being rescued, at any rate.

Then he explained they were going to perform some more tests, using a camera to reach the hollow spaces that were accessible from the outside, to catch any signs of life. The device that they were going to use had a small camera attached at the end of a wire. The handheld display monitor would show them the surroundings of the unreachable cavities.

The team members proceeded to look for various spots to locate the appropriate hollow space where the wire could be inserted.

They kept climbing higher over the rubble to look for the right spot. They would stay at one specific spot only for a few minutes, then move on to the next.

All around us, the crowd stood silent and with folded hands, in anticipation. And Punal, Raghu and I kept looking for spaces in the debris in an effort to help the team.

After trying for about half an hour or so, the IRC team told us that they were unable to pick up any signal from inside, because there wasn't any space for the wire to reach inside the structure. They would come back the next day when there was more visibility, and when some more excavation was done.

I thanked them many times for their tremendous work as they climbed back to the ground with their equipment.

During the next hour while the excavation continued, I changed into a fresh pair of clothes that my father's driver had brought for me from his home.

Dinesh uncle who was very close to my mother and to the rest of our family came near me, insisting that I eat. "You haven't had anything in the last five days. Eat *something*, my dear.

"I can understand how you must be feeling right now, but you need to eat something so that you have enough energy to stand where you have been standing for the past few hours."

But I didn't feel like eating. How could I? Knowing that my family members must be struggling between life and death, only a few feet away from me.

In the quiet space that followed, he cleared his throat— then told me his thoughts about our family. . .and that everyone thought there were only two persons who might survive something like this.

"After seeing the devastation, we couldn't help but think about the worst-case scenario. We all thought that whatever happened, you and your father were the only ones who could survive through something like this. May God help them wherever they are," he concluded, barely controlling the tears.

It had started getting dark, and it was becoming difficult to see since it was about an hour after sunset. The excavator now had its two rectangular flood lights switched on. The lights were high up, and focused only on a small area in front of the machine. Even so, it was very difficult for the operator to see anything due to some of the long, extending concrete slabs that spanned dark shadows underneath the bright light. I was only a few feet away from the steel claw, but I could not see anything clearly.

The next half-hour went by, watching painfully over the machine doing its job, and making sure that its large steel claw did not end up hurting someone inside. The helper in the excavator, one of the neighbors, Punal, Raghu, Bijal, and I were helping the operator by watching the arm very carefully.

After some more time, the machine was shut down. The driver told us that there wasn't enough light for him to continue his work, and that he was extremely nervous of hurting someone stuck inside.

"Pull an electrical cable from somewhere. Get a generator," I argued. "Do whatever it takes to keep working. My family is out here. Do you understand? They cannot wait for anyone. They are inside and they are between life and death right now!"

"*Sahib*, I am just an operator. I don't know where to get the lights. There is no electricity in the town yet."

Even though I'd seen the devastation of some of the town I hadn't fully grasped the situation here. Raghu and Punal told me that there was no electricity in town, and that there were no shops or a place where we could get a generator or anything that would help us. Nothing in Bhuj was functional.

"The whole town lacks basic necessities like food and water, Viral. People are homeless all over the town."

The situation was bleak. We had to work with what we had.

I still continued to ask the operator to keep working, and I was able to convince him to work for some more time for us. I told him that there were five people to guide him, and that he didn't need to be nervous.

"We will watch very closely. Please do it for us. *Please*."

The operator now worked very cautiously due to the lack of light. Within just a few more minutes, however, the machine was once again shut down.

"Viral, we have to come back tomorrow now," Raghu said.

Punal and Raghu once again tried to explain the situation to me.

"We have to get the generators from the government offices, nearby homes, somewhere!"

"Not a single building is spared, Viral. Government offices are trying to manage the situation by keeping their desks outside the broken buildings."

Frustrated energy took hold of me. I did not know what to do. I wanted to break everything that came in my way, but we had no other option except to stop working until daybreak.

Within a few minutes it had become totally dark. The broken columns stood there in the blackness. It looked like an abandoned and dead structure standing in the night, broken.

The excavator operator left after convincing us that he was going to be at the site early in the morning. I thanked him several times and requested him to come back without fail, and not to run away. He assured us he would not fail us.

I thought about how difficult it must have been for all my relatives to be here, with nowhere to go even to get some sleep. All of my uncles were close to 50 years of age or above and none of them had seen any hardship in their entire life. They had left their families back home in such a situation only to help our family.

Dinesh uncle told me that one of the religious temples nearby had setup a relief camp, and that we were now going there to get something to eat. I did not want to join them, but I was forced to since everyone was going.

"I will not force you to eat, just come with us, Viral," Surendra uncle insisted.

Sitting next to uncle in the SUV, we all headed to the temple. As we passed through the street, I once again saw devastation. It looked as if someone had crushed the town, and crushed the confidence of the masses. There were no lights anywhere I looked. The only bright lights were our vehicle's headlights. I saw people walking with flashlights in their hands and a lot of people sleeping by the sidewalk or sitting by bonfires trying to get warm. It was about 15° C, and the temperature was dropping quickly.

"All these people have nowhere to go. They have all become homeless," the driver told us.

People were all over the place, and yet it looked like a ghost town. I looked at the devastation in awe. This was just one of the streets in the city, and I had only seen what was visible in the darkness. I did not know what the rest of the city looked like.

Everyone was quiet during the ten-minute ride to the temple. Once we reached there, we saw a very large gathering of people—at least a few thousand. I could hear the announcements that were being made on the loud speakers, about food being offered to everyone. We parked the vehicle about 500 feet away and walked through the dusty path toward the temple.

There was a very long line of people standing in the cold and dark winter. Punal told me that it was the line for making phone calls, and that he had stood in that line for hours to get a message out to Ahmedabad. This is the only telephone booth that was working in the town, and this was the only place where they had generators working so that there was enough light.

I followed where my cousins told me to go as we joined a horde of people heading toward where food was being served.

Even though there were thousands of people there, there was silence. People were quiet. Most of them had lost someone in their family or they had lost their home. I overheard some of the locals talk about their experiences, and about their loss.

Fresh food was being served on sheets of newspapers that were cut to 10 by 12 inches. The food was kept in big metal drum barrels, and there were volunteers who were helping serve.

Khichri (a preparation made from rice and lentils) and *bhajiya* (fried Indian snacks) were served to everyone in limited quantities.

Dinesh uncle and Surendra uncle insisted that I have something to eat, many times, but I refused.

"You need energy to work tomorrow, Viral. You haven't eaten in days. Eat *something*."

I really did not feel like eating, not only because of the situation but also because I had convinced myself that food was a vice, and that it was a bad thing. With their insistence, however, I accepted a small serving of *khichri*—though I could not finish most of it.

After everyone else ate, we headed back toward where our tent was. Once we reached there, I saw a large tent that was about 30 feet long and about 15 feet wide. Holding a flashlight in hand, we entered the tent to see that there were some blankets lying in the corner and the ground was covered with a thin cloth.

"We need to go now," I insisted.

"Where do you have to go now?" Dinesh uncle asked.

"I have to go back to the site to see if I can hear anything."

"Viral, we will all go early in the morning. There is no light out there," Punal reminded me.

"Yes, I know that but I will carry the flashlight. I have to go there—*right now.*"

"Then let me come with you," Raghu offered.

We headed back to the site with the driver. No one talked.

Please God, make me hear someone's voice from the debris, I prayed silently.

We reached the site within a few minutes. During the day, there were hordes of people, and now there was not a soul to be seen. It was late in the night, and in total darkness I could only see the outline of the leaning tower, in the sky. When I looked at the ground, I could barely see anything in the pitch-darkness.

Raghu and I walked slowly and cautiously toward the location from where I'd been evacuated. It was extremely difficult to walk even a few feet in darkness, and it took maybe ten minutes to walk through the debris and reach near where the excavator was parked.

I flashed light inside every hollow space I could find.

"HELLO! *KOI CHE*! (Is anyone there?) HELLO!"

Raghu and I shouted many more times in the hollow spaces. And after each shout, we would wait to hear something or someone. There was no response.

"Punal and I have shouted hundreds of times in the last few days, Viral," Raghu informed me.

No one had responded then either.

But I was inside at that time! And no one could hear me. Not even the machines. After spending some more time at the site in total darkness, we drove back toward the tent. I asked the driver to be ready at 7:00 AM for us.

When I stepped back inside the tent I saw that everyone was asleep. I heard snores in the darkness, and looked for a place to sleep.

There were two spaces with folded blankets where Dinesh uncle was sleeping. I laid on my back on the ground next to him. The ground was cold, and I could feel the little sharp pebbles underneath the thin cloth covering the ground. Looking in the void I was thinking about what had suddenly happened to my life and what I was going to do now.

Even though I was outside the building, I was still shouting to find my family, and there was still no one who was replying.

I woke up several times during the night because of unstoppable thoughts running in my mind. The thoughts were about getting to the site and evacuating everyone. I had many other thoughts that were about evacuation and nightmares about waking up late.

Even though days had passed, I still thought that once I opened my eyes, everything was going to be normal. I wanted to wake up and get a shower so that we all could then go to the resort.

The box-shaped tent we were sleeping in did not have any kind of shutter. It was a tent that had an opening as wide as its width. It was a very cold night and the cold breeze made a whistling sound as it passed through the gaps in the tent. I looked around and saw that everyone had their faces covered.

I am going to find everyone tomorrow, I promised myself.

All through the night, this was the only thought I had.

22

I KNEW. . .

"Some days the dragon wins."

—ANONYMOUS

The news about my being found alive had spread. My rescue was shown on TV, across the nation and on all the major international networks repeatedly. Various news agencies gave me various names. "Miracle Boy" was one of the terms used repeatedly.

When the news about my survival reached all my relatives in Ahmedabad, the atmosphere changed at my grandmother's home. Not much, but a little. Even though it had been five days after the earthquake, there was now new hope that our entire family would be found alive.

Mahendra uncle had just reached home from the Lord Hanuman's temple when he heard the news about my rescue. Even though the other members were yet to be found, his happiness knew no bounds. He knew God had just replied to his prayers. God was listening.

Each one of my close relatives was going through different emotions. No one had seen anything like this before. Bharat uncle, my maternal uncle, who was now in Reno, Nevada, called every few hours to get some news about us. He had always been very close with our family, and all he could do was wait helplessly for some good news.

Meanwhile, in Bhuj, my own tension mounted.

The digital display on my watch showed 6:00 AM. Everyone else was sleeping in the tent. I could see the sky starting to light up in the far distance. It was freezing cold and windy, and I still had the blanket wrapped around me. The date display on my watch showed 31 JAN. I was scheduled to leave back for the United States on February 5th. I still thought that it was possible to find everyone today, just like I was found. I couldn't think of a reason why it was not possible.

After seeing what I saw yesterday, I now knew that I had to rely on the heavy machinery for excavation. I was also starting to understand how difficult it was to clear the debris and how hard it was for people to even survive in the town.

"Viral, go to sleep, dear. There is still time," Dinesh uncle said, when he saw that I was awake.

"No uncle, I am awake now. Don't we have to go back to the site now?"

"It's still too dark, and the machine operator will be there much later. You should get some more rest before daybreak."

I waited for some more light. Punal had told me that the tent belonged to the owner of the home next to it, and that he was kind enough to let us use anything that we needed from his house.

About half an hour later, the ground started to become more visible. Surendra uncle woke up and he took me to the nearby home. I met the owner of the house whose tent we all were sleeping in. He told us that he had known my father, and he knew that my family was still inside the building and had not yet been found. He told us that he was there to help all of us in any whatever way possible.

"The least I could do is help. Please feel free to use anything in the house. Please," he insisted.

When I entered his new home I saw a plush home with marble flooring and expensive furniture. The walls of this new home had cracks that were about an inch wide, and the flooring had visible cracks in various places. This gentleman's family was sleeping on the beds that were put in the garden, since the home was unsafe to inhabit, especially when frequent aftershocks were still taking place.

He was preparing morning tea for everyone inside the tent, and told us that his two bathrooms were available for use.

I was provided with two large buckets of hot water in the bathroom. It had been six days since I had taken a bath. In the bathroom when I poured water over myself, all I could see on the floor was soiled brown water. I washed myself from head to toe as well as I could. I cleaned my teeth with my finger. I then dried myself with my own clothes, cleaned the bathroom as well as I could, redressed in the same clothes, and left as quickly as I could.

It was remarkable to see how people came together to help one another in this time of need. Through his actions this gentleman had earned so much respect from me. I wanted to spend time with him and thank him for everything he had done for me and my relatives. I wanted to thank him for the tent, and for the support and for his kindness, but I knew time was running out for everyone still trapped under the debris and I had to go.

"Please pray for my family," I said, before I left his home.

"May God be with you."

Surendra uncle and I left for the site first, after we decided that others would join us once they were ready. The driver had had his morning cup of tea and was ready to drop us off.

We were among the first few to reach the site. There were a few neighbors' faces that I could recognize. More people had started to come in as minutes passed. The excavator was still parked where it was left yesterday. I was scanning the faces in the crowd to find the excavator helper or the operator. They were nowhere to be found.

When I walked toward the debris an unpleasant smell hit me, and I covered my nose. I recognized this stench. It was very similar to the smell coming from the comforter when I was trapped inside. And this was very strong and difficult to bear. I did not know if this smell was coming from a dead body and could only hope that it was not coming from any of my loved ones.

It was 7:15 AM, and there was now enough light to start work, but the excavator operator was still missing. Had he run away just like the other operator? What were we going to do if he didn't show up? Would another day be wasted?

That was *not* going to happen. I started to plan things in my mind without wasting any time.

The other groups of neighbors also were desperately waiting. I spoke to them and tried to get more information about the driver's home. No one had any information other than the name of the village that he came from. We all planned to wait 15 or 20 more minutes, after which I planned to go to the government office to request another operator.

I felt a surge of impatience go through me now. Extremely crucial time was being wasted.

Once Punal, Raghu and a few other relatives arrived at the site a few minutes later I explained the situation.

"The operator should be here in the next 15 minutes or so, Viral. That is his usual time," Raghu told me.

The usual time! This is not a usual time. People's lives are at stake. What was everyone thinking?

Each minute felt like an hour.

At 8:05 AM, I saw the driver and his helper walking hurriedly toward us, leaving small clouds of dust behind. Both of them wore the same clothes from last night. I was extremely relieved to see them.

Still, reading my look of worry, he said, "I gave you my word, *Sahib*. How could I break your trust?" Then he rushed on to explain.

"I came as early as I possibly could. The village where I live is in shambles, and I didn't get home till past midnight. Then I started back here again at 5:00 AM, but it was very difficult to hitch a ride. I had to walk until someone picked me up and brought me here."

All the other relatives arrived in the next hour, and together we watched the excavator start to break the mountain, piece by piece, going much faster now that there was daylight.

As he worked, everyone remained alert for signs of dead bodies or sounds, though over the noise of the machine even shouts were hard to hear.

I found myself squeezing my hands into fists, holding on to hope with all my might.

The excavator was shut down a few minutes past 1:00 PM. It was time for the operator to take a break. I, however, continued to comb debris, along with Raghu and Punal, looking for anything from our home—pieces of granite, the large metal cupboards, the dressing table, the bed, comforters, pillows, shoes, jackets, handbags. . .anything. There was nothing. I saw some new hollow spaces that had opened up. I shouted aloud a few more times inside these spaces. There was no response.

Though everyone urged me to eat, I could only reply, "If I cannot stand anymore, I will come here and ask for food."

I had no idea what kind of energy I was carrying. I only knew I could not stop.

When the operator returned, he continued breaking the pieces for the next hour. Shortly, Punal, and Raghu called me to where my other relatives were.

As I walked closer, Punal came toward me, put his arms around my shoulder, and walked me away from everyone else. I thought he was now going to advise me to have some food.

But he didn't.

"What's the matter?" I asked.

"I need to tell you something." He still had his arm around my shoulder, and his voice was serious, reluctant.

I looked back and saw that all my other relatives were looking at us.

"We have found Roshan," he said.

A hundred thoughts ran through my mind. Was my brother found on the other side of the building? Was he in the hospital? How could he be found when I was watching the excavator every single minute? Where was he now?

"Where is he?" I demanded.

Punal took his hand away from my shoulder and pointed at the excavator. "He is there. . ."

"Where?" I could see nothing.

"We found his body yesterday—before we found you, Viral. He is underneath sheets and comforters from where you were found."

"That is an air conditioner, Punal *Bhai*. Where is *Bhai*!"

He was silent.

"Why you didn't tell me yesterday!" I shouted.

Dinesh uncle had come up beside me, his eyes full of tears. "We could not bring ourselves to tell you yesterday, *Béta*. We didn't know how you would take it. You had just come out of the rubble. We just could not tell you."

I now understood why Raghu had prevented me from going toward the pile of comforters.

"But why was he kept there yesterday!"

"His body is still stuck underneath the rubble, Viral. And since yesterday the excavator operator has been trying to clear the rubble so that he has enough space to work and get the body out without damaging it anymore. His body was crushed under tons of concrete. . .and most of it is still under the rubble."

Numbness spread through my whole body.

Dinesh uncle then told me that all the relatives were certain that it was one of us, even though the face was not yet visible.

"A big section of wall had to be pulled down to get Roshan's body out safely. But once that wall was pulled down, we heard *your* voice! We left everything and worked only to get you out safely first, Viral."

As he spoke I felt so much of the hope I'd held onto drain from me.

The truth was, after seeing the diamond ring and the gold bracelet, I had known in my heart since yesterday that Bhai was no more. But I was not ready to hear what I was hearing now, and I felt as if I was going to lose balance and fall.

Closing my eyes, I pulled myself together and remained standing. It felt like I had just lost a part of my own body.

"Does the excavator operator know that there is a body underneath the comforters?"

"Yes, he knows."

"Have you found anyone else?"

"No. We only found Roshan. That was the first body we saw after three days of work. You don't know, Viral—it's only a miracle that you survived in such a situation," Punal said.

Now what remained was to try to retrieve Roshan's body today by trying to raise the slab above it.

Dinesh uncle apparently saw me becoming numb, and he said, "I have seen your father do the impossible every single time it was required of him. He is a man of extreme strength, Viral.

"I am not saying that no one else will survive. We are hoping for the best, but it is extremely difficult for anyone else to survive like you without food or water."

I knew what he was saying was true. It would be very, very difficult for my mother or sister-in-law or my small nephew if they were still in the rubble. But—having gained a little strength—I could not give up hope. Not yet. I had to hold on to possibility.

It was possible that there was a hollow space where some of my family members were stuck the same way that I was. It was possible that they had water to drink, since they were near the dining area when the earthquake occurred. It was possible that they were stuck in the stairway chamber. When I could have easily stayed inside for another day or two, surely anyone else could do the same.

Surely.

23

A FAMILY

Courage isn't having the strength to go on – it is going on when you don't have strength.

—NAPOLEON BONAPARTE

All my friends at Fairleigh Dickinson University now knew about what had happened. Later I learned that my roommates in New Jersey had known that my family was missing, and now they came to know that I was found alive, unscathed.

Alpesh, who had dropped me off at the New Jersey's Newark airport only a few weeks back did not know how to react. He had just heard about me while he was in Mumbai. Sheetal, my other roommate and a close friend, was speechless. He had spent more time with me than any of the other roommates, and knew my nature and personality, but he did not know how I was going to handle something like this. The atmosphere in our apartment in New Jersey was tense. Everyone hoped for the best, and wished that my family would be found alive.

It was about 6:00 AM, seven days after the earthquake, when I opened my eyes inside the tent. This night had been the worst night of my life. I had gone to sleep knowing that Bhai was no more, and had not been able to sleep all through the night. I had kept my eyes closed, and wished that I could get some sleep. With an achingly disturbed mind, I had only been able to manage a few bouts of sleep, during which I felt as if I was awake. I had no dreams. It felt like my body was getting rest but my mind was not. Images churned in my head. I could not in my worst nightmares imagine what I had already been through—and what I had performed last evening.

I had cremated *Bhai*.

How could something like this happen? With eyes wide open I lay flat on the ground inside the tent. It was a cold and windy night, but I did not want to feel the warmth of the blanket. I wanted to bear the cold weather. It was as if I did not care about anything, and as if I wasn't scared of anything anymore.

How could this happen to someone like *Bhai*?

After all, he'd survived a motorbike crash so recently, which could have seriously injured or taken him from us. He was always so full of life, so invincible. Or so I'd imagined.

The only brother I had was gone. Lying there I knew I would have to live with this fact for the rest of my life. This was the first day of that life.

I was too full of grief at that moment, and only much later would I think, *We need to base our lives in that which is greater than our human existence, that is, in the spirit.* For now, I was lost in despair.

Bhai was cremated at about 5:00 PM. This was the first time in my life that I had performed the rites of cremation. This was the first time I had cremated someone from my family.

It had taken an excruciating and aggravating two hours to take *Bhai's* body out of the pile of debris without hurting it anymore. The whole time my soul was in torment. It had taken every bit of courage and mental strength for me to help recover his body. A lot

234

of people were watching from a distance, but they did not have the courage to get close and help.

Punal, Raghu, Bijal and I had done our best to direct the excavator operator so he could more efficiently move the big concrete slabs. Every single time the excavator operator lowered the steel claw close to *Bhai's* body my breath stopped. The operator was extremely careful, but he couldn't see as well as we all could. There was the chance he could mistakenly pull rebar or any other big piece of concrete slab from above or below the body by mistake.

It was not possible to pull *Bhai's* body out the way I was pulled out, since it wasn't in a hollow space. We had to continue to keep breaking the pieces around him so that we could have enough room to pull him out, without hurting him.

Bhai's body was taken to a waiting ambulance, which drove directly to the cremation ground.

There, along with my family members, I performed the final rite.

Words cannot express or can ever describe the waves of pain, misery, frustration and anger, disappointment and grief that went through me. My body was wracked.

Given that I still needed to find the rest of my family, I did not have time to grieve for long at the cremation ground. In fact, not even one minute. The excavator was continuing its work at the site, and it was possible that someone else from my family was found while I was away.

Tormented, almost breathless, I rushed back to the site.

"No, *Sahib,*" the operator replied, in answer to my anxious question. "No one was found during the hour you were gone."

Then the excavation work was stopped for the day after it became dark. None of us knew what to say or do. Dinesh uncle cried. Punal cried, while he held onto my shoulder. And then there were those who felt more pain, because they could not cry. I was one of them.

Now I lay on the ground thinking over every detail of what had happened that day and how it happened, all of it etching itself on my mind. I knew these memories would stay with me until the day I died. . .and maybe beyond.

As I lay there I felt my body surge between numbness and burning anger.

How could God do something like this?

I was now waiting for the sun to rise. I had to go back to the cremation ground, to collect the ashes, before I went back to the site.

Surendra uncle, Dinesh uncle, Punal and Raghu came with me to collect the ashes, and I brought *Bhai* back in a small earthen pot.

Later, a few minutes after 7:30 AM, I reached the site along with Surendra uncle. It was a cold morning, and I could smell smoke in the air. This smell was coming from the roadside bonfires by locals who wanted to get some relief in this cold weather.

Only a handful of people had gathered around the broken structure that day, and there were still some media personnel around. As we waited for the operator to arrive again, I realized that every passing moment was making it much more difficult for anyone to believe we would find someone alive.

To our great relief, the operator showed up again. . .and for me another agonizing day began.

For the next two or three hours, the steel claw continued to dig deeper into the broken structure where I had been trapped for days. We saw pieces of furniture, crushed appliances, and things that were crushed beyond recognition. And then, I saw something familiar.

It was my tote bag, which I had been looking for during the five days when I was inside. Once I told the excavator operator about it, it took only a minute to free the bag from the rubble around it. Even though it was badly crushed, somehow the cellphone inside wasn't damaged. It had some battery charge left, but there was no wireless signal in the town yet.

Inside the bag, I found a pair of clothes and my wallet, my camera and a sweater. Dad had bought one sweater for Bhai and he had kept one for me while I was in the U.S. He had gifted it to me on the 25th of January, a day before the earthquake.

During the next few moments I saw more things. Things that tore my heart. I saw perfume and cologne bottles I had brought for Mom and Dad from the U.S., still in sealed boxes, and I saw gifts that I had brought for them with so much love, lying in the debris, smashed.

The large cupboard that was in the room was recovered next. It was made of steel, but now it was squashed nearly beyond recognition. Valuables that my family had safely kept were found inside what remained of the cupboard, now filled with cement and sand. Scattered around the debris were the pens that my father collected and safely kept in the cupboard.

While I stood in the hot sand, wearing boots that the army truck driver had lent to me, my father's lug shoes, which were kept a few feet away from where I'd been trapped, were recovered next. This was the first time when I stepped into my father's shoes.

Throughout the day, work continued in fits and starts. More hours went by—and then the moving arm of the excavator abruptly stopped after the excavator operator's helper shouted.

I went closer, as he pointed toward the debris and shouted.

"I CAN SEE A HAND!"

An explosion went off in my heart.

Oh dear God. . .! Please let this be someone else, God! Not someone from my family, my Lord!

Hearing the shout, many other people gathered near the excavator, the atmosphere suddenly becoming quiet and tense. The rattling machine was shut down and a terrible silence fell.

As I walked toward the mountain of rubble I did not know what to wish for. I was desperate to find the rest of my family, but I wanted to find them alive and well. I continued to pray for their safety.

When I was close enough, I could barely see the hand coming out of the cement structure. My heart pumped so fast it felt like it was going to explode, and I felt my ears getting warm and my head had suddenly started to hurt.

As I looked closer at the hand I tried to take a deep breath but I could not. I again tried to take another deep breath as I moved closer, but I still could not. The hand was covered with cement and dust. The palm faced upwards, and a little part of the wrist was visible. I saw that the individual was wearing a golden bangle. I was looking at the thickness of the wrist and the size of the palm.

At once a surge of terrible relief came over me. I could most positively say that this was *not* someone from my family.

Thank God. . .

My heart continued to pump hard, and I tried to calm it down by taking deep breaths. And a few moments later I descended back toward the ground where the excavator was.

Even in my personal relief I felt the sad truth. It wasn't someone from my family, but it was someone from someone else's family. The life of this person was as valuable as the life of any other human being. The only difference was that I didn't know this individual.

The body was later identified by one of the neighbors in our building who had been watching the excavation with us. Everyone around who had the courage and the heart to help helped. Most of the people watching from a distance continued to keep their distance. It took us about an hour to take the body out of the debris.

Once the body was outside, and was being taken to the cremation ground, a few people from the crowd asked about who it was. Someone from the crowd asked how old the person was, and then someone asked if it was a male or a female.

I was getting more and more agitated with the questions from people who were only there to watch but not lift a finger.

"Go see for yourself if you have the courage! Stop making this a spectacle! If you cannot help, then don't—but shut up!" I shouted.

No one asked any questions after that.

From a distance I saw the family members of the neighbor grieving and carrying the body to the ambulance. I looked away. I did not want to give up the hope of finding my family alive. I walked away from everyone else and while looking at the site I prayed for everyone's life. I did not want anything else in the world for me.

Once the excavation work continued I found myself thinking about how I was going to tell my father about *Bhai*. How would I explain to him that I couldn't save his eldest son?

Mom would not be able to survive after hearing this.

What would I say to her?

I was horrified at the thought of being the one to break the worst possible news to my parents.

And what was I going to tell my sister-in-law, and what was I going to say to my dear little Shalin. How would that little soul even know what he had lost?

I wanted to think about everyone's reactions, because I wanted to convince myself that they were alive, somewhere.

Two more bodies were found in the next two hours, followed by efforts to remove them. The location of the bodies was about 30 feet away from where Bhai and I were found, and thus I was certain that they were from the neighbor's family.

While a group of people continued to help us, another group of people had formed a few feet away. More bystanders were joining them to see what they were discussing. I was told that they were talking about someone else being found on the other end of the building.

Without any thought, I ran toward that group. I stumbled a few times on the loose pieces of concrete lying on the ground.

"They found someone on the other side of the building," Punal confirmed.

Listening to that, I did not even want to ask if the person found was dead or alive. I ran toward the other side of the building, with Punal and Raghu on my heels.

Our building had fallen in such a way that I had to walk through the other properties around the building. As I jumped across one of the broken walls on the other side of the building, I saw a group of people who had gathered near the front of the building that I was familiar with.

"Viral *Bhai*, we found someone here," a person said. He had covered his mouth with a disposable mask.

As I got closer, I saw the crushed pillars below the building where the parking space was. The structure above seemed intact, but the entire building had settled. I saw that there were a few inches of gap between the settled structure and the ground. And when I looked through the gap I could see someone's leg.

Blood surged in my arms, legs and face as my heartbeat kicked up. There was a roaring in my ears, and my face felt hot.

I could not see the whole body, all I could see was the foot and the calf. It was a male. I then saw that the throw blanket lying near the leg was. . .ours.

It was painfully difficult to look at someone's leg and try to tell if it belonged to someone from my family. But looking at the skin tone I thought that it was someone else. I still could not say that with confidence, however, because that was most definitely our blanket lying next to the body.

Punal and Raghu were seeing what I was seeing.

"This is our blanket, Raghu. I used it about two or three years back, when I was in India."

"But how can your blanket be towards this side of the building?"

Once again I forced myself to look through the cavity and peer at the foot more closely. There was no cement or debris covering it, and it was clearly visible even with limited amount of light inside the cavity.

And once again I felt a terrible kind of relief.

I was now positive that it was not someone from my family, even though it bothered me to see our blanket next to the body.

"I think my mom would have given the old blanket away to someone in the watchman's family, whose daughter worked as our maid and helper at our home."

We spent a few more minutes with this group of people and then returned to the other side of the building. There, the two bodies had already been recovered. I had a quick look at the bodies and did not recognize them.

And then someone shouted, "There are three people!"

That was impossible. I had only seen two bodies. But my steps quickened, along with my pulse.

One of the bodies, that of a woman, was wearing a heavy, silver bangle on her ankle. Someone identified her as the watchman's daughter.

And now the other woman, who had been found with her, was recognizable.

It was Jaishree *Bhabhi*, my sister-in-law.

And then came the next shock. The women's bodies had been lying on top of a little child, whom they had apparently been trying to shield and protect.

It was Shalin.

24

THE PILLAR OF STRENGTH

"Life teaches you things.
One of them is to never give up."
—VIRAL DALAL

Hope.

To me hope meant an expectation, a wish, a prayer. I always thought that faith and hope walked hand in hand. If you had strong conviction and true faith in something and you wished for something with your true heart and gave it the best that was humanly possible, nature would have to answer your wish.

Even after the discovery of two more family members' bodies I continued to try to cling to it.

No thoughts were running in my mind the morning after we'd found *Bhabhi* and Shalin, as I was once again waiting for the excavator operator and his helper to arrive. I did not know how this day was going to unfold, and I was not even anxious about the excavator operator running late.

I felt torn, as if the earthquake had broken and pulled apart the ground of my soul in its destructive wake.

A small part of me thought that it was better if he came late, because I was not ready to face any more pain—while a big part of me told me that my father was going to make it out alive.

The images of what I had seen in the last few days flashed in front of my eyes, however, while I stared at the barren ground with no emotions. I had not yet fully realized what had happened with me and with my life. Mentally, physically and emotionally I was nearly lifeless. If the darkness inside the pile of rubble had been great, the darkness growing inside me was greater.

The only thing that gave me the energy and the courage to still work harder was that I knew in my heart that if my father was trapped in an enclosure the way I'd been trapped, he would make it out alive even a few days from now. Of this I had no doubt. That hope, that belief, brought moments of light.

I tried not to think about what would have happened to my mother. I prayed that she was not in any kind of pain, wherever she was. I did not know what else to pray for.

If my prayers were answered, though, would surviving bring her any form of happiness—given that her son, her daughter-in-law, and her only grandson had passed? No matter. I prayed for her peace and happiness anyway.

Then I shook myself out of my grief and lethargy.

Today, I have to do whatever it takes to find my parents. This is the only time that will matter in my life. Nothing else is worth anything.

The work started about an hour later than usual since the excavator needed a diesel fill-up. I'd had heated arguments with the operator and his helper, because I thought that the fill-up could have been done the previous day after the daylight hours. I knew that for someone who was inside, this waste of time could mean the difference between life and death. I was tired, angry, frustrated, helpless—and I had already lost three members of my family. It was extremely crucial that we not waste even a minute.

Punal, Raghu and I continued to keep an eye on the excavator for the next three hours. There were no traces of anyone. Everyone gathered under the shadow of the same tree to get something to eat.

I left the site briefly for one *thepla*, a type of flatbread eaten as a snack, a small cup of tea and some water, then rushed back toward the debris.

Carefully, I climbed on top of the highest point of the debris, where the broken structure had settled. I had looked here the day after I'd been evacuated and had found no clues of anyone, but I wanted to go through the same spot once again to make sure I had not missed anything earlier. I continued looking for any visible gaps or hollow spaces, so that I could shout or peek through. All I saw was crushed pieces of concrete. There were no big pieces or columns there, and thus there were no hollow spaces.

Then I scrambled toward the destroyed elevator shaft that was in a tilted position and leaning against the only wing of the building that was still standing. There I came across a very strong odor of rotting bodies. Covering my nose with a mask I looked for any signs of a body for the next few minutes. The smell of decay was extremely strong, and I kept holding my breath for long moments. While I did this I remembered my position seven days back, when I was holding my breath to make sure I was not using up all the oxygen. Suddenly that time seemed very distant to me—like it had happened a very long time ago.

Mentally and emotionally, it was as if I was in a tunnel. Everything before this moment seemed far, far in the past. Everything ahead seemed—well, there didn't seem to be anything ahead. Nothing beyond the goal of finding my parents.

The work once again began after the lunch break. I was extremely desperate, and kept standing next to the excavator in the sun. Raghu stood a few feet away and Punal *Bhai* was sitting on the same mound of dirt nearby, keeping his focus on the excavator.

Some of the relatives had left the previous night, as they had left their families alone in a crisis situation.

The mound of debris was still about 40 feet high. The excavator's claw could only reach about 15 feet. Once a few feet of debris was cleared, the loose pieces of heavy concrete, cement or columns that were not reachable would crash to the ground with massive force without any warning. If anyone was alive inside, how on earth would they survive the rescue effort?

I could not let myself think about this.

At about 3:00 PM on what had become a very hot afternoon I was standing with my hands on my waist and focusing only on the excavator and its steel claw. I could see that the excavator operator was clearing the debris much faster today, and I thought that was because we'd had an argument, and maybe he once again understood that someone's life depended on him. Some of the rounds of clearing the debris were noticeably faster and at times I could not keep up with it. All of us had to focus really hard and make sure that no one was hurt inside the rubble. For this same reason the excavator operator seemed extra cautious as well.

I kept changing my position, since the soles of my shoes kept getting hot while I stood in the hot sand. And as I continued to look at the steel claw, I suddenly saw my father's face. . .

"STOP STOP STOP! STOP IT! STOP THE MACHINE! STOP!" I shouted.

Hearing my shout, the excavator was stopped immediately. The helper looked at where I was looking. Everyone who heard me looked in the direction I was looking at.

"What happened, *Sahib*?" The helper asked while he turned and looked again where I was staring.

I blinked hard. I focused hard where my father's face had suddenly flashed. There was nothing there. Only concrete pieces and some broken furniture near the steel claw.

"No. . .I am sorry. I thought I saw something," I said, then added, "Just be careful. My parents are in there."

This was the first time in my life that an image like this had flashed in front of my eyes. I could not understand how it happened. Maybe the stress and extreme fatigue caused it. I could not even imagine my father being deceased. To my mind that was impossible.

The excavation continued.

But the image that had flashed in front of my eyes had shaken me.

Now it was about 4:00 PM, and it seemed like everyone was tired. There was significant work done but no one had been found yet. The excavator operator took a few minutes' break so that he could get something to drink. I walked back to where my uncles were sitting, to get some water.

I walked back toward the site with the excavator operator, and told him that he had made significant progress today.

"I am doing the best I can, *Sahib*," he replied.

Then he stepped back on the excavator and waited for the helper to join him and kept revving the engine. Seeing that we all were waiting for him to start, he honked a few times for his helper. I saw the helper waving his hand and running toward us while holding a bottle of water in the other hand. Once he came close, he quickly jumped onto the excavator.

"Go on! Go on!" he shouted.

The first hit on the rubble loosened a few big pieces of broken concrete.

For me, the world stopped.

Clearly visible was my father's body.

25

THE CREATOR

"You can never step into someone else's shoes.
Never, ever."

—VIRAL DALAL

Dad. The strongest man I knew.

And now it was the morning after I had cremated him. And I was on my way to the cremation grounds to collect his ashes.

Something supremely powerful had gone out from me. I knew what it was.

The way I saw the world around me. The way I thought. The way I treated people. The dreams and the passions I had. The way I spoke. Even the way I drove my car and the way I polished my boots. Every single big and small thing in my life was influenced by my father. Every single thing I knew was not just something that a child sees and learns from parents. These were some of the things that were taught to me, and to me they were the right way to be because my father was a very learned man and he knew how to do things the right way.

Everything had to be clean, very clean, spick and span. If someone touched one of his things, he would know if it had been moved even a millimeter. My father was known among everyone as a perfectionist. Every single thing that came in contact with him had a designated place. Every person he knew had a designated place, and was respected. Each person that he could extend help to, he did. Every person that he met remembered him distinctly.

Dad was more than a perfectionist, though. Perfectionists can be difficult. He was as impeccable in his treatment of people as he was of things he owned. People relied on him, and they looked up to him. He was someone who could get things done. Anything. He was a very strong man, and a very hard-working man, with a brightly shining soul.

In my mind's eye I'd envisioned him living more than 100 years. How could this happen to my hero? My soul burned from inside when I saw his body. The hope of finding him alive, which had kept me focused and living for the last eight days, shattered into a million pieces, and then it burned to ashes.

Dad had to be alive still. He had to be. His spirit was too big for him to be gone. A big part of me refused to believe what had happened. I couldn't even think of talking about him in past tense. I knew that he was there, somewhere, watching me. When his body was recovered, there wasn't a scratch on him. It seemed as if he would talk any moment, but he didn't.

I looked at the watch at midnight, lying in the tent. It was *Bhai's* birthday. We'd been scheduled to celebrate it at the Taj Ummed Palace Hotel in Ahmedabad. The birthday party and dinner was going to be hosted by Dad, and the custom invitations had been presented to all of us in the family. Dad's work. I was named as the Guest of Honor.

The pain was unbearable. I could never have imagined that *Bhai* would not be there to see this day, nor would the host of the party. After a horrible night full of turbulent thoughts, though, I was completely numb.

Early in the morning on this day, which was supposed to be a day of celebration, I was now returning from the cremation grounds. . .carrying my father's ashes.

It did not occur to me to focus on myself right now, though something huge was taking place inside me. The person I had been, with all my vital energies, was draining out of me. Perhaps it was a good thing that at the moment I didn't notice how dead and empty I felt.

It felt like the darkness was winning.

I could not let that happen.

There was another hugely important task to focus on— loathe as I was to do it. Somehow I found myself back at the site of our collapsed building, knowing I had to continue trying to find my mother somewhere inside the rubble. It had been a few hours since the excavation work had begun. Two bodies had been found since early morning. They belonged to a neighbor's family.

I was now sitting far away on the mound of soil where Punal sat before. I had not given up the hope of finding mom alive, but even if such a miracle happened, I did not know how she would continue to live, knowing that she had lost her husband, her son, her daughter-in-law and her only grandson. It would be impossible for her to survive if she found out about how our lives had been altered, forever.

While I watched the machine in the distance, the only thoughts running in my mind were about my father and my mother. I hadn't spoken to anyone since morning. I avoided speaking to anyone who came closer to console me, and told everyone to stay away from me. I had talked harshly with everyone who tried to talk to me since last night, and now I was sitting all alone thinking about who did this to our family and why.

Tears blurred my vision. I did not wipe them. I let them fall on the barren ground as I closed my eyes. More and more tears filled my eyes as I thought about each one of the loved ones that I had lost. Tears poured out of my eyes as I struggled to keep a straight face, and looked toward the excavator with anger.

Crying did soothe some pain when it really hurt, I had learned this in life. I had also learned, though, that it never solved any problems.

This was the ninth day after the earthquake. The number of people at the site had significantly gone down. Only three days back, there were hundreds of people here, and there was no space for people to even stand. There were hordes of bystanders for the next few days. Media crews, cameramen, army personnel, and also the Minister of Defense, George Fernandez had visited the building site. They were all gone now. The people who remained at the site were either the rescue workers or the people who were looking for their family members in the rubble. Raghu approached. "Viral, eat something, dear. You have not eaten anything."

"I don't want to eat."

"I understand, but you should eat. . .something. We all did what we could. Everyone is worried about you now, dear."

"Tell everyone not to worry about me. I will deal with this, Raghu. I am my father's son."

Biren, Punal, Raghu, and my uncles each took turns sitting with me as hours passed, and then they went away. During the break time I once again climbed the mountain of rubble and looked for any signs of life. I shouted in the hollow spaces that I could find. I spent some time looking closely for any signs of life.

Again, I could not see that signs of life were leaving me, as well. Nothing made sense, and my thinking was numb. I did not know what *good* or *bad* meant anymore, since everything good and beautiful in my life was gone for no good reason.

I no longer knew what to pray for, but I did pray quietly and I prayed hard. I knew that for my mother, facing the reality would be much more painful than anything else in the world. I still prayed for her life.

So I prayed to God to give her the strength to face what had happened. I prayed for her to be happy, wherever she was.

I couldn't think of anything else that I could pray for.

During the next hour, the excavation was stopped many times to make sure that no one was hurt inside. The excavator operator was working very hard, and had cleared a significant amount of rubble since morning.

And then, the excavator was once again stopped.

It was now around 3:00 PM, and the operator's helper shouted that he saw something. The helper went closer to the site to look closely, and then he called everyone to have a look at what he was seeing.

I stood from the rubble heap on which I was sitting, and I ran. In an instant, my forehead was moist and my heart started pumping very fast. It was beating so fast that I thought that I would suffer a heart attack.

As I rushed closer to where the helper was, I prayed for the wellness of my mother. Once I reached the spot, I looked between the rubble and dust—and I saw Mom's arm.

Whatever vital energies remained in me all but drained away. I thought that every single cell in my body died.

The darkness had won.

26

THE SHINING LIGHTS

*"When you think that the light inside you has gone out,
what you don't know is that your guardian angels
are watching over you, guiding you. They are the
light that's inside you."*

—VIRAL DALAL

fam·i·ly (noun) : A social unit consisting of one or more adults together with the children they care for.

My dad was the one who had made me *who* I was. My mom was the one who made *me*.

Strength shined through my father. Life shined through my mother. She was the only friend with whom I had shared all my life. She was a strong lady with a very soft heart, one that loved to put smiles on other's faces. Her life was her family. She was the living heart of our family.

The adult males in the house, my dad, *Bhai*, and me, did not always talk about everything to everyone, but each one of us talked about everything to her. She was the glue of the family that kept us all together. She was everyone's sweetheart. It was her radiant soul, her emotions, her love, her care, and her laughter that made our home a very happy home.

She was also the mischievous one—and yet she carried herself with true elegance. People loved her. Whether they were friends, neighbors, our relatives, or even the caretakers working for us, the love for her always poured in, because she cared for them. Nieces, nephews and other relatives loved her back, and couldn't get enough of her.

Whereas my dad taught us how to live and how to think, Mom taught us how to *feel*. She was the sentimental one, the one who felt all the emotions, and expressed them. Every emotion I had inside my heart was a gift from my mom.

Then there was *Bhai*, of course. Quick intelligence and great humor shined through him.

All. Gone.

Unstoppable tears continued to fall on the ground after I performed my mother's cremation.

Now I felt as if the ground beneath me had collapsed into a chasm, and the shelter of family in which I'd lived all my life had crashed down and the strong pillars of support around me had turned to ashes.

In my bleakness I did not care about the world around me anymore. The world, for me, had finished. Inside, my soul was in turmoil. Boiling thoughts about what had happened made me ache with futile rage. I was in terrible pain, and I was burning from inside with enormous anger. Words to describe the grief did not exist.

I had lost everything of value in my life, and there was no way of getting it back.

The torment was made worse by the hundreds of images that flashed in front of my eyes. I saw images of my mom reading me a book during my childhood, the time when I annoyed her when I was little, and about how sad she had been to see me leave for the

U.S., and then how thrilled she was on the phone to hear that I was coming back to India for a vacation. And then I saw the image of her being found underneath the rubble.

"You will remember me when I am not there," she had said, just the night before the earthquake.

Why had she said that?

Images of my dad followed. How he had travelled overnight from Bhuj to meet me, just to give me a surprise. How happy he was when he had first heard that I was going to the U.S. for higher studies. How he had put a comforter over me only minutes before the earthquake.

Images of *Bhai*, *Bhabhi* and Shalin flashed in front of my eyes. I thought about how *Bhai* had recently escaped a serious injury during the kite flying season. How happy he was to receive the gifts that I had brought for him. How happy *Bhabhi* was to receive me at the airport, and how Shalin played peek-a-boo with me the night before the quake.

These thoughts did not stop. They continued to pour through my head and heart for hours. Childhood memories of vacations, birthdays, celebrations, little fights and arguments, jokes, and every memorable incident passed through my mind as if it was on a tape. Everyone who was on that tape was gone—except me.

The terrible irony was that the very people who would have helped me bear my pain were all gone. Yes, all my other close relatives could feel the tremendous pain I was going through, but they were as helpless as I was.

Adding to my misery was this fact: The drive to find my family was over, and suddenly I felt I no longer had any purpose. There was nothing left to do, nowhere to go. There were no other members of the family who were to be found, and there were no more dead bodies to be recovered.

Sitting on a cement platform, far away from all my relatives, I continued to look at the burning pyre. With eyes bloodshot, I mourned in silent, unspeakable agony.

In the last four days I had lost five members of my family.

I now had no family.

I was not a person. I was only a living ache.

27

ALONE

"No one saves us but ourselves.
No one can and no one may.
We ourselves must walk the path".

— B U D D H A

*Mom. . .*So many memories flooded in as I sat at the cremation grounds. It was strange, the one that stood out. . .

"Your father is going to take you to foster care today, and leave you there," Mom had said to me earlier during the day.

I thought that it couldn't be true, even though I had caused a lot of pain to my parents during the previous weeks. She was only trying to scare me, like she had at different times before, when I had been unmanageable.

But later during the day while I was playing with my toy cars I heard my father start his motorcycle, and before I could think of anything else, my mom came rushing inside my room.

"Papa is waiting for you on his motorcycle. Now get ready to leave. You have to go," she said hurriedly.

"Go where?"

"You have not even packed your clothes. You need more clothes for your days at the foster care."

She picked some of my clothes from the wooden shelf, and shoved them inside the suitcase hurriedly.

"Hurry up now! Your dad is waiting"

"But Mom, I don't want to go," I said in a breaking voice.

"You have to go now, *béta*. You have given us a very tough time in the past few weeks. We now have no other option but to send you to foster care. We will visit you every few weeks."

"But. . .I want to stay home."

"Okay, then go and tell that to Papa, and apologize to him first," she said, holding my arm. I noticed that she did not put down the small suitcase she'd packed, as we walked toward the doorway out to the driveway, where my father was waiting.

A bad feeling was twisting in my stomach.

Dad was waiting outside for me on his large motorcycle, which was running. He did not look at me.

"Hop on now," was all he said.

Something like lightning shot through me, and I swallowed hard. I was going to the foster care for real, because of my bad behavior and because of throwing tantrums about going to school. As soon as the realization hit, I cried aloud and in seconds my cheeks were wet with running tears. My legs couldn't seem to carry my weight, as mom tried to pick me up from the ground while still holding the little suitcase filled with clothes.

Mom, too, had tears in her eyes. She set the suitcase on the pillion seat of the motorcycle, while I struggled to stay put on the ground. When she finally managed to lift me in her arms, she placed me on the pillion seat behind the suitcase.

In a torrent of words I began apologizing. The horrible thought I was about to be taken and left at foster care was intense.

"I will go to school every day mom," I cried.

"I will go to school happily."

"I will not cause any more trouble."

I made every other promise about good behavior I could think of.

Dad had looked at me only once, and he seemed dead serious. He had not let go of the motorcycle's handlebars. Had I convinced him? I didn't know. It seemed as if he was all ready to take me to the foster care. Was he really going to take me away from my family, so I'd never see them again?

I continued to sob and plead, but it didn't seem to be working, and I tightly gripped dad's shoulders, pulling myself up to standing on the motorcycle seat. They seemed to be totally serious about taking me away—but once I stood up on the seat it was scary to jump from that height.

"Please!" I sobbed. "I promise!"

And suddenly my ordeal was over.

My mom lifted me up and held me in her arms. My dad casually rubbed his beard, and shut the motorcycle down. Mom calmed me down and told me that I wasn't going to the foster care after all because I had promised not to bother everyone anymore. She walked back with me inside my room, where I cried, and so did she.

The little heart inside me thought that my parents failed to understand my feelings. I did not want to go to school only because I liked staying with everyone at home. After that day, however, I went to school obediently. It was only years later when I grew up that I learned all of this was staged.

"Why were *you* crying that day then, Mom?" I had asked.

"I couldn't see you in pain."

That was my mother.

I could not cry now, much as I wanted to, as I sat staring into my mother's burning pyre until late night.

It was late in the evening, and I was planning to spend the night there—but Dinesh uncle and Surendra uncle came and told me it wasn't considered good to stay all night at the cremation ground.

Later that night as I lay on the ground under a blanket, there was unsurmountable pain that made my heart seem like a piece of stone. I did not make any effort to stop the thoughts about my loved ones and all I had been through in the past nine days. The darkness of the night was nothing compared to the darkness within me.

Seeing the faces of my family, hearing voices, I felt myself slip down and down into a zone where there was no feeling at all. My soul felt dead. My present life didn't matter anymore. Everything that was precious to me lay only in the past. Future didn't matter.

I fell asleep finally sometime after 5:00 AM, and I then woke up after about an hour. It was time to rise and go collect Mom's ashes from the cremation ground.

After I returned, there was no reason to stay in Bhuj anymore. By the following afternoon, after showing gratitude to the owner of the home who had allowed us to use his tent, we all left.

It was over.

Everything was over.

I'd been wondering how my mother would survive if she was rescued only to find that most of her family was gone.

But now—how would *I*?

Sitting in the front seat of the SUV, looking at the highway in front of me, I could only stare with empty eyes and an even emptier soul. We all were now heading back to Ahmedabad. Surendra uncle, Dinesh uncle, Punal and Raghu were with me in the vehicle.

The rest of my family was with us now in the form of ashes, kept safely in separate earthen pots.

I struggled to keep a straight face while I could barely see the blurry highway. Unlike my tears as a little boy still under my parents' roof, now they failed to sooth any of the ache. Unlike the ordeal of the threatened foster care, which had been staged, this one was real and it had no end.

Everyone in the vehicle talked about things that they had seen in the past ten days, and about how massive the earthquake was and then about the situation and the cold nights. Punal and Raghu talked about their frustrations and about what they had to go through during the initial days. I gazed at the highway for hours while memories continued to churn inside my mind. Not only memories, but questions.

What was I supposed to do now? How would I go on, when I felt so numb?

So dead and dark.

We had one tea break during this eight or nine hour drive to Ahmedabad. As the SUV entered the city of Ahmedabad, things started to become more real. I had left home with family, and now, I was returning with their ashes.

It was late night when our SUV reached outside my grand-mother's home. Several vehicles were parked outside the main gate, and then I started to see familiar faces of people standing outside the gate, wearing white clothes, waiting for our arrival.

When others greeted me, I did not know how to react or what to say. I walked inside the house with my head down, passing through the walls of relatives, who all fell silent as I passed.

"*Giriraj Dharan ki Jai* (Praise the Lord!)," my grandmother chanted as soon as she saw me. Throwing her arms around me, she broke down.

Other relatives broke down and cried as well.

I knew they were happy that at least I had survived and returned to them. But they seemed distant, like figures in a dream.

"Throw away these stupid pictures of god!" I shouted in anger, looking at the large picture frame of Srinathji on the wall. I wanted to smash it, but I did not. "You see what he has done? Throw these pictures away!"

Sidhant, my very good friend who was also there, hugged me tightly. "Shalin use to walk on his toes when he had just learned to walk. He was so cute, Viral. . .," he said, and broke down crying.

I did not cry. I had a glass of water and walked away from all the relatives. I wanted to be alone. I did not know how to face everyone and what to say. I spent the next hour sitting inside the room with Sidhant and Deval, my friends. My relatives wanted me to be at peace and so they let me do what I wanted to and what made me comfortable.

Later, I went out with my friends to a place nearby to get some air. We spent hours as I talked about what had happened. They all listened. They told me about the devastation in Ahmedabad, and that thousands of lives had been lost in the entire state.

Now that I was back in Ahmedabad, I wanted to go back to my home. My relatives weren't sure about my mental state, and about what I was going to do now. They all only knew one thing—that I was not going back to my home that first night under any circumstances.

"*Baa (Grandma)*, let me go home. I just want to be alone," I said to my grandmother.

"I cannot let you go, my dear," she cried.

"Just let me be alone. I am not going to kill myself. Let me be."

"No. I cannot let you go tonight. We cannot."

"We will bring anything you want from your home, but you are staying here, with us."

I argued, and then I understood their worry. I stayed. Not for me, but for everyone else's peace of mind. It dawned on me that I was starting to become a responsibility.

My friends stayed overnight at my grandmother's home. My entire life had changed in the last ten days, and I was now lying on the bed in darkness, looking at the ceiling fan in Dinesh uncle's room. It looked just like the ceiling fan in our apartment that swung like a pendulum while its blades scraped the ceiling violently.

I slept, not knowing what the morning was going to bring. What was I going to do after I woke up?

When I woke up—late—I took a warm shower, and then saw that more and more people had started arriving at my grandmother's home. The living room was full of relatives, friends and acquaintances who had come to see me and to pay their respects to our family. I was reluctant at first, but I made the effort to see everyone, because they cared. There was no talking, though.

Later that day Dinesh uncle told me that an obituary had to be placed in the local newspaper for the memorial service and so we needed pictures. It was mid-afternoon when I went to our home with him, for the first time after the earthquake. When I looked at our home from outside, it looked just like the way we had left it. I unlocked the iron main gate and immediately felt that Mom was going to open the large teak main door. And then when I turned the keys to open the main door, I still secretly wished that my family would greet me. My mind had not even partially absorbed what had happened.

Inside our home, a thin layer of dust had settled over the white marble flooring. Otherwise, everything else seemed untouched. Nothing had changed. There was no sign of the massive earthquake that the city had suffered. The living room was mute. Shalin was nowhere to be found. Mom was not waiting for me near the dining table. Dad was not sitting on the sofa reading the newspaper. *Bhai* was not rushing down the stairs to his office. *Bhabhi* was not running behind Shalin to get him to eat something.

I went upstairs to find the pictures for the obituary. There were hundreds of pictures that sat in various cabinets, but I knew exactly where the latest pictures were. They were in my room, in my drawer. These were the recent passport pictures that Mom and Dad had gotten done to get their passports renewed, so they could visit me in the U.S. in the near future. The passport applications lay next to the pictures in the form of broken dreams. I collected pictures of *Bhai*, *Bhabhi* and Shalin from other photo albums, and before thinking any further, I locked the house and we left.

I stayed at my grandmother's home the rest of that day, and once again requested her to let me go home later in the night.

"Let me go, *Baa*. I am going to be fine. Just please let me go."

After I repeatedly told her that I was going to be okay and that I really wanted to go to my home, she agreed. I promised her that I was going to be back at her home for lunch the following morning, and I told her that I would stay there for the whole day.

Later in the evening, Dinesh uncle came to drop me to our home. He spent some time with me, and knowing that I was going to be all alone, he did not want to leave, but with a heavy heart he did.

It was now February 5th, 2001—the day I had planned to leave for the U.S. I would never forget this day: my first night at our home, completely alone.

After Dinesh uncle left, with all the anger that I had inside me, it was time for the collision that had been approaching.

A collision with God.

28

THE HOUSE

"When I have been unhappy, I have heard an opera. . .
and it seemed the shrieking of winds;
when I am happy, a sparrow's chirp is delicious to me.
But it is not the chirp that makes me happy,
but I that make it sweet."

— JOHN RUSKIN

"The resort we are visiting tomorrow is suitable for people who are popular, *Bhai.* Do you know that my name was in the newspaper few days back?" I teased Roshan, referring to the welcome note that my father had placed in the newspaper at the time of my arrival in India.

Roshan took out his wallet and pulled out a small newspaper clipping and showed it to me.

"Roshan Dalal, an assistant manager with Celforce in Ahmedabad, was injured during the season of Uttrayana in Satellite area of Ahmedabad. . ." it read.

"See? Here is the news about me in the *Times of India*. If that helps.

"Dad had to *pay* for that message of yours. Has your name ever been printed in a newspaper without someone *paying* for it?"

I had no answer to that and we had all laughed.

Reading my name in the news reports, I distinctly remembered this conversation, which happened at the Prince Hotel, the night before the earthquake.

My rescue had made it to the front page of the *New York Times* and various other newspapers. My friends and roommates back in the U.S. now knew about everything. They also were in touch with my uncle in the U.S. who had all the information.

Various national and local U.S. news agencies held a news conference at my alma mater, Fairleigh Dickinson University at the Teaneck-Hackensack campus in New Jersey. Dr. J. Michael Adams, the president of our school, was deeply saddened after hearing the news about the earthquake, and about my family, and yet he was happy after hearing about my survival. He termed it an accident of life. When interviewed, emotions ran high, and he only had a few words to say.

"Today we feel a sense of joy, yet tremendous grief. The entire university community shares the elation that comes from knowing that a member of community, a student of unbridled potential, has been rescued from the brink of disaster. . ."

Being thousands miles away, he was trying to find a way to help in whatever way possible.

". . .If that means counselling we will provide it, if that means helping with transportation costs, we will be happy to do so. If that means an increase in our financial aid or helping him with tuition expenses, we will gladly consider that."

Emotions were clearly visible on my roommate Sheetal's face, when he was interviewed by the news reporters.

"He loved his family a lot, and I don't know how he is going to face the loss for his whole life. We friends are always there for him. . .but family is a big loss. I don't know what he is going through right now."

"Without him there is no noise in the house," he concluded.

Nilay, my other roommate, told the news reporters his feelings:

"We are like a family. We have been living together for more than a year. We are looking forward to seeing him in the U.S. with us."

We roommates had lived through the initial tough years in the U.S. together. We were very close.

During the days that followed, when all my roommates were together, they often talked about what I was going to do now. Some thought that I would return to the U.S. and never go back to India, because of what had happened, and some thought the opposite. They only hoped that I was stable mentally.

As for me, I was now alone at home. I spent the first night looking at the empty spaces in the house. Even imagining that none of my loved ones would be coming back here made me think that it wasn't possible. It was a mistake. It had to be undone. I wanted everyone back. I desperately wanted to tell them that I was alive. Did they even know that?

Upstairs, when I entered my parents' bedroom I felt the lifeless silence. The large bed where we all had celebrated birthdays past midnight was empty. The images of all the family members flashed in front of my eyes in this large room. The dresser, the large metal cupboards and other furniture in the room stood still and mute. It seemed as if time had stood still in this room. Every single thing around the room was telling a story. Everything in the room had become invaluable.

When I walked inside *Bhai's* bedroom, it looked like a hollow space. It was a big room that now looked even bigger, and it felt empty. The new furniture in the room seemed muted and the lights felt dim. This room echoed with Shalin's playful giggles and constant joyful banter, but now the room looked like a vacant room in a hotel. I switched the lights off and walked toward my room.

Inside my room the colorful posters and pictures on the wall looked frivolous and only made me feel more grim now. I saw my large suitcase that was kept under the study table. I knew that *Bhai's* birthday present—a wristwatch—was still kept inside the suitcase. It hurt when I thought about it.

I should have given the present to him earlier.

That thought erupted into a host of other regrets that flew out of my soul. And another wave of grief.

Later, when I went downstairs I sat on the marble steps in the drawing room for a long time, looking nowhere. While I sat there, I felt that my mother was looking at me right at this moment. I couldn't see her, but I knew that she was there, looking at me, looking over me.

I looked hard at the corner seat of the sofa where my father used to sit. Maybe he was sitting in the same spot right now. If he was, he must be observing me closely at this time. He must be watching how I would handle this situation. He would be sad, but he still wouldn't show it.

When I walked inside the kitchen, the silence hummed in my ears. The once bustling kitchen now looked like a weird room with utensils and crockery. Mom's favorite china crockery set was visible through the dark glass panels. Placed besides it were the crystal glass goblets that I had brought recently.

When I walked inside the TV room, I saw *Bhai's* favorite chair— now forever empty. The remote control next to it seemed worthless. And then when I looked around, I saw toys lying on the floor.

The image of Shalin lying in the rubble flashed in front of my eyes.

The pressure that had been mounting became unbearable.

WHY? I raged within my soul.

WHAT DID HE DO WRONG? NOTHING!

WHO DOES THIS OR ALLOWS IT TO HAPPEN TO A TWO-YEAR-OLD CHILD?

I felt as if my veins were going to burst with uncontrollable outrage, while my heart was in intense pain. There was nothing I could do, and there was no place to vent my fury.

But something deep inside me resisted.

I reached a point in my life where I had started to understand what a trap looked like—and instinct told me that feeding the uncontrollable anger was a trap.

I walked out of the room. . .

After that I did not focus on the fury. Instead, I decided to soothe my pain. It wasn't easy, but I could do it.

I decided I would speak to everyone in my family—Dad, Mom, *Bhai* and *Bhabhi*, Shalin. . . And I did so, for a long time. I talked about what I felt and what I was going through. I paused many times, because I knew that I didn't need to tell them everything, because they were there besides me, well aware of everything that was happening. I didn't tell them what I was going through. They knew that.

मातृदेवो भव । पितृदेवो भव ।
(Matru Devo Bhava. Pitru Devo Bhava.)
—TAITTIRIYA UPANISHAD

May the mother be thy God. May the father be thy God.

My own gods were not *with* me anymore, at least not physically. But they were alive *in* me.

And so I continued to look at the old picture albums all through the night, and then slept on the floor past sunrise. I did not want the comfort of a mattress.

271

This was the time when I thought that I had crashed to the lowest point of my being.

It also was the time when my being had nowhere else to go but to rise. Could I?

Hundreds of people attended the memorial ceremony at our home two days later. Everyone came. Relatives, friends, neighbors, colleagues, acquaintances and each and every person who knew any one of the five members of our family came to pay their respects. People broke down in tears, and the ones who didn't, felt the pain. There was shock and there was disbelief.

As people came and left, I was deep inside my thoughts. Everyone wanted to see me, give me some words of comfort. And when they did, they used words that were dead. This was another difficult day for me. Looking at the newly framed pictures of my family, while my vision was blurred, I had started to see things more clearly. I had started to realize that the path of my life had been altered, forever.

A few days passed.

People continued to visit our home and my grandmother's home. For me, the next few days weren't any different than the first day after I returned from Bhuj. I would sleep late, wake up late, and go for lunch at my grandmother's home, late. My relatives continued to perform religious chanting each evening for our family. This would bring peace to the souls of the departed, they told me. I would spend some time with my grandmother and all the other relatives, and have dinner there.

Grandma would often hug me, as if she was hugging everyone from our family. She did not know why God had done such a thing to her daughter's family. She was fighting her own battle with God.

And then it was time for some of my relatives who had come from distant cities to leave.

Surendra uncle and my aunt Jaishree aunty had left their two daughters—my cousins back home—in the care of their neighbors in Hyderabad. It was time for them to leave. Surendra uncle was inconsolable before leaving. My father was his only brother.

My maternal aunt, Jyotsna aunty, hugged my grandmother and Panna aunty, and with tears in her eyes, she hugged me.

"Take care of yourself. Your loved ones will be unhappy if you are."

"Always remember how happy your mother used to be."

The situation in the city had started to improve, just a little. People had started to gain some confidence after the frequency of the tremors decreased. TV stations now relayed other news besides the news about the earthquake and the death toll. The debris and the rubble was now being cleared at a much faster pace in the city. People had started returning to the high-rise buildings from places that they had fled to. Some of them would hang wind chimes or a homemade alarm system of some sort under the ceiling fan or the chandeliers so they would know if the ground shook. People slept in the night with their main doors open, keeping necessary items in grab-and-go packs close to them.

Mahendra uncle, Panna aunty and their daughter Hiral moved back from my grandmother's home to their 11-storey apartment building during this time. I was now going to their home for meals instead of going to my grandmother's home, as their home was closer.

Life wasn't the same for all my near and dear ones after they saw what had happened to our family. People who were close to us lost interest in what they enjoyed in life. *Things* did not give them pleasure anymore. Things seemed worthless.

Panna auntie's family had always been very close to ours. Every single day I would reach their home hours late for lunch and for dinner. My aunt would not complain. She would patiently wait with my cousin Hiral.

Hiral was then studying for her M.Com (Master of Commerce) Part II. Until now, she had always been someone who did well academically, but things had started to change inside her. She was extremely close to our family, and had seen both my father and my mother work very, very hard all through their lives. And now when it was time for my parents to sit back and enjoy the fruits of their struggles and their hard work, they were gone, in an instant.

Being very close to our family, Hiral lost interest in achieving anything. For her, life had suddenly become fragile, and there were no guarantees.

Excel academically—for what?

She was much closer to Roshan than to me, and she had spent more time with Shalin during the last year than I had. It was a personal loss for her.

Every evening after dinner I would spend time with her, in their apartment balcony, on a swing. I would talk and she would listen.

"How did you survive inside?" she would often ask.

I would tell her things, but not everything that I had been through. I didn't have to. I knew that if I did, it would only make things much more painful for her.

This was a difficult time for each one of us in the family, so I tried to keep my pain to myself, as much as I could. Each and every person that knew about me felt sorry for me.

I did not.

Something was stirring in me. And I knew that—just as I had made choices while inside my cement coffin—I had choices to make now.

I was not sure that I could.

274

29

THE LIGHT

"Our greatest glory is not in never failing,
but in rising up every time we fail."
— RALPH WALDO EMERSON

My personal struggle wasn't over yet. Far from it.

As more days passed, things started to become more difficult. Other than going out for meals, I was mostly alone at home. Dinesh uncle and a few other relatives still visited me regularly to offer their support and to make sure that I was coping well. The frequency of other visitors at home had gone down, though. Apart from Prabhu, our household helper, only one other person visited daily—Mona aunty, our next-door neighbor.

Mona aunty and Mom usually met over the boundary walls of our homes to chat. Their relationship had always been cordial and loving.

Rajen uncle, Mona auntie's husband, had met me only a few weeks back at the doctor's office after *Bhai's* accident during the kite flying season. He nodded in greeting when he saw me, but like everyone else he was at loss for words after what had happened. They often talked about me, but they did not know what to do.

Knowing that an amicable neighbor's entire family had perished, they wanted to help. Mona aunty was also very clear that she would continue to provide meals during the day and make sure that I was okay. She was worried about me.

"I will take care of his lunch from now on," she told Panna aunty after a few days.

Panna aunty did not want Mona aunty to be burdened by any responsibility. Mona aunty on the other hand did not think of it as a burden or a responsibility. From the look on her face I knew her heart ached every time she saw me. She had made a decision that she was going to help, and so during the next few days she was finally able to convince Panna aunty that she would be taking care of my morning and afternoon meals.

I was least bothered about these discussions about food and my comfort. I did not need any of this. I was lost, angry and searching for answers. I wanted to be left alone. How was I going to convince them to let me be?

I had always been independent, and I wanted to be that way now, and soon I talked to Panna aunty and with Mona aunty about my meals and my wellbeing. "If I feel hungry I'll go out and eat."

As expected, that discussion did not go well. Panna aunty told me, "You must come to my home at least once a day," she insisted.

Mona was also very clear that she would continue to provide meals during the day and make sure that I was okay. "Don't eat if you don't like it, but freshly cooked meals will be served from our home."

When she told me this, she had tears in her eyes, and I knew she felt hurt that I was trying to refuse her kindness. I did not say anything after that. I knew that she cared, and so did Panna aunty.

Every day I would wake up at different times, mostly after noon, and whenever I would open my veranda door toward the lawn I would see a thermos filled with tea, set on the cement boundary wall that divided our homes. Within minutes of taking that thermos inside the house, Mona's auntie's household help would knock on the door and serve me a freshly cooked meal. He would then come back again to place cold coffee, some fresh snacks, and fruit juice in the refrigerator. Most of this was never eaten.

Once I closed the door, the struggle would come on full force. I would dwell over the unanswered questions.

- *Why my family?*

- *They had never done anything wrong or hurt anybody? Then why them?*

- *Where are they now?*

- *Are they at peace?*

- *Do they know that I am alive?*

I would find myself thinking about these questions for hours. I would try to think of a reason behind what had happened. I would try hard to think if my family had ever hurt anyone. I wanted to know who did this to us, and why. "It was an accident" wasn't a good enough answer.

In a way, it was as if I was still back in the darkness of the fallen building, but surrounded now, not by cement but by huge and weighty questions that felt as if they were crushing the life from my soul.

Later I would realize that when you lose someone, it is normal to think about the time you spent with them and what that person meant to you. You think about that person's love and sacrifice, and you think about how that person had an impact on your life. You think about the things that you will not be able to do with them for the rest of your life.

I had spent my entire life with my family, of course, and so the thread of memories was long and beautiful. One thought would lead into another, and then another. I would travel through this endless loop of thoughts for hours at a time. I would be sitting in one place looking in the void while I would continue to go down memory lane. I would reach Panna auntie's home for dinner hours late, and come back late in the night. Every single day I tried to force myself to go to bed before sunrise, and every single day I failed.

I would collect the morning newspaper later in the afternoon or in the evening, and throw it in the bin. The same helper from Mona auntie's home would come and replace the old coffee with new, and replenish the refrigerator with fresh snacks. I would then drag myself to get a shower, and get ready. And then I would find myself looking at the photo albums once again. I knew what I was doing—trying in vain to hold onto everything and everyone that was gone—but I did not care.

I often remembered Jyotsna auntie's words when I was in sorrow.

"They will be happy if you are happy."

I knew that it was true. I tried, but there was no on-off switch for happiness. How could I be happy when I was not? I believed that happiness came from the same place where love or sadness or other emotions came from. It came from within. What defined happiness for me were things that gave me pleasure, or my personal accomplishments or absolute peace of mind. All of it had become insignificant to me because my soul was in turmoil. The highest form of happiness for me came from being with my family. I was not going to *try and feel happy.*

What I wanted was an answer. A way forward, when there seemed to be none.

It was as if my body had been freed from the cement coffin I'd been trapped in, but my soul had remained imprisoned there.

I continued to live the same life for the next few weeks, and I became more and more careless. Making the bed, planning the day, meals, sleep, shower, and many other daily activities were performed at absurd times. A big part of me was doing all of this on purpose. I wanted to be careless and see what happens. I wanted to do nothing and see how it was going to hurt me. I wanted to stay hungry and see if it was going to hurt me in any way. Something always told me that it was not right, but I ignored it because I did not care anymore. I had a "what does it matter?" attitude toward everything, while I continued to burn from inside.

I had dreams. I had goals in life. I had plans, and I had a direction. Yes, I had them, but moving toward them was a different matter.

Now I didn't even bother moving off the sofa I was lying on in the middle of the day. A big part of me had died in Bhuj. Only a small part of me was still alive, though it was agitated and ready to fight. But how? Where would the strength come from?

Our *Pooja* room became a war ground. I went there to fight with God. I would accuse him of what he had allowed to happen. I would accuse him of taking the good times away from my parents, who deserved to enjoy the fruits of life and who had worked extremely hard all through their lives. They deserved to sit back and enjoy. I asked him why he had taken *Bhai* and his family away. I accused him of taking thousands of innocent lives. I fought with him with all the anger that I had inside me.

But again I had self-restraint. I did not cross my limits even when I abused the higher power. I wasn't scared, but I hadn't forgotten how I had prayed to the same higher power for my life at the time of my evacuation. At that time I knew that only one granule of

279

sand in the wrong place could have made the concrete slab settle over my body and crush me. I remembered that I had prayed hard for my life, to the same God that I was fighting with.

After what had happened with my life, it would not have been difficult to become an atheist. But I was not going to make any decision as yet. Every time that I fought with him, I thought about one thing.

How could I break all ties with my own Creator?

My dad's words echoed in my ears. "Always bow down to your Creator."

Everyone who knew me told me that I was an example of God's miracle, and that God had saved my life. No one truly understood what I was going through at this time—that I was fighting with this God, hard.

And so, while I continued to be focused on the darkness that had befallen me, I failed to notice and recognize that despite everything I'd been through, the light had not fully gone out inside me. Almost, maybe, but not quite.

As more days passed some of my concerned relatives told me that I had to begin getting things in order, slowly. There was some movable and immovable property that belonged to my family. There were things like bank accounts and the monetary investments, insurance, bonds, and many other things that needed to be taken care of. Whenever my relatives enquired about how I was going to handle these things, I told them that I was doing the needful. To me, all this didn't matter. In reality I was going down fast in a downward spiral of sadness. I was just like a rogue planet floating in the galaxy without any direction or gravitational pull. The planetary system that I was a part of didn't exist anymore. I knew that I had to find my path, and I thought that I had the ability to find my path, but right now I did not care.

I would go for lunch at the home of my father's elder sister, Malati aunty, on Saturdays. She had always been very close to my father. I would spend hours talking to her about Dad's childhood, about the earthquake, and about how I was coping. Malati aunty had read the remembrance tribute that I had placed in the newspaper 30 days after the earthquake:

"MAY THEIR SOUL REST IN ETERNAL PEACE," it read at the bottom of the family picture.

"Viral, you should chant mantras. The energies of your mantras will reach them and give them peace, and to you."

A mantra is a sacred utterance, a numinous sound, a syllable, word or phoneme, or group of words that has psychological and spiritual powers. She instructed me to chant the mantras 108 times each day for all the loved ones.

While I was driving back home that day I decided that I was going to chant mantras. Later during the night I entered the Pooja room, once again, and I looked at God's picture in the eye. I did not need anything for myself. All I wanted was peace for the departed souls.

My logical mind started asking questions. *Is this going to work? How will I even know if this was working? Why 108 times?*

I did not start looking for ultimate answers at this time. At that moment, my duty was to do whatever I could to bring peace to my loved ones. In some small way, maybe, to light their way to eternal rest with my prayers, if such a thing was even possible.

Each night, then, I would chant mantras for hours. I would concentrate and think about the family member I was chanting mantras for. When I chanted these mantras with true heart I knew that *I* felt better. I could only hope that it brought peace to them. This newfound peace made me feel better but it would not last very long, though. Thoughts, anger and helplessness would take over once again and pull me down. I would once again crash back to the ground.

During the rest of the day I did not do a single thing that would move me forward. These days were a downward spiral, and I knew that if I did not do something the darkness of it all would take me beneath the ground.

Secretly, I knew that when I wanted to stand back up I would. Right now I wasn't trying hard enough, because *I* did not want to. What I didn't know was that the time had come when I *needed* to stand back up.

One night, after I returned home late after dinner from Panna auntie's home, I watched TV for some time, recited the mantras, and prayed for peace. Then I sat back on the sofa thinking.

My eye was drawn to Dad and Mom's pictures that were kept on the corner table. These photos were taken a few years ago during *Bhai's* wedding, and tonight I could not take my eyes away from them.

When I'd looked at these pictures before, the radiant faces in them had warmed my heart. In a way, these photos aligned me inwardly and made me feel good.

But at this moment things went differently.

Today, when I looked Mom and Dad's faces I found that I couldn't look into their eyes. Instead, I had to look away. I tried hard, but when our eyes met I kept looking down. I looked at *Bhai's* family picture, and I could not look into their eyes either.

What's wrong? Why can't I look into the eyes of anyone in my family?

I tried again. This time I *tried* to feel good when I looked at their pictures, but the once bright and glowing faces looked sad. Very sad.

Of course I knew that these were pictures, and the images hadn't changed. I couldn't help but see, though, that my family looked sad. How could that be? And why couldn't I face them without looking away?

My deeper self knew the reason. The spirit inside me was trying to tell me something that I had known, but it was something that I did not want to hear.

I knew that I now had a home to live in, and I surely could manage without working very hard for anything in life. I was not answerable to anybody. I knew that if I slept all day, there was nobody who was going to tell me to even wake up or move a muscle. Just because I could afford to lie on the couch, I did, and I didn't bother to stand back up.

The truth was this: my family had always been the shining lights of my life. What had drawn me back home to them excitedly from college were all the strong and beautiful traits that shone from within, traits I had also discovered in myself—gifts that had transferred from them to me. It dawned on me that the shining light that was in them had already jumped inside me during my ordeal in the darkness. In fact, it was their life, their strengths within me that had kept me alive. Even though I was still feeling extreme pain over losing them I suddenly knew this:

I had no right to do what I was doing with my life, which was to waste it—after all I'd been given by my family and by God—lying here in this coffin of pain and anguish and not moving forward.

A great awareness dawned. I was on the wrong path, and yet I was not stopping myself. And in my head I could hear myself asking— or was it my family? Or maybe even God?

WHAT ARE YOU DOING, VIRAL?

Would they approve of what you are doing?

Are you making them proud? Or are you wasting what they've given you throughout your life?

I could hear my father's voice in my ears.

"*Shu che ema?*" (What's the big deal?) Dad would often say this, meaning, "Why are you giving such importance to problems? Life is full of problems." By which he also meant, "Stop complaining, keep going."

"*Akhand Rehvanu.*" (Stay unbroken.)

Another voice came to mind.

"*I never have to worry about you, Viral. You can manage in any situation,*" I heard Mom saying what I'd so often heard her say to others about me.

"*He can get anything done.*"

I felt broken, though. I was not that person anymore.

I'd been standing there, staring at their photos, and I went across the room and slumped on the sofa. I had to get away from this inner onslaught.

More thoughts flooded my mind, though.

Did my family teach me to be the way I am now?

Did they teach me to be weak?

Who is this person lying on the sofa, almost lifeless?

I knew the answer: That person was *not* me.

I would not give in to darkness and weakness. I would choose the light.

Suddenly, I flung my feet to the floor and stood up, wanting to distance myself from the lifeless being that I had become. I took a step away and wandered around the living room, still clueless as to what I should do next.

But I was on my feet. Standing. Feeling a surge of strength returning. As if all the energy of those I loved was coming back to join their strength with my own.

How could I have sunk to that level?

What have I become?

Is this why you are alive, Viral? To waste the rest of your days in pain and anger?

Questions pricked me like needles.

There were wounds on my soul that only I could understand. These were not nicks or scratches, they were gashes. Everyone I could share that kind of pain with had gone. But now, something else was even more painful—the feeling of being unable to look into my family's eyes. I wanted to be able to see into their eyes. I wanted to see their radiant smiles. Period.

My inner self shouted at me.

ARE YOU MAKING THEM FEEL PROUD?

I would remember this day very clearly for the rest of my life—this day when my soul once again started to move forward. This was the day when I started to care once again. It was the day when I wanted to walk back into life once again.

No, it was not as simple as making a decision and standing back up again. I had to ask myself the right question. This question was the key to moving me forward. It was like a toe hook that was going to pull me out of the spiritual coffin that I was cemented in.

What would make my family happy?

No answers came, because my mind was still processing what was happening inside me. And then, a flood of thoughts rushed through my mind the next moment. Out of all the thoughts that came to my mind, only one stood out. The important one.

Then I heard myself say: "Don't stop. Finish what you started."

It was my family's dream to see me excel in my career and earn a Master's degree from a U.S. university. It was a collective dream. I imagined how happy they would have been if they had seen me graduate. How deliriously happy it would have been to share that feeling with my mom and my dad, who were always worried about my going to school. How terrific *Bhai* would have felt seeing me achieve my goals. How magnificent it would have been to celebrate that day with the entire family. . .

This was the day I decided I would return to the U.S. to

complete my degree, first. I decided that I would not stop moving in the right direction, and I was not going to alter anything in my life or my lifestyle because of what God had allowed to happen to my family and to me. I decided that I was going to make my parents happy, and I vowed that I was going to bring back their lost smiles. I promised myself that I would keep it that way.

That same night I started to make a plan.

I knew that it was not going to be an easy task to get everything done that I needed to accomplish here in India.

I started to look for information about bank accounts that belonged to all my family members, where all the investments were made, where all the paperwork and information was kept. I started to gather information about the vehicles, insurance, cellphone lines, land lines, gas lines, property papers, tax bills and many more other things that came to my mind.

Looking at the overwhelming amount of work, I knew it was going to take time.

Without taking any rest I continued to work that night, because now that I was up and moving I did not want to stop. I wanted to keep going as long as I could, and I continued to work for hours, working on a rough draft of things that I needed to get in order and take care of.

When I lay down, I thought that I had tried and stopped a large boulder that was rolling down the hill. What I didn't know was that I could hold it there only until I had the energy. Only later would I realize that it was going to take much more than stopping the boulder in its path.

This was the first step into a profound inner journey that I was about to embark on. I was on a journey that was going to bring me fully back to life.

30

AWAKE, ONCE AGAIN.

"Arise, awake, stop not until your goal is achieved."
— S W A M I   V I V E K A N A N D A

The next afternoon I joined the local gym that I had been missing for more than a year. A day later I registered myself at the local skating rink. I had always wanted to learn to skate, and there was no better time than right now.

During these days I would carry bunches of large folders full of documents in my car. With a long list of tasks on Post-it Notes on the dashboard, I would spend time going from one government office to the other, one financial institution to the other, carrying bunches of certified copies of death certificates, news reports, and applications. Days and days were wasted chasing bank and government officials and trying to find someone who could help.

Once again, it was Mona aunty who would often come to spend some time with me after I would return in the evening. Later during the day I would spend a long time talking to Mahendra uncle and Panna aunty about the struggles of the day. Raghu would often come to visit, and then there was Hiral, whom I would spend time with, on the swing in their balcony before going back home late in the night.

I wanted to complete all the legal work before the fall semester began. Looking at the pace at which things were moving, it didn't seem likely that I would be able to accomplish that. It was not easy to get anything done. There were times when various little tasks like cancelling a cellphone line would consume the whole day.

Months were spent going to the banks, government offices and investment houses, and everywhere I went, more and more paperwork was required. Time dragged because of improper rules and regulations and the red tape, and then there were bank holidays and national holidays that would consume even more time.

I would often voice my frustrations when I was with my friends. Sidhant and his wife Seema often came to spend time with me. I met my ex-colleagues Kandarp, Raji and Pratyusha often. All of them would patiently listen to the struggles I had been facing, but there wasn't much they could do besides being by my side.

The list of these incomplete tasks that kept growing daily made me extremely angry each passing day. Often I had to push people to work and get things done. The hindrance made me extremely angry each day, and I knew then that I had to divert my attention to something else, quickly. I thought about it, and the next day I bought a full-size punching bag and a pair of boxing gloves. I did not plan to vent all my frustrations and anger on this bag, but I wanted to divert my mind onto something that I always wanted to do. I learned more about the sport, and often used this punching bag to practice in the night. Venting anger was a bonus.

Understanding my growing frustrations with the work of cleaning up family affairs, Rajen uncle spoke to me. He then got in touch with the right people in his office, and designated an attorney who was now going to help me procure the required court orders needed in such circumstances. It took some time, but once I got these papers in hand, things started to become a little easier.

Not a single day went by when the situation did not try to drag me to the ground and pummel me. But every single day I fought, with every ounce of energy that I had. Some days I was beaten, but I rose with more energy the next day. No, it wasn't easy, and I did not give up, but I realized the truth.

Deciding to stand back up was not going to be as simple as just making one great decision to move forward. Moving in the right direction meant moving in the right direction every time, every moment. Every time I paused, I slid back. Every time I stopped, I fell.

No, I did not give up—though at some deeper level I knew a much greater shift needed to take place. In some way I could sense this was true, but I had no clue what that shift might be. My goal, in any case, was to complete everything that I possibly could, so that I could head back to the U.S. and complete my studies.

I continued to spend time thinking about my loved ones and spent time in their rooms. Now, however, I had become aware that my feelings and emotions had the power to take control of my life if I allowed them to. There was no easy way to know when these emotions were taking control, but I learned a few things.

First, I realized that *inaction* was a big indicator of something else taking control of my life. Whenever I found myself doing nothing, I shook myself up. I also realized that if I was looking into the void for more than a few minutes—feeling the great emptiness left where my family had been—there was a problem. I would try to pull myself out of it, but often I would catch myself in that state much later. As time passed, I learned to catch myself earlier by becoming more and more self-aware.

Still, late in the night if I wasn't able to get any sleep, I would go to the local cyber café where I would browse the internet for hours. I did not own a personal computer then, so this was the only way for me to connect to the rest of the world.

It was during this period that I read the emails from my friends in the U.S. and also from the president of my school, Dr. J. Michael Adams. I clearly understood from the wording of Mr. Adam's email that he was deeply sorry to hear about my loss, and that he wanted to know how I was coping. In his email, he mentioned that he was looking forward to seeing me back in New Jersey, and that the university was willing to support me.

"I am planning to be back in the fall semester of 2001," I wrote back to him.

My relentless, restless pace continued.

At night I would often go for a drive on the highway, or just drive around town for hours. Anything to keep moving. Sometimes I would go skating in the wee hours of the morning after being awake all night. I was doing all this to try and calm down the turbulent waves and thoughts inside me and not get caught by them.

I would often compare my situation with Forrest, in the movie Forrest Gump, who starts to run, after his girlfriend leaves him. He runs for three years across the country, not knowing why he is running. In real life, I was doing the same thing. I was running, and running, and running. . .away from that dark void I did not want to slip into.

Apart from all of this, which I did late at night, there was one other thing of which no one was aware.

I was looking for answers. This was the time when I started to learn who I was, and this was the time when I started to learn more about life, and more about death. This was the time when I started to uncover what was hidden in books and the religious scriptures. I would read every book that I came across that had the potential to enlighten me or bring me answers. All night I would watch Aastha, a spiritual television channel in India, trying to learn from the gurus and the maharishis. I would spend time reading about earthquakes, disasters, human evolution, human psychology, and about all forms of emotions. I read every book that I could that might bring me understanding and answers. I also started to attend seminars and joined various discourse groups.

This was the time when I started to read the *Bhagavad Gita*, a beautiful segment of the Hindu scriptures. I started to look for books that described the *Upanishads*, a collection of texts that contain some of the central concepts of Hinduism.

None of the books made any sense to me, however, not the first time I read them or the second. Nothing could convince me that I would find answers here. Halfway through a sentence I would close the book and put it away.

Later, I would realize that this was not the right time to find spiritual answers, because I was not open to hearing them. This was only the beginning of the journey that would be the rest of my life. This was also the time when I had started to write about what had happened with my life, and how I was dealing with it.

I wanted my family back. How could I even allow myself to read about *karma*, and death, and the next life, when all I truly wanted was to have them back here with me in *this* life?

Unbeknownst to me, life itself would prove to be the answer I needed.

31

A COLLECTIVE LITTLE DREAM

"Life isn't about finding yourself.
Life is about creating yourself".
—GEORGE BERNARD SHAW

August 28th, 2001, seven months and two days after the earthquake, I was ready to leave my home once again to complete my studies. Carrying two suitcases, and a handbag, only *I* could feel the heavy weight of the real burden that I was carrying with my soul.

All my relatives, Mona aunty, and my friends came to see me off at the airport. It was tough for everyone to see me go like this. There was no one from my family to see me off this time. When I waved goodbye to everyone at the airport gate, I still searched for my family members' faces in the crowd. *Bhai's* face flashed in front of my eyes. I remembered him peeping inside the airport window to catch a last glimpse of me. I remembered Dad and Mom waving at me the last time I had left for the U.S.

All I could think of through the flight was what I had been through. I spent time remembering my family, but I did not let any of the thoughts pull me down.

I was heading toward where I wanted to go. Where my life was calling me.

I had a five-hour scheduled layover at London Heathrow Airport. This was going to be my first time at Heathrow, and I was eager to see the airport as I had heard praises about it. Impatiently I walked through the jet bridge to see what it was like to be in London. The airport did not disappoint.

After spending some time in the lounge, I went inside one of the shops and browsed. I then picked up a little soft toy for purchase. Even though months had passed since the earthquake, I realized only a few moments later that I did not have anyone from my family to send gifts to. I put the toy back and walked to the lounge.

Alpesh and Keshma (my ex-roommate Apurva's wife) came to pick me up at the airport in New Jersey. We hugged. The ride in the car toward our apartment was quiet.

My friends and roommates wanted to know what had happened in Bhuj and what I had been through, but none had the heart to openly talk about it because they thought it best not to.

I realized that a lot of people I knew hesitated to talk about my experience because they thought that it was going to hurt me, or it was going to bring back memories that I did not want to recall.

I did not want to try and purge a part of my experience from my life and pretend that such a thing never happened. I was able to express what had happened. I was able to talk about the memories that had left an indelible mark on my soul.

A few days later I spoke to all my roommates and ex-roommates one evening. Alpesh, Apurva, Keshma, Nilay and Sheetal heard about what took place in Bhuj. I did not share everything, but I shared enough. I did not want sympathy, so that day I talked about the facts and not about the scars.

During the last seven months I had worked very hard internally to be the same guy I had always been. I couldn't deny the scars, but I did not want that to affect me or the people around me in any way.

Only years later did I learn that my roommates had often discussed me when I was in India. I also came to know much later that they had all agreed on a few things before I came back to the U.S.:

- Behave normally in front of Viral.

- Don't leave him alone in the apartment.

- Don't ever ask him about what happened in Bhuj.

- Don't make phone calls to your family members in front of him. He may feel a void.

Later, my roommates also told me that none of them had expected to see a smile on my face after what I had been through, and they had expected me to have changed in a drastic way. Only when they met me again did they realize that they were wrong.

Once I settled a little, I went to meet the president of Fairleigh Dickinson University. I had never met him before. After a momentary wait in the reception lobby of his office Dr. Adams came to see me outside.

The first thing I noticed once I saw him was that he was a very tall man. Overjoyed to see me, he shook my hand and then he tried to hug me by bending down a little. It did not work. We both laughed. He then held my hand in his hands and invited me inside his office.

"Welcome back, Viral!" he greeted me heartily.

"We all at FDU thought that there was a very high chance that you would decide not to come back to pursue your studies, but I am glad that you chose to complete your studies."

Dr. Adams spent a few more minutes with me talking about some of my experiences underneath the rubble and then how I dealt with the pain afterwards. It felt good when I shared my thoughts with him, and it felt as if I was talking to a friend.

"If there is anything I can do, please do not hesitate to ask. We are here to support you, Viral," he concluded.

Before I left his office he was kind enough to present me with a leather-covered pocket book and a pen. He then walked me to the exit door of the building.

"Get in touch with me if you need anything," he offered as I left him that day.

During the next few years, I went back and forth to India many times, and stayed there for long periods of time before completing my studies. All my relatives, Rajen uncle's family and my friends stood by my side whenever I was in India. They were always there for me.

On May 21, 2003 Dr. Adams stood on the podium handing degrees to the hundreds of new graduate students. I was one of the students waiting to be called. As I walked onto the podium, Dr. Adams recognized me instantly. He shook my hands with warmth, and asked the cameraman to take an additional picture with him. He later sent the picture to me in the mail with a note: *Viral, I thought you would enjoy this.*

This was the day I was able to fulfill my parents' dream and mine. My parents would have been so proud.

Mom, Dad, Bhai and I - Srinagar, India - 1978.

Bhai and I - Tadoba
National Park, India - 1978.

Mom and Dad - Nepal - 1986.

Mom, Dad, and I, the day I left for the U.S.
for further studies. August 1999.

With Friends at the World Trade Center - September 11, 1999.

Mom, Bhai, Bhabhi, and I, just before leaving
for the U.S. August 1999.

Alpesh and I - New Year's Eve - Times Square,
New York - 1999 - 2000.

Bhai, Bhabhi and Shalin in Bhuj, India - 2000.

Mom, Dad and Shalin at Vijaya Vilas Palace, Mandvi, Gujarat, India - 2000.

Dad and Aamir Khan, at our home in Bhuj - 2000.

Family, in Ahmedabad - October 2000.

Sahjanand Tower, Bhuj.

The plastic electrical fitting
(called ceiling rose) that I used
as a cup. (Not original)

The wristwatch
that saved my life. (Original)

Sahjanand Tower, Bhuj.

International Rescue Corps.
Looking for me.

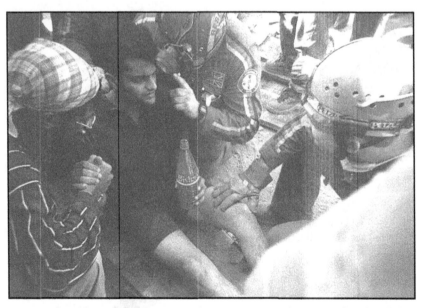

Rescued. With James Livingstone, Simon Drayton and Ranjit Jadeja (Raghu).

The International Rescue Corps team in camp. Mark Baker, Sheena McCabe, Alan Turner, UN Rep, Brian Davison, Ray Gray, Robert Barrie, UN Rep, David Egan, Simon Drayton, Paul Wooster, David Maddock, David Dawson, Stuart Kinsey, James Livingstone, Mark Wilson North, John Anderson, John S Anderson and James McElwee.

Searching for family
in the rubble.
(Associated Press)

The location from which I was rescued.
February 1, 2001.

Bhai's cellphone.
Recovered from the
debris. (Original)

The late Dr. J. Michael Adams - former president,
Fairleigh Dickinson University, and I - May 21, 2003.

With friends - from the top: Apurva Zaveri, Nilay Shah, Sheetal Chudasama,
(myself), Maulik Shah, Gopu Baskaran, Alpesh Shah. December 2001.

*Additional photographs and link to the rescue footage
can be found at www.viraldalal.com*

32

LEARNING FROM THE LIGHT

"Winning starts with beginning"

— ANONYMOUS

Over the years I continued to excel in my career as a software engineer. I continued to learn and I continued to grow. It took time for things to change inside me even slightly, but I did not stop moving away from the deep darkness and toward light. The gash on my soul was so deep that I thought nothing was going to bring me any comfort. But bit by bit, what I was learning about myself and about life started to make a difference.

This was a solo journey, and I had no mentors.

While moving through this dark tunnel, I learned about the things that brought me peace and brought life back into my life. There were innumerable lessons I learned during this time.

After what I had gone through, I was looking for answers. This search for answers led me to many places, and I happened to learn a few things. My experience or what I learned doesn't make me an expert on any of the things that I am sharing here today. I am no expert on any of the religious scriptures, nor am I trying to preach any particular religion or way of living, or about how to live life.

I am simply sharing the things that I learned, and the things that became my strength. I am sharing how I pulled myself out of a black hole that had the ability to consume my life.

LISTENING TO YOUR GUT

I cannot express how grateful I am to have been able to spend the last days with my dear ones. I fail to imagine what I would have gone through if I had lost my family while I was in the U.S.

I was able to see them and be with them because I listened to my gut. I left my career—my first job in the U.S.—to be with them.

I continue to make decisions that are driven by my gut, knowing now how important that is. So much "light" for living comes from this instinctual level of our being.

THE PRESENT MOMENT

Bhai's accident on the day of *Uttarayana* had shaken me up, and only a few days later I found myself struggling between life and death.

I knew that life was unpredictable, but I also happened to think that such a thing could never happen to my family or to me. Only after going through these personal losses, I realized that anything could happen to anyone, at any time. There were no guarantees.

This experience made me realize that the present is much more important than the past or the future. Present moment is real. Present life is real.

The past was inaccessible, and I didn't have the ability to mend it, but I had the ability to change my present. I planned for the future, but I continued to focus on the present.

It wasn't easy. I had to drag my mind out of the past, over and over again each day, and bring my focus to the present moment. I learned to live in the present, much more than ever before. Present was the only thing that was in my hands, and I learned to sculpt it. It would eventually become my past.

WILLPOWER

You have strong willpower.

People told me this often. All I know is that I sincerely believe in what I believe. I have genuine faith in my own self. I have faith in the voice that's inside me and I don't fight with it. The voice inside me is my ally because the voice inside me is my own. I am one with that voice.

When I was inside the rubble there was nobody around me to tell me that it was a tough situation, or that it was impossible to survive. There was only me, with my inner voice. If I wasn't one with my inner voice at a deeper level, I wouldn't have survived.

The strength, the willpower or the confidence inside me was built over years, one block at a time. It was a result of my parents' trust in me, and my trust in what they said to me, and about me.

"I am never worried about Viral. He can do anything."

My mother often said this, and I believed her.

FEAR

When people ask me if I was scared when I was inside the rubble, I always have one answer.

No.

I couldn't explain why I wasn't scared when I was inside the cement coffin, though. Books and websites on the internet only explained what fear was, and about its external causes, and about how to overcome fear. I couldn't find any information about why someone would *not* have fear. Only through introspection did I learn something else.

Every single life experience played an extremely significant role in what I am today. Looking up to my father, I had learned to be strong, very strong, like a rock. He was fearless. Looking up to him all through my life, I became strong and I grew up with a lack of fear.

There is a feeling of fear in every being. I interpreted that feeling as something that needed to be resolved. For me, fear was raw information. I wouldn't have been here today if *the feeling* of fear had entered my mind. I believe that fear is nothing by itself. We create it, ourselves.

Why didn't the feeling of fear enter my mind? Was that even possible?

Yes.

Because there was something more important:

My family.

When we are living for something beyond ourselves, fighting for someone else, fear is replaced by courage.

THE BODY, MIND AND SOUL

Words will never be able to describe the intense feeling of hunger and thirst that I experienced when I was inside the rubble. It was one of the most agonizing feelings I had experienced in my life. Not a day goes by when I don't think about those days inside the rubble. Each drop of water that I drink and each morsel of food that I put in my mouth is a true privilege, and is invaluable to me.

Through my experience I learned that it was possible to stay alive without food or water for days if I applied the powers of my mind. I was able to manage my bodily needs using my mind, at least for some time. Deep within, my mind was calm and in control when I was inside the rubble—but later, things changed.

Because of what I had gone through after being rescued, something inside me changed. . . After I returned home I had allowed the turbulence on the surface of my life to affect the deep calm inside my mind. This was the time when things started to go out of my control.

I learned that mind was a tremendously powerful thing. It had the ability to put you on the highest pedestal in the world, or sweep you into destruction. It was like a horse that could take the chariot of your life anywhere. If you lost the slightest grip over its reins, it would take you where it wanted to go.

It took me some time to realize what was happening around me, but soon my higher self, my *Atman* (soul), was able to reclaim control and clutch the reins firmly.

Let the *Atman* direct your mind, and let your mind direct your body. Your mind is the seat of the *Atman*. There is nothing impossible for *Atman*. *Atman* is supreme.

ASKING QUESTIONS

I got no answers when I asked questions while being trapped inside. That did not stop me from asking questions. If I had not continued to ask myself questions, I may not have been able to find a way to stay alive.

After I was rescued and after I learned that no one from my family had survived, there was no reason for me to survive, but I did. I also knew that mere surviving was not enough, and I knew that the right thing to do was to perform action, but I couldn't do it. I didn't feel like doing it.

At that time, once again there was only one thing that came to my rescue. Questions. I asked myself the right questions. The answers guided me through.

I realized the power of questions. And I learned that

your higher self will always find answers. . .*if* you ask the right questions.

I wanted to get my life back to where it was before. It took time, but I learned how to do it.

I asked questions and continued to correct every single misstep.

HAPPINESS

"You are a very lucky man," a press reporter had told me only a few hours after I was evacuated.

"I don't think I am lucky. I would call myself lucky only if I live a happy life," I had told him then, knowing that my family was still missing.

For me, happiness was a sense of being that came from within. A beautiful blue sky or a pot of gold cannot bring true happiness to someone who is not receptive to being happy. I believe that the outside *things* that bring you happiness are only an extension of your inner self, a mere reflection of how you *want* to feel. The *things* that make you happy are not the true cause of happiness. The root of happiness is within.

But truly, happiness didn't come from inside 24/7. I had to work to make happiness a way of life, and not an end goal.

How did I become happy?

One step at a time.

Every time I thought about happiness, I thought about my mother, first. She was such a happy being. Her demeanor and her attitude toward life often came to my mind when I thought about happiness. She could make anyone roll with laughter with her wisecracks. She knew how to be happy and stay happy in any situation.

And then there was *Bhai,* whom I had always looked up to. He always wore a smile on his face. How did he manage to do that?

These thoughts made me focus on positives, and on the things that pulled me up. I tried to look at the past with a smile.

I observed that when I wanted to be unhappy, I could be, and nothing could stop me from being unhappy. I used the same "formula" to stay happy. No one was going to stop me from being happy either.

The thing was, I had always liked being happy. I did not have to make new pathways in my brain or train myself to be happy. These pathways of happiness were there, but they were blocked.

So even though I wasn't stuck inside a concrete box anymore, I continued to work hard on opening up these blocked pathways inside my brain, one scratch at a time. I did not realize at the time that it was an inner engineering feat.

"Consistent drops of water falling in the same spot can make a hole in the toughest rock known to man," I remembered my father saying.

With persistence and determination I was eventually able to clear these blocked pathways of happiness.

BHAGAVAD GITA

I learned, from everywhere around me. *Bhagavad Gita* happened to be the first religious scripture that I read after the earthquake. I read various versions of it over time.

Bhagavad Gita is a part of *Mahabharata*, one of the two major epics of ancient India. The literal meaning of *Bhagavad Gita* is "Song of the Lord." It is a 700-verse, Hindu scripture written in Sanskrit (an ancient Indian language), which came into existence in the 3rd or 4th millennium BCE.

Bhagavad Gita, also referred to as *Gita,* is set in a narrative framework of a dialogue between Prince Arjuna, the seeker, and his guide and charioteer Lord Krishna, the knower. It is a dialogue between a man and God.

Once I became more receptive to the knowledge hidden in the *Bhagavad Gita*, I learned, and I understood.

DEATH

I am going to die.

Such a thought never occurred to me. When I was inside the rubble, not even for a fraction of a second did the thought of death penetrate even one cell of my body.

I wasn't controlling my thoughts, if such a thing was even possible, but the thought of death never occurred to me naturally. I believe that if such a thought had occurred, I may not have been able to survive even a few hours inside the rubble. I am here today because such a thought did not occur.

I believe with all my heart that a thought with the right intensity, even if it has occurred in the past, is enough for an event to take place.

Over time I learned more about death. I learned that death would not come to you if you don't give up, in some way or form. Death occurs when one gives up, consciously or subconsciously, and when the pain of taking another breath weighs more than the pleasures that life has to offer.

Everyone has a different theory about death, and it is often based on what is believable for them, and what brings them peace. For me to believe in anything was difficult at first.

I had always known the description of death, but that wasn't enough. I wanted to know more. Everything that I learnt about death brought me back to the same thing, over and over, only through different routes.

There were no other answers, but the truth.

अच्छेद्योऽयमदाह्योऽयमक्लेद्योऽशोष्य एव च ।
नित्यः सर्वगतः स्थाणुरचलोऽयं सनातनः ॥ २४ ॥

acchedyo 'yam adāhyo 'yam akledyo 'śoṣya eva ca
nityaḥ sarva-gataḥ sthāṇur acalo 'yam sanātanaḥ

The soul is indestructible; the soul is incombustible, insoluble and unwitherable. The soul is eternal, all-pervading, unmodifiable, immovable and primordial.

Death was not the end. The soul that was in the body continues its journey, and unites with the eternal power.

नैनं छिन्दन्ति शस्त्राणि नैनं दहति पावकः ।
न चैनं क्लेदयन्त्यापो न शोषयति मारुतः ॥ २३ ॥

The soul can never be cut to pieces by any weapon, nor burned by fire, nor moistened by water, nor withered by the wind.

ATTACHMENT

I had heard this before. But I had never truly paid attention to these verses about attachment in the Bhagavad Gita. I was paying attention now.

ध्यायतो विषयान् पुंसः संगस्तेषूपजायते ।
ंगात्सञ्जायते कामः कामात्क्रोधोऽभिजायते ॥ ६२ ।

Meaning:

While contemplating the objects of the senses, a person develops attachment. From such attachment develops desire, and from desire arises anger.

क्रोधाद् भवति सम्मोहः सम्मोहात्स्मृतिविभ्रमः ।
स्मृतिभ्रंशाद् बुद्धिनाशो बुद्धिनाशात्प्रणश्यति ॥ ६३ ॥

From anger arises delusion, and from delusion arises

313

bewilderment of the memory. And when memory is bewildered, all intelligence is lost, and when intelligence is lost one perishes.

The meaning of these two verses was deep and profound. What I understood helped me understand the root cause of my pain. This is what I understood:

All of our suffering came from different forms of attachments.

I was in pain because I was attached to my family. And because they were taken away, a massive inferno of anger was burning inside me.

Understanding these versus did not mean anything at first. I understood the meaning, but then what? How was it even possible to detach myself from my parents and my family? How was it possible to not be attached to them? No answers came, for a very long time.

It took years before I could *truly* understand and absorb what I was trying to learn. What I understood was that I did not just *love* my family, but I was *attached*. Attachment was natural, but it was bringing me extreme pain, love was not. Attachment was pulling me down, love was not. Attachment made me sad. Love made me look back with a smile. I learned that attachment was transitory and love was not.

I learned the difference between attachment and love. And whenever I thought about the past, I learned to think about it with love and not with a sense of attachment.

I discovered that love is the most powerful thing in the world, attachment is not.

PERSPECTIVE

Sometime after the earthquake:

Once when I was at a traffic light I looked at the gentleman inside the car next to mine. He looked at the red light, banged the steering wheel a few times. Then he looked at it again and shook his head and mumbled something. He then honked a few times, though the lights were still red. He seemed to be in a hurry and quite upset.

Later that day, while I was with one of my colleagues during lunch I observed that his day wasn't going well either. He spoke about the bad weather, and then about how crummy the food was at the local joint, then about the awful traffic, and a few other things that were bothering him. He sounded very unhappy with everything around him.

That morning during the rush hour I had been running late, too. I also had challenges at work. I sat in the same traffic jam just like everyone else, and the weather was no different for me.

In this day and age, when a traffic light that doesn't turn green fast enough can ruin someone's day, I cannot help but think: why are people so unhappy with their *perfect* lives. What is everyone *really* upset about? *Where* is the problem?

After what I went through in Bhuj, the definition of "problem" changed for me. I know what a real problem looks like.

I wish people could see just a glimpse of life through my eyes...

When I was inside the concrete enclosure, trapped for days without any certainty of living another day, a single drop of water or a tiny of light would have given me the amount of happiness that one cannot even fathom.

All I can say is that if you are alive and well, you are very lucky. If you have a loving family around you, you are living what some people can only dream of. Life in itself is a beautiful thing. Everything else is a big perquisite. Give it a hug. Every day.

FAMILY

I was lucky by birth. And extremely lucky to have been born to such parents who instilled knowledge and strength in me over the time that I had the privilege to spend with them. I was lucky to have parents who made me what I am today.

Not everyone is lucky to have parents who guide their children in the right direction. I have seen parents who hurt their children, and who do not make an effort to nurture their own children or teach their children what's important. *"You don't have to bow down to anyone in the world, but you should respect your parents, because they created you."* This is what my dad used to say.

DHARMA

Having spent most of my life in India, I thought that I knew what *dharma* meant. *Dharma* meant duty. *Dharma* meant conduct. Dharma meant "the right way." Over time, I read more about *dharma* and tried to understand its true meaning. While looking for answers, I tried to relate my situation to the situation of Prince Arjuna, the seeker from the epic *Mahabharata*.

Arjuna was about to fight a war, after tremendous injustice had been done toward his family. All diplomacy had failed to prevent this war.

But before the epic war was about to begin, Arjuna was unable to even stand on his feet, or hold his mighty bow. He was about to give up even before the battle. His mind did not allow him to fight because all he could think of was the aftermath of the war. What was he going to achieve by winning the war?

Facing his duty as a warrior to fight the righteous war, Arjuna is counselled by Lord Krishna to fulfill his duty as a warrior and establish *dharma*.

How was this story related to my life?

I wanted to know "the right way," *my dharma*, after I came back home.

I learned more about *dharma* from what Lord Krishna told Arjuna.

What was *my* dharma?

My dharma depended on who *I* was. I had to find out who I was first.

According to the *Rig Veda*, the most ancient of Hindu scriptures, Hindus were divided into different classes, and based on these classes the duties of each individual were defined, like this:

- Brahmins: The duty of Brahmins was to perform spiritual and priestly activities.

- Kshatriyas: The duty of Kshatriyas was to perform the responsibilities of a warrior.

- Vaishyas: The dharma of the Vaishyas was to perform trade and agriculture.

- Shudras: The dharma of Shudras was to perform manual work.

All of this was meant for ancient India, and even though these classifications are still prevalent in some parts of the country, my parents had never taught me to classify.

I was trying to find out who *I* was, because I wanted to know what *my* dharma was.

As time went by, the answer presented itself. It had always been in front of me.

I exist because of them. My *parents* were, in a practical sense, my God.

To me, nothing mattered more than their wishes, their dreams, their likes, their aspirations and expectations. They wanted happiness for *me*. They wanted *me* to grow, to fulfill *my* dreams, and perform good deeds.

My dharma was to please my God.

That was it. That is what I was going to do.

I did not think. I did just that.

Make your parents proud of you. Be what they want you to be. Do what they want you to do. You are here because they made you.

CHOOSING LIGHT

After what I experienced in my life, I could have chosen to gripe for eternity and live in the shadow of darkness all through my life.

The choice is always in our hands, and over darkness, I chose light.

NEVER STOP LEARNING

September 2010, nine years after the earthquake, Virginia, U.S.A.

I had always wanted to skydive, and I couldn't hold back the urge to do it any longer. I found a well-respected skydiving school in the area and signed up.

Once there, I took the required training, signed the paperwork and agreement that said, "I UNDERSTAND THAT I CAN DIE" on each page. The last page had the same words in the largest font size possible. I signed it with a smile. I wanted to fly.

This was my first jump, so it was going to be a tandem jump, A tandem jump means that I was going to be attached to an instructor during the jump, and he would be doing the needful maneuvering of pulling the ripcord to launch the parachute, or I could do that under his supervision.

Soon, while waiting for the plane near the drop zone, I saw the professional skydivers jump out of the plane and land a few feet away from me. While I struggled to shut down the chatter of my mind, which told me not to do it, I wanted to do it—very badly.

Wearing a professional jumpsuit I boarded the plane. It took 20 long minutes for the plane to reach an altitude of 14,000 feet. And then, it was time. The large airplane door was opened in the middle of the sky.

I had never seen anything like this in my life before. As my instructor and I headed toward the door, I saw a carpet of grass a few miles below. My mind told me not to do this.

"I am ready!" I said to the instructor.

And then we jumped. . .

Wind hit my face at more than 100 miles an hour as I fell. I had no clue what was happening, and I was tumbling beyond control.

Instantly I thought I had made a bad decision.

And then from nowhere, came the cameraman, who had jumped at the same time that my instructor and I had jumped. He flew close to us, took hold of my hand, and aligned me so he could take video and pictures while we all plummeted toward the ground together.

At that moment I knew I was not falling. I was flying. And it felt incredible!

My body was now in a horizontal position, and it felt as if the wind was trying to hold the weight of my body, while I flew like a bird. The skin on my face fluttered like a plastic bag while I continued to shout aloud and posed for the camera. The exhilarating experience consumed all the nervousness I was experiencing just before jumping out of the airplane.

In moments, it was time to pull the ripcord to deploy the parachute. As the instructor pulled the cord, I felt a very sudden and strong pull that tried to stop my fall. I thought that the harness was going to break and I would fall to the ground like a piece of rock. I had nothing to hold onto other than the harness on my own torso.

As soon as our parachute flung open, instantaneously our pace slowed down. Within moments, we were gliding toward the ground, very slowly. It had become very calm, very quickly. It seemed like the exciting part of the rollercoaster ride was over, and we were returning back to our station through a serene ride.

And then, while talking to the instructor I heard a fluttering sound in the background. The instructor looked up at the parachute and then he looked at his altimeter.

"I think we've got an issue here."

I heard him say this at more than a mile up in the air. It did not sound very good.

"What's the issue?" I asked.

"We may have to cut the chute."

"Okay. Let me know what you want me to do," I said without wasting any time.

"Make the arch position for me, so I have some space to cut the chute off."

I did just that, quickly. The next moment, the instructor cut our chute off!

We both fell at the speed of gravity, and this time we were falling vertically. It felt as if I had just jumped off a very tall building and was falling toward the ground very fast.

The few seconds that I was falling from the sky felt like a very, very long time. The ground suddenly seemed so close. And then, once again, I felt the jerk and the pull from the emergency parachute that had just deployed.

"EVERYTHING OKAY?" I shouted.

"Yes, we're fine."

"Okay. What happened?"

"The lines of the main chute had gotten tangled. We now need to make sure that we land safely."

"What if *this* parachute goes bad?" I asked.

"Then we die," he said, in a calm tone.

We both laughed.

During the rest of our descent, we talked about what happened, but otherwise we were mostly quiet. We hoped that no gusty wind would topple or tangle our only emergency chute now.

Within the next few minutes we were able to land safely to the ground. We shook hands and hugged. The instructor told me that things turned out in our favor because I was calm, even though it was he who had brought both of us back to safety by handling the situation professionally. I was just glad that both of us were back on the ground safely. We thanked each other and parted.

After an hour or so, I was driving back home. This was the day when I learned one more very important lesson in life.

You are invincible when the higher power, or the universe, or good luck is by your side. No one knows how much or what it takes for these powers to be by your side, every single time.

Don't test these powers.

In the end what I want to say is this:

Life is extremely, extremely precious. It only takes a split second to throw a very precious life away. I learned not to take life for granted. I learned to value it, much more. And once again I learned that my life and the power to make the right choices will always be in my own hands.

EPILOGUE

GOOD THINGS HAPPEN.

"The purpose of life is to be happy."
— DALAI LAMA

I was in India a few years after the earthquake, once again trying to complete some pending work. During this long period of time I made contact with a girl who was from India but was working in London. I had come to know her through my cousin Manor and his good friend Divyang, both of whom lived in the U.S. We met, this girl and I, over the phone and via webcam.

I had never met this girl before, but one thing was certain. The conversations with her were always quite pleasant. When we spoke, I felt free to say what I wanted to say. I could be myself.

This girl already knew about me and what I had been through. We talked about the earthquake, but we did not discuss it at length. Time flew by as we continued to talk to each other for a few weeks over the phone. Weeks turned into months, and very soon the time came closer when I had to head back to the U.S., back to work.

I told her that I was leaving for the U.S. soon, and that we would only be able to meet each other the next time we were in the same geographical location, which was going to take some time. We wanted to meet, but I was stuck trying to do a lot of things at once.

After one conversation, I later learned, she made a decision.

"I am leaving for India tomorrow," she told her roommate when she woke up the following morning. She had decided to meet me. Period.

She quit her job that day, and then called me.

"I am coming tomorrow, Viral."

When I heard this I stared at the phone. I didn't breathe for a few seconds. How could she do that? Quit her job and leave the country overnight to meet *me*?

"Are you serious?" I responded.

"Yes. I'm getting on a plane within the next few hours."

The next evening she was standing at my doorstep. She had not bothered to think about her visa status in London or her leased apartment. After quitting her job, she had handed everything over to her roommate and left England for good.

I was amazed. How could she just. . .*do* that?

This was the first time we'd met face-to-face. And we both knew that we wanted to see each other again, and so we continued to meet each other over the next few weeks.

February 14th, 2006, Valentine's Day. Sitting in the car together I turned to her and took her hand.

"Would you marry me?"

First, she cried. Then she said, "Yes."

We got engaged in 2006, and we were married in 2007.

Her name is Margi. Simply put, she is the most wonderful girl that I have met in my entire life, and she is the most beautiful thing that has happened to me. The love that she has poured into my life over the years, and the sacrifices she has made for me cannot be described in words.

I often asked her about how someone could leave a country, a life, and a career behind to rush to meet someone whom she had only known for a few weeks?

During a conversation before we got married, Margi told me that she wanted to meet me, and that was it. She knew my story, and so she initially expected a sad and serious tone over the other end of the phone. But after only one conversation between us she realized she was talking to someone who seemed. . .*fun*. She wondered how that was even possible, knowing what I had been through. How could someone be happy after going through such a tragedy? I told her that it's the blessing of my parents that gives me the strength.

We did not know whether things were going to work out between us or not, but it was she who left everything behind to meet a person who had been through a tough time in life. A very tough call.

She later told me that she had read every single webpage she could find on the internet that had news about me. And she had made a decision to meet me.

It wasn't a difficult decision for her. To this day I think that it was a decision that very few people would ever dare to make.

Margi is selfless, simple, and yet a very strong individual who happens to be an amazing life partner. I often think about how someone could do what she did. I still joke and tell her that I doubt her at times, and often ask her if she had come back to India for a vacation, and thought of meeting me while she was at it. She has gotten tired of my questions, and has stopped explaining.

"You still haven't paid me for the air ticket," she often tells me.

Margi gifted our family with a baby boy in March 2012. It was the proudest time of my life, the day my son was born. His name is Arjun.

Arjun looks at our family picture and recognizes everybody. "*Shalin Bhaaaaai!*" he shouts, looking at the family picture.

Last Christmas, the only gift Arjun asked for was a toy car wash. My dad would have been so happy to learn that.

My mom always wanted a baby girl in the family, and so came along our little princess. Margi gave birth to our little baby girl in July 2015. Her name is Anokhi. It is a Hindi name, and it means "unique." My mom would have fulfilled her wishes of dressing her up the way she always wanted to.

Looking at both of our children I often see a reflection of my dad, my mom, and *Bhai*.

And so in the way I often see vivid images of my family when I close my eyes. . . and when I open my eyes they are not gone at all.

That is because, through choosing light and being open to life's ongoing miracles, I now see a reflection of them in front of me.

GLOSSARY

Asana: A yogic posture.

Baa: Grandmother.

Bachao: Help

Béta: Dear son.

Bhabhi: Sister-in-law.

Bhagavad Gita or **Gita:** Literal meaning: "Song of the Lord". It is a 700-verse Hindu scripture in Sanskrit that is part of the Hindu epic Mahabharata.

Bhai: Brother.

Bhajiya: A spicy fritter containing pieces of vegetables made usually with a batter of chickpea flour and deep-fried.

Chachu: Uncle (Father's younger brother).

Fua: Paternal uncle.

Kaka: Paternal uncle.

Karma: Action or deeds.

Khichri or Khichdi: A nutritious preparation made from rice, lentils and vegetables, which is usually served hot.

Kurta: Long collarless traditional Indian shirt.

Mala: A string of beads used for counting mantras while meditating.

Mama: Maternal uncle.

Mandir: A Hindu temple.

Manja: An abrasive thread colored and coated with powered glass to facilitate kite wars.

Mantra: A sacred utterance, a sound, or group of words in Sanskrit believed to have psychological and spiritual powers.

Memsahib: A respectful form of address for an lady.

Namaste: A respectful form of greeting among Hindus.

Pooja or **Puja:** The act of worship or prayer.

Prana: Life force.

Pranayama: Regulation of the breath through certain techniques in yoga.

Sahib: Master.

Sanskrit: An ancient classical language of India and of Hinduism.

Saree: A garment worn by Hindu women, consisting of a long piece of cotton or silk wrapped around the body with one end draped over the head or over one shoulder.

Tasla: A large bowl shaped container used to pick up heavy dirt or other construction material by workers.

Uttrayana or **Uttrayan** or **Makar Sankranti:** A festival celebrated in various parts of the Indian subcontinent to observe the day that marks the shift of the sun into lengthening days. This day is celebrated by flying kites with friends and family.

ACKNOWLEDGEMENTS

I started writing about my experience long ago. During these years I had to live through the disaster many times. It wasn't easy, but the story had to be told.

There were numerous things that happened prior to the earthquake that played an extremely important role in saving my life: my childhood habit of keeping the wristwatch on while sleeping, my father gifting me an iridium wristwatch only months before the disaster, and my father telling me to switch from the mattress on the floor onto the bed only minutes before the building collapsed.

When our building started to shake, there wasn't a single piece of brick or mortar that touched my body. Not even when our wing crashed to the ground and turned into rubble. The amount of space that I was trapped in was meant for one human being, no more, no less. Even a scintilla of sand in the wrong place would have closed the cavity I was trapped in.

After my struggle inside the rubble for days, getting me out of a hole that was sandwiched between layers and layers of massive concrete slabs, totally unscathed, was no less than a miracle.

I know that I could have been crushed and killed at the time of the earthquake or when I was being rescued.

Thank you, God for listening to my prayers at the time of my rescue.

Thank you, God, for giving me a new life.

I am grateful for the infinite blessings of my grandparents, the late Mr. Parmanand Dalal, the late Mrs. Jasoda Dalal, the late Mr. Ratilal Kothari, and the late Mrs. Savita Kothari. I couldn't have done it without your blessings.

For the unending shower of blessings, for the courage and the strength that resides in me, for the willpower and the ability to handle a tough situation, for the compassion, for the smile that I still possess, and for the heart that beats inside me, I humbly bow down to my mother, the late Mrs. Jaimati Dalal, my father, the late Mr. Girdhari Dalal, and my brother, the late Mr. Roshan Dalal.

Thank you, Mom, Dad and Bhai, for your endless blessings. I am here today because of your blessings.

This book is dedicated to the volunteers of the International Rescue Corps. They saved my life.

Because of the joint efforts and dedication of Ray Gray, John Anderson, Rab Barrie, Paul Wooster, Jimmy Livingston, Mark Baker, Brian Davidson, Davy Dawson, Simon Drayton, Dave Egan, Stuart Kinsey, Dave Maddock, Sheena McCabe, Jim McElwee, Alan Turner and Mark Wilson-North, I once again saw sunlight after January 26, 2001.

It is because of these men and women at IRC that I have the privilege of living a beautiful life. It is because of their selfless devotion and humanitarian effort that I am able to enjoy the infinite wonders that life has to offer.

I don't have words to express my gratitude for these men and women who put their lives at stake and who leave their homes to save the lives of people in trouble in different parts of the world.

Thank you. . . I will forever be indebted for what you did for me.

My uncle Bharat Shah, my cousin Biren Parikh, my cousin Punal Kothari and my cousin-in-law Ranjit Jadeja were among the first ones to reach Bhuj. The search and rescue work at Sahjanand Tower would not have started for days if it hadn't been for them.

Over the years I've heard only bits and pieces about what these men had to go through in Bhuj while I was still trapped inside the rubble.

All of these men had to suffer the pain of living in a town that had turned to shambles. With a lack of every human need, these men continued to stay in the town.

For everything you did for me and for my family I can only humbly say thank you, Bharat Fua and Punal *Bhai*, and thank you, Raghu. I will never be able to thank Raghu enough because of the things that he has done for our family. They will not be forgotten.

Biren Parikh is not with us anymore. He is survived by his wife and two wonderful children. I posthumously thank Biren *Bhai* for his help and for what he did for me over the years.

I humbly thank my uncle Surendra Dalal and my uncle Dinesh Kothari. I cannot thank them enough for the help and moral support that they provided to me in Bhuj and later over the years. They were always there for me when I needed them. Thank you, Surendra *Kaka*, and thank you, Dinesh *Mama*.

When I was still trapped inside the rubble, all of these people were in Bhuj to help: my uncle Kiran Desai, my second cousin Jatin Desai, my cousin-in-law Bijal Shah, my cousin-in-law's brother Viraj Shah and my cousin's cousin Rupesh Dalal. They drove toward the epicenter of the earthquake leaving their families behind, only to look for us. Some of these men are my distant relatives whom I hadn't seen in years. They were there for *us*. Thank you, all of you, for being there for our family.

In the days following the earthquake, there was only one place in Bhuj where thousands of people were served food each day at no charge. It was at Shri Swaminarayan Mandir.

My relatives and I were among the thousands of people who were able to get something to eat in a place that had turned into a ghost town. I thank the Swaminarayan Sampraday for this true form of selfless service.

Indian Army jawans were called from different parts of the country to serve during this national disaster. With limited machinery and equipment, these jawans continued to help in whatever way they could. I salute and thank these jawans for their sacrifice and selfless service.

After I returned to Ahmedabad, help poured in from every direction and from everyone who knew our family. My uncle Mahendra Parikh and my aunt Panna Parikh continued to provide support during the months that followed, and for many more years to come. They provided me the warmth that I needed the most.

In addition to the countless things that they did for me, I cannot forget the evenings that this family waited for me for hours at the dinner table, and never complained. They understood what I was going through and they let me be.

Thank you, *Masa* and *Masi*. You will always be loved and respected for your kindness and for what you have done for me.

Their daughter Hiral Parikh was quite young at the time of the earthquake, and she was shaken up by what had happened with our family. During this time she continued to stay by my side. Thank you, Hiral, for the love and the care.

From the day I returned from Bhuj to Ahmedabad, until today when I visit my home in India with my family, there is one family that has always looked after all of us. This is the family that had supported me then, and supports us now in ways that cannot be put into words.

Rajen Shah, Mona Shah and their son Jaishal Shah are not my relatives. They are much more than that.

My relatives often say this:

"Even a close relative wouldn't do what the Shah family continues to do for you. You are blessed to have them."

I agree.

What Mona aunty and Rajen uncle have done for me and my family over the years is unprecedented. They are the ones who continue to be there for us. They are the ones who fill our home with unending love and affection.

Today, years after the earthquake, the refrigerator in our Ahmedabad house still happens to be loaded with beverages and refreshments by Mona auntie's household helpers when we are in town. Mona auntie's focus now happens to be finding the right treats for our kids. My children know that these are a bunch of exceptional people.

Thank you, Mona aunty and Rajen uncle, for being there for us. Always.

This incident affected each one of my relatives deeply. Most of my relatives never could express their feelings in words, but they did so by offering help. I thank all my relatives from the bottom of my heart for the help and support that was offered to me in various ways during the years following the earthquake.

I want to express my gratitude to Madanmohan Parikh, Malati Parikh, Niranjan Parikh, Usha Parikh, Geeta Shah, Leela Shah, Jaishree Dalal, Kamalkant Parikh, Jyotsna Parikh, Asha Kothari, Bharat Kothari, Priti Kothari and Rekha Kothari for their continued support and for their love and affection towards me and my family. Thank you for being the strong pillar of support for me.

My friend Sidhant and his wife Seema stood by my side when I was going through a rough phase. Deval Shah, Kandarp Trivedi, Raji Trivedi and Pratyusha Mehta were among the ones who were there when I needed them the most. Thank you, guys, for always being there.

I would like to thank Mr. Gautam Thapar, Chairman of Avantha Group, who took personal interest at the time of the earthquake and offered to help with any official matters in Bhuj. I very much appreciate it.

I would also like to thank Mr. Gajendra Trivedi, who was always there to support me during this difficult time and shared his knowledge and supported me in various ways.

Once I returned to the U.S. I thought that I did not need anyone's help, and yet each one of my roommates and friends tried to help and support me all along. Thank you, Alpesh Shah, Bijal Shah, Apurva Zaveri, Keshma Zaveri, Nilay Shah, Sheetal Chudasama and Snehal Thummar. Thank you, guys. Thank you for not putting it down in our Black Book. Thank you Maulik V. Shah and Divya Reddy for your help during this time.

In the U.S., I had made a new friend. It was Dr. J. Michael Adams, who was the President of Fairleigh Dickinson University.

Dr. Adams is not with us anymore.

I want to express gratitude for the kindness of this man, the late Dr. J. Michael Adams, who not only offered financial support on behalf of the school, but who took personal interest to enquire about how I was doing in my life.

I would like to thank the wife of the late Dr. Adams, Mrs. J Michael Adams for helping me procure permission for the picture taken on my graduation day. I would also like to thank Karin C. Hamilton from Fairleigh Dickinson University for the help and coordination.

I am grateful to Fairleigh Dickinson University for the support, and for the help that was offered during the time of personal tragedy.

When I completed the first draft of my book in 2014, it was more than 700 pages long. David Hazard was the man who looked at it and told me that it was a large block of marble that needed to be sculpted.

David did a tremendous job guiding me through the process of writing my story, and he made sure that the power of the story was captured. David also happens to be the man who understood my story and suggested a title for my book that resonated with it.

David, I learned a lot from you, and more importantly it is because of you that my story's got a heartbeat. Thank you for your help all along the way. You are truly an amazing individual.

I would like to thank the beta readers who spent their valuable time reviewing my story. Thank you, Steven Proulx, Jeffrey Brunk, Ketan Parikh, Sonali Parikh and Nirav Parikh for your opinion and your suggestions. Your inputs helped me tremendously. Thank you, Mahima Bedi Lobo, Gauri Popli, Vidya Shankara and Abhilasha Ratna Padhy for taking out the time to read my story, and for sharing your point of view.

I needed a book cover that resonated with my story. George Foster and his wife and creative partner Mary read my story. George came up with three unique book cover designs, all of which were very, very good. The collective opinions and suggestions from George, Mary, David Hazard and my wife Margi Dalal got us to the final book cover. Thank you, George for your hard work and for the beautiful book cover. Thank you, David, Mary and Margi for your suggestions.

Claudia Mueller did a great job proofreading the manuscript. Thank you, Claudia, for doing a great job and answering my infinite questions.

I would like to thank Peter Gloege who did a wonderful job designing the interior of the book.

There is one person without whose patience, sacrifice and extraordinary support this book would not have been possible. That person happens to be my wife, Margi Dalal.

Margi is the one who has sacrificed the days and the months and the years when I was focused on writing my story. She always knew how important it was for me to tell it.

With a smile on her face, she would take care of our two powerhouses of energy—our children—singlehandedly, when I would be busy writing. Never did she complain when I would make her review my writing, often after midnight.

Thank you, Margi, for your incredible patience, your invaluable inputs, for being an outstanding partner that you are, and for being a truly wonderful mother to our children.